DICTIONARY **OF**
Allusions

JULIA CRESSWELL

HarperCollins*Publishers*

HarperCollins*Publishers*
P.O. Box, Glasgow G4 0NB

First published 1997

Reprint 10 9 8 7 6 5 4 3 2 1 0

© Julia Cresswell

ISBN 0 00 472054 7

Printed and bound in Great Britain by
Caledonian International Book Manufacturing Ltd, Glasgow G64

For my son Alexander Cresswell:
may he find it useful.

Introduction

The major difficulty in writing this book has been choosing what to go in and what to leave out. The English language is so rich in allusions that it was impossible for everything that ought to go in, to fit into a book this length. I have been collecting material for this book for several years and have several thousand quotations on filing cards, and in the end I took the coward's way out and relied on this evidence. So if an allusion was well-enough supported by quotes it went in; if not, however obvious a candidate, it did not, unless it related to something that was already in. I hope in the future to be able to bring out a longer version of this work that will be able to include a wider range of material, so if the word you want is not here, please be patient.

No-one can write a book like this in isolation. I have had to consult many reference works to check the facts included. In particular I have made extensive use of David Pringle's *Imaginary People* (1987), and of Jeff Evans' *The Guinness Television Encyclopedia* (1995). Since I have only included information which is relevant to the use of the entries as allusions, readers looking for further information might like to turn to these books first. I also wish to thank a number of people. Anna Leinster has supplied me with hundreds of allusions from her reading, and Constance Fishwick has also supplied a good number. Fred McDonald has, as ever, been a constant supply of support and information. My husband, Philip, has patiently put up with my questions about books,many of which he had not read for years and been a wonderful source of obscure information, and my son Alexander has helped with children's TV and reading. The people at HarperCollins in Glasgow have made useful suggestions, Alice Goldie has helped with science information, Helen Moore helped with the Demon Headmaster, and my editor Edwin Moore has been a constant support and source of sanity-saving phone calls.

Julia Cresswell
Oxford, 1997

AB FAB see ABSOLUTELY FABULOUS

ABEDNIGO see SHADRACH, MESHAK AND ABEDNIGO

ABEL see CAIN AND ABEL

ABELARD AND HÉLOISE [*History*]
Abelard and Héloise were real-life lovers, and almost as famous as ROMEO AND JULIET. Peter Abelard (1079–1142) dedicated his life to learning and was the leading scholar in Paris when, at 38, he became a tutor to the equally brilliant 17-year-old Héloise. Almost inevitably they fell in love, and were secretly married. As a married man Abelard's career was blighted, for learning and the church were linked in those days. For this reason Héloise publicly denied they were married, despite the fact she had borne Abelard a son. In revenge for her disgrace Héloise's uncle had Abelard castrated – not only as a fitting revenge for the seduction of his niece, but because castration was as much of a bar to Abelard's career in the church as marriage. After this Abelard became a monk and Héloise a nun, but they continued to write to each other, and these touching letters survived. When Abelard died Héloise had him buried at her convent, and when she died her body was placed by his.

ABERFAN [*History*]
A mining village in Wales which was the scene of a disaster in 1966 when it was engulfed by a landslide from the local pit's unstable slag heap. The village school was directly in the path of the debris, and 116 of the 144 people killed were children. The Aberfan disaster shook the country, and led to reforms in the treatment of such tips. 'One man is concerned about a building site at the end of the close, a favoured playground for children. It's a mini-Aberfan, he says, anticipating injury or worse' (*Radio Times* 20–26.7.96).

ABILENE see WILD BILL HICKOK

ABSOLUTELY FABULOUS [*Television*]
An immensely successful BBC TV comedy (1992–96) showing the chaotic life of two friends: **Edina**, a PR agent and **Patsy**, a fashion-magazine editor. Insincerely calling everyone 'sweetie' or 'darling', they drink and take drugs, shop compulsively, throw tantrums, chase after celebrities and generally behave badly, much to the disapproval of Edina's strait-laced daughter **Saffron** (Saffy).

ACHILLES [*Mythology*]
Achilles was one of the great warriors of Greek myth. The son of the sea-nymph **Thetis**, he was the chief hero on the Greek side in the TROJAN WAR. When he was born his mother dipped him in the River STYX to make him invulnerable. Consequently, no weapons could pierce him, except at the place on his heel where his mother had held him during his immersion – hence the term 'Achilles tendon', and the expression 'to have an Achilles heel', meaning a weak spot. Needless to say, Achilles was shot in this weak spot, and, as it was a poisoned arrow that wounded him, he died. The fate of his fabulous armour, made by **Hephaestus**, the Greek smith-god, was the cause of a great quarrel among the remaining Greeks.

ACORN ANTIQUES see MRS OVERALL

ACTION MAN [*Popular Culture*]
A popular boy's toy, Action Man seems to come in for a lot of mockery, probably because when it was first introduced dolls for boys were a novelty and the early versions were notoriously limp-wristed and difficult to pose.

ADAM AND EVE see EDEN, GARDEN OF

ADDAMS FAMILY [*Television, Popular Culture*]
A fictional comic and macabre American family. Originally appearing as a series of newspaper cartoons by Charles Addams, the Addams family have also appeared in a TV series, animated cartoons and in film. They comprised **Morticia**, **Gomez**, **Pugsley**,

Wednesday, **Uncle Fester**, **Cousin Itt**, various other family members and their butler **Lurch**, living in their spooky American Gothic house on **Cemetery Ridge**. See also THE MUNSTERS.

ADLER, IRENE see SHERLOCK HOLMES

ADONIS [*Mythology*]
In Greek myth Adonis is a beautiful young man, loved by APHRODITE, who is killed by a wild boar while hunting. The red anemone is said to have spring from his blood. The term is used to mean a classically handsome young man.

AEGIS [*Mythology*]
An aegis was the term for a shield (or in some versions a goatskin) carried by both ZEUS and ATHENE. Thus to be 'under the aegis' of someone means to be under their protection.

AENEAS see DIDO AND AENEAS

AFGHAN TRIPEHOUND see DENNIS THE MENACE

AGAMEMNON see CLYTEMNESTRA

AGATHA, AUNT see BERTIE WOOSTER

AGGIE, AUNT see DESPERATE DAN

AGUECHEEK, SIR ANDREW see MALVOLIO

AHAB, CAPTAIN see MOBY DICK

ALADDIN [*Fable*]
A character from one of the stories in the ARABIAN NIGHTS. The story of the poor boy Aladdin and his magic lamp is most often found allusively in the term 'an Aladdin's cave' for any assorted collection of rich things. For some reason it is particularly popular with journalists describing a store of stolen goods.

ALAMO see DAVY CROCKETT

ALBATROSS [*Literature*]
After its use in Samuel Taylor Coleridge's poem *The Rhyme of the* ANCIENT MARINER, an albatross is used for something unwanted that someone cannot get rid of. One of the Mariner's punishments for shooting an albatross is to have the bird's corpse hung round his neck as a sign of shame. Thus, 'George Bush's "Read my lips, no new taxes" was ... always an albatross waiting to land on his presidential neck' (*Independent* 11.1.94).

It is an alternative to a **millstone**, an expression based on the words of Jesus: 'It were better for him that a millstone were hanged about his neck and he cast into the sea, than that he should offend one of the little ones' (Luke 17.3).

ALBERT SQUARE [*Television*]
The decaying Victorian square which forms the setting for the action in the BBC's highly successful TV soap opera, *Eastenders*.

ALCIBIADES [*History*]
Alcibiades (450–405 BC) was a charismatic and beautiful Athenian nobleman. He was the ward of the great politician **Pericles** and a friend of the philosopher SOCRATES (whom he is said to have tried to seduce). At first he was the golden boy of Athenian politics, but he was an unstable character, and after being exiled from Athens turned against the city and joined its enemy, SPARTA. He eventually died a lonely exile. The ancient world was fascinated by his story, and several lives of him were written, concentrating on his personal charm and attractiveness, and ultimate failure.

ALDERSHOT [*Military*]
A Hampshire town which is the site of the largest military camp in England. Established in 1854, Aldershot (and the nearby officer-training establishment of **Sandhurst**) has come to represent the British military establishment in general. From the poems of John Betjamen it also represents the idealised, leisurely life between the two world wars, thanks mainly to *A Subaltern's Love-Song* (1945), where the tennis-playing MISS JOAN HUNTER DUNN is 'Furnish'd and burnish'd by Aldershot sun'.

ALECTO see FURIES

ALFRED see BATMAN AND ROBIN

ALGY see BIGGLES

ALI BABA [*Literature*]
A character from one of the stories in the ARABIAN NIGHTS. Ali Baba is a poor woodcutter who observes the secret of the **Forty Thieves'** cave in which they hide their booty and the magic words '**Open Sesame**' which open the doorway. He takes their gold and becomes rich, but the robbers plan their revenge. They hide in oil jars in Ali Baba's courtyard, waiting to kill him in the night, but are discovered by his faithful slave-girl **Morgiana**, who kills them all by pouring boiling oil on them.

ALICE IN WONDERLAND [*Literature*]
The name commonly used for one of Lewis Carrol's two books about Alice. *Alice's Adventures in Wonderland* (1865) and *Through the Looking-Glass and What Alice Found There* (1871) – better known as *Alice in Wonderland*, and *Alice Through The Looking-Glass* – depict a fantastic world where the strangest things can happen, and the only sort of logic which operates there is the logic of a dream.

ALOYSIUS see BRIDESHEAD

ALPHAVILLE see DAN DARE

ALTAMONT [*History, Popular Culture*]
A rock festival which took place on 6 December 1969, Altamont was the first major free festival after WOODSTOCK and events there marked the end of Hippie hopes of love and peace. While the Rolling Stones were performing on stage, a group of Hell's Angels who were acting as the festival's security staff beat up and stabbed to death a spectator, an event that was captured by film cameras.

AMALTHEA see HORN OF PLENTY

AMBRIDGE see ARCHERS

AMIN, IDI [*History*]

Dictator Idi Amin (1925–) was the Ugandan head of state from 1971 to 1979. He was notorious for his cruelty – which even extended to eating parts of his enemies' bodies – mass executions, self-aggrandisement, including awarding himself the Victoria Cross, and general mental instability. Unfortunately for Ugandans, his erratic and ridiculous behaviour made him an international figure of fun, which reduced international outrage at his appalling behaviour. He currently lives in Saudi Arabia. 'I can only describe the ethos of my school as like working for Idi Amin – I never know if I'm going to be smiled upon or be verbally clubbed to death' (*Independent* 11.4.96).

ANANSIE [*Folklore*]

Anansie is a cunning, tricksy spider in West African and Caribbean folktales, always out for what he can get and getting the better of the other, less intelligent, animals.

ANCIENT MARINER [*Literature*]

The central character from Samuel Taylor Coleridge's mystical poem *The Rhyme of the Ancient Mariner*. In it, a wedding guest is stopped at the church door by an old, half-mad man who insists on telling him the story of how on a voyage he shot an ALBATROSS, and of the weird punishments which followed. Meanwhile the poor guest, unable to escape, hears the wedding take place without him. The poem is the source of the expressions 'A sadder and a wiser man' and 'water, water, everywhere, Nor any drop to drink' (usually misquoted as '... and not a drop to drink'). The Ancient Mariner is usually used allusively with reference to someone insisting on telling something, even if the hearer wants to get away – 'Ever since, I have been going around London like the Ancient Mariner buttonholing my single girlfriends ... ' (*Evening Standard* 9.8.96) – or for confessing one's sins: 'A couple of years ago, she had such a compulsion to confess her affair with a married man she made the Ancient Mariner look reticent' (*She* June 1991).

ANDROCLES AND THE LION [*Fable*]

The legend of Androcles and the Lion tells of how Androcles, a

Christian Roman slave, ran away from his master in North Africa and hid in a cave. There he found a lion, helpless because its paw was swollen and infected by a thorn. Androcles took pity on the beast and took out the thorn. Later Androcles is captured and thrown to the lions in the circus at Rome. However, one lion does not attack him, but fawns on him – it is the lion he had earlier saved. When the story comes out, Androcles is pardoned.

ANDROMEDA [*Mythology*]
Andromeda was a princess who was chained to a rock as a sacrifice to a sea monster and rescued by the Greek hero PERSEUS. Her name was given to a constellation of stars. The term **Andromeda Strain** for a rapidly mutating micro-organism comes from Michael Crichton's 1969 novel, where this is the code-name given to an organism brought back by a satellite from the upper atmosphere and which threatens to wipe out mankind.

ANGRY YOUNG MAN [*Literature*]
The Angry Young Man was the British equivalent of the REBEL WITHOUT A CAUSE, although the literary writers of the time would probably have been horrified by the comparison. The term was used to describe both a group of writers and the characters they portrayed in their plays and novels. They were rebellious or downright anarchic, alienated, and felt that post-war society had let them down. See JIMMY PORTER.

ANIMAL FARM [*Literature*]
George ORWELL's 1945 novel *Animal Farm* is a satire on revolutions. In it, the animals on Mr Jones's farm revolt under the slogan 'Four legs good, two legs bad', and drive out the humans. Soon the pigs have taken over, and their leader, NAPOLEON, has become a STALIN-IST dictator. Although everything is supposed to be shared equally among all the farm animals, the pigs take everything for themselves according to the doctrine that 'All animals are equal but some animals are more equal than others'.

ANTICHRIST see APOCALYPSE

ANTIGONE see OEDIPUS

APHRODITE [*Mythology*]

Aphrodite is the Greek goddess of love and beauty. The Romans called her **Venus**. Unlike most of the Greeks gods she was not a child of ZEUS: instead, she was born from the sea-foam caused by Zeus's throwing into the sea the genitalia of his father, **Chronos**, after he had castrated him on deposing him. Aphrodite is often painted being carried to land on a cockle-shell after her birth. She was married to **Hephaestus** (Roman **Vulcan**), the lame smith-god, but preferred the handsome **Ares**, the god of war. Once Hephaestus trapped them in bed, catching them with a net of brass and exposing them to the ridicule of the other gods. ADONIS was another lover.

APOCALYPSE [*Religion*]

The Apocalypse is the Greek term for the biblical book which is otherwise known as the Revelation of John the Divine (or The Book of Revelation), in which St John sees a series of visions of the future, particularly the coming of **Antichrist** and the SCARLET WOMAN, the end of the world, and Heaven and the **New Jerusalem**. **The Four Horsemen of the Apocalypse** appear in chapter 6. The first horseman who rode a white horse, carried a bow and went forth to conquer is usually interpreted as Pestilence; next came War mounted on a red horse and carrying a sword; then Famine riding a black horse and carrying a pair of scales, and finally, St John says, 'I looked, and behold a pale horse: and his name that sat on him was Death, and Hell followed with him.' See also NUMBER OF THE BEAST.

APOLLO [*Mythology*]

Apollo is the Greek god of the sun and the arts. He is usually shown as a blonde young man carrying a bow, and he became the type of the handsome young man. As the God of **Delphi** and its oracle, and of serious art, he is the type of the rational person (compare DIONYSUS). His temple at Delphi bore two inscriptions 'Know thyself' and 'Nothing in excess'.

APPEASEMENT see MUNICH

APPLEBY, SIR HUMPHREY see SIR HUMPHREY

ARABIAN NIGHTS [*Fable*]

The Thousand and One Arabian Nights is an ancient Oriental collection of stories. A series of tales, including those of ALADDIN, ALI BABA and SINBAD, are set in a framework which tells of a sultan who, disillusioned with women, takes a new bride every night and has her strangled in the morning before she can be unfaithful to him. He meets his match in the wise and beautiful **Scheherazade**, who tells him a bedtime story, but does not finish it. The sultan, in order to hear the ending puts off her execution, and the process is repeated night after night. Finally he relents and abandons his murderous ways.

ARABS, FOLD TENTS LIKE [*Literature*]

H. W. Longfellow's poem *The Day is Done* (1844) contains the lines 'The cares that infest the day / Shall fold their tents, like the Arabs, / And as silently steal away.' So this term can be used to refer to anyone making a silent exit.

ARACHNE [*Mythology*]

In Greek myth Arachne was a woman who dared to challenge the goddess ATHENE to a weaving match and, inevitably, lost. She was turned into a spinning, weaving spider, which is why today the scientific term for spiders is 'arachnids'.

ARAMIS see D'ARTAGNAN

ARBUTHNOT, SIGISMUND see NIGEL MOLESWORTH

ARCADIA [*History, Mythology*]

Arcadia means a pastoral paradise, an ideal region of rustic peace, of a gentle life where shepherds and shepherdesses play their pipes and tend contented sheep. Arcadia was a real area of ancient Greece, the mountainous region of the central Pelopennese. Its natives were said to be the earliest settlers in Greece, and became associated in Greek poetry with the life-style of the GOLDEN AGE.

ARCATI, MADAM [*Drama, Film*]

Madame Arcati is the eccentric, strikingly dressed medium in Noël Coward's 1941 comedy *Blithe Spirit*.

ARCHERS, THE [*Radio*]
The Archers, on BBC Radio 4, is a long-running (1950–) radio soap opera. This 'everyday story of country folk' was originally conceived as a means of getting across the Ministry of Agriculture's advice to the farming community, but has long since left this remit behind, although it does still have a didactic element. Set in and around the village of **Ambridge**, the series got its name from the original central characters **Dan** and **Doris Archer** of Brookfield Farm, and it still deals with their descendants and their neighbours.

ARCHIMEDES [*Science*]
Archimedes (c. 287–212 BC) was one of the great mathematicians and engineers of the ancient world. He discovered the relationship between the volumes of the sphere and the cylinder and invented Archimedes' screw, a means of raising water for irrigation that is still widely used in the Third World. He is best-known for running naked through the streets, crying '**Eureka!**' ('I have found it!'). The story behind this is that Heiron, Lord of Syracuse, had given a goldsmith some gold to make him a crown. The finished crown weighed the same as the original lump of gold, but Heiron suspected that the goldsmith had stolen some of the gold and replaced it with base metal, and he told Archimedes to find a way of working out if this had happened. When Archimedes got into a full bath and noticed the water slop out, he realised that the volume of a complex shape like a crown could be measured by the amount of water it displaced, and, too excited by his discovery to remember his state of undress, he rushed out crying 'Eureka!' Archimedes died when the city he lived in was captured by its enemies, and is said to have been killed by a soldier who found him too engrossed in a mathematical problem to have noticed what was happening.

ARDEN, DALE see FLASH GORDON

ARES see APHRODITE, MARS

ARGO, ARGUS [*Mythology*]
The *Argo* was name of the ship in which **Jason** and the **Argonauts**

(i.e. those who sailed in the *Argo*) went on the quest of the GOLD-EN FLEECE in Greek fable. It was a magical ship that could talk. It was called *Argo* after its builder, **Argus**, but he should not be confused with two more famous bearers of the same name. One of these was the faithful hound of Odysseus (see ODYSSEY), who waited faithfully for his master for 20 years; although nearly blind with age, Argus was the only one who could still recognise Odysseus when he returned. He lived long enough only to greet him, and then died. The other Argus was HERA's hundred-eyed watchman who could not be outwitted because some of his eyes were always open, even when the rest slept. When HERMES killed him by trickery, Hera placed the eyes in the peacock's tail.

ARIADNE [*Mythology*]

Ariadne was a Cretan princess who fell in love with **Theseus**. When he was going into the deadly and hitherto inescapable **Labyrinth** to fight the MINOTAUR, Ariadne gave Theseus a ball of thread. He secured one end of this at the entrance to the **Labyrinth** and unrolled it as he went. Once he had defeated the Minotaur he was able to follow the thread back, thus being the only man to find his way out of the fatal maze. The old word for a ball of thread was 'a clew', and this, respelt, gives us our word 'clue'. Ariadne fled Crete with her lover and they landed on the island of Naxos. What happened next comes in two versions – either Theseus heartlessly abandoned her, or else the god DIONYSUS warned him off, and he left Ariadne to him. Whichever, Ariadne was left lamenting on the shore of Naxos, and was comforted by and married to Dionysus. The crown he presented to her at her wedding was later placed among the stars as the constellation of *Corona Borealis* (the Northern Crown).

ARIEL see CALIBAN, PROSPERO

ARK see NOAH

ARTFUL DODGER [*Literature*]

A character in Charles Dickens' OLIVER TWIST (1838), the Artful Dodger was the senior member of FAGIN's gang of child pickpockets. His name was gained through his skill at the job.

ARTHUR, KING [*Mythology, Folklore*]
King Arthur and his Knights of the ROUND TABLE are the great
national heroes of British myth. Originally shown as British warriors fighting the invading Saxons, they soon mutated into
knights in shining armour living in a dreamy, mystical world of
vaguely medieval times, fighting tournaments and righting
wrongs. King Arthur himself did not die, but sleeps with his
knights, waiting to return to rescue his country once again at its
time of direst need – hence his title of 'The Once and Future King'.
Some say he waits in AVALON, but there are hills all over Britain
which are claimed to be his sleeping place. (See further under
CAMELOT and individual characters from the stories).

ASHLEY, LAURA [*Retail, Popular Culture*]
A chain of British clothing and interior furnishings shops, named
after their founder. When Laura Ashley shops first became well
known in the 1970s it was for selling milk-maid dresses in floral
prints. Later, the shops were very successful selling a cottagey,
chintzy country look for interior decorating, and these styles have
become firmly linked with the name.

ASLAN see NARNIA

ATHENE [*Mythology*]
Athene (or **Athena**, in Latin **Minerva**) was the Greek goddess of
wisdom, war and the crafts. She gave mankind the olive tree, the
first one of which she planted at Athens, the city named after her.
Her birth was extraordinary. The king of the gods, ZEUS, had
learned that any son Athene's mother, **Metis**, bore him would be
greater than his father. Zeus was afraid of the consequences, having deposed and mutilated his own father (see APHRODITE), so he
turned the pregnant Metis into a fly and swallowed her. Months
later Zeus had a terrible headache, so bad that he ordered that his
immortal head should be split open. From his head sprang his
daughter Athene, mature and fully armed. See also AEGIS,
ARACHNE.

ATHOS see D'ARTAGNAN

ATKINS, TOMMY [*History, Popular Culture*]
Tommy Atkins is the source of the expression '**Tommy**' for a British soldier. The term goes back to the 19th century, when the name Tommy Atkins was used on guides printed to show soldiers how to fill in official forms.

ATLANTA see STINGRAY

ATLAS [*Mythology*]
In Greek myth Atlas was a giant who stood on top of the North African Atlas mountains holding up the sky on his shoulders to stop it crushing the Earth. Early books of maps often carried a picture of this, giving rise to the term 'atlas' for a collection of maps.

ATLAS, CHARLES [*Popular Culture, Advertising*]
Charles Atlas (see ATLAS) was the name taken by Angelo Siciliano (1894–1974), a body-builder who won the title of 'The World's Most Perfectly Developed Man' in 1922. For many years he promoted his body-building courses in advertisements with the slogan 'You too can have a body like mine', claiming that he had once been 'a seven-stone weakling'. The advertisements' strip-cartoons featured one such seven-stone weakling who loses his girlfriend after a bully kicks sand in his face on the beach, then gets his own back after building himself up with Charles Atlas's course. The cartoons became so famous that they have entered the national folklore.

ATTILA THE HUN [*History*]
Attila (c. AD 406–453), nicknamed 'The Scourge of God', became king of the Huns in 434, and had soon united under him a number of other nomadic barbarian tribes and controlled an area which stretched from the Rhine in Germany to the borders of China. In 447 he ravaged the lands between the Black Sea and the Mediterranean and defeated the Byzantine Emperor. In 452 the Pope had to pay him large sums not to sack Rome itself. There are various stories of his death. Some say he died from a nosebleed, some from drunkenness, possibly bringing on the nosebleed, and some, since he died just after marrying a beautiful princess, from

other forms of indulgence. 'Slightly to the right of Attila the Hun' is used to describe someone perceived as fanatically right-wing or militaristic. See also GENGHIS KHAN.

AUDREY [*Music, Film*]
This was the name given to the carnivorous plant whose constant plea to the employees of the florist shop was 'feed me' in Howard Ashman's *Little Shop of Horrors*. Originally an off-Broadway musical (with its best-known song, *Mean Green Mother from Outer Space*), it is more widely known from the 1986 film, described by one critic as being 'The best movie ever made about a man-eating plant'.

AUGEAN STABLES [*Mythology*]
The term Augean Stables for something that is abominably filthy or something that desperately needs cleaning out, comes from one of the labours of HERCULES. He was ordered to clean out in one day the vast stables of King Augeas of Elis which had not been cleaned for 30 years. Hercules does this by diverting the nearby River Alpheus and using its waters to flush out the muck.

AUNTIE [*Television*]
A nickname used in affectionate reference to or gentle disparagement of the BBC. It is a hangover of the corporation's more paternalistic, Reithian days (see LORD REITH).

AURORA [*Mythology*]
Aurora (in Greek **Eos**) is the goddess of dawn. She fell in love with the human **Tithonus** and begged the king of the gods to grant him immortality. However, she forgot to ask for eternal youth, and Tithonus grew older and older and more and more senile until at last the gods took pity on him and turned him into a grasshopper. By him she had a son, **Memnon**, who was killed at the TROJAN WAR by ACHILLES. The dew is supposed to be the tears she sheds for him.

AUSTIN, STEVE see BIONIC WOMAN

AVALON [*Mythology*]

Avalon is the wonderful earthly paradise where KING ARTHUR is taken to recover from his head wound after battle of **Camlan** which ends his reign; from Avalon, some say, he will return to save Britain. Tennyson describes it as a place 'Where falls not hail, or rain, or any snow, / Nor ever wind blows loudly; but it lies / Deep-meadowed, happy, fair with orchard lawns / And bowery hollows crowned with summer sea' (*The Passing of Arthur*, 1869).

Avalon means 'land of apples', an important feature in Celtic myth, and it is probably a version of the **Tir na Nog**, 'The Land of the Young People', an Irish earthly paradise peopled by heroes. Others connect it with Glastonbury which has strong Arthurian links and where monks claimed to have found Arthur's body in the 12th century.

BABEL, TOWER OF [*Religion*]

A biblical tower which was a manifestation of pride and a catalyst of divine vengeance. According to the story told in the Bible (Genesis 10), at one time everyone on earth spoke the same language. They began to build the town of Babel (the name is a form of BABYLON), and to build a tower to reach up to heaven as a memorial to themselves. To punish their pride God made them all speak different languages, so they were unable to continue building, and mankind has been left with the curse of different nations being unable to understand each other.

BABY JANE see JANE, BABY

BABYLON [*History, Religion, Popular Culture*]

An ancient city and the capital of the Babylonian Empire (in what is now southern Iraq). It once held the Jews in captivity, so it is mentioned unfavourably in the Bible. In the book of Revelations the **Whore of Babylon** is generally interpreted to mean Rome (the Emperor NERO is the great villain of Revelations), and this led to the term's being used by Protestants after the Reformation for the Roman Catholic Church, or the pope. From this, Babylon passed into Afro-Caribbean speech to mean racist white society, with **The Babylon** meaning the police. The term is now spreading more widely, and coming to mean uncaring society in general. 'You shame us all before the world, hiding half the wealth of Britain behind your snobbery and elitism while leaving the homeless in doorways, lost in the granite of Babylon' (*Evening Standard* 13.8.96).

The Hanging Gardens of Babylon were one of the seven wonders of the ancient world. Tradition says they were built either by the legendary Queen **Semiramis** in the 9th century BC, or else by

King Nebuchadnezzar II (reigned 604–562 BC), who built them for his Median wife, Amytis, because she missed the mountains and greenery of her native land. They were probably a series of terraced gardens on an artificial mound, and archaeologists have found what could be their remains.

BACCHUS, BACCHAE, BACCHANALIA see DIONYSUS

BADER, DOUGLAS [*History*]
Douglas Bader (1910–82) was one of the great RAF heroes of the Second World War. A daredevil and show-off, he lost both legs in a flying accident after a foolhardy stunt, but nevertheless grittily taught himself to fly again with artificial legs. He was shot down and taken prisoner, but made repeated attempts to escape. A biography of him, *Reach for the Sky* (1958), made into a very successful film in 1962, spread his fame and portrayed him as the personnification of jocular, stiff-upper-lipped heroism. He was knighted in later life for his work with the disabled.

BADGER see TOAD OF TOAD HALL

BAGGINS, BILBO AND FRODO [*Literature*]
Bilbo and Frodo Baggins are two **Hobbits**, the heroes respectively of J.R.R. TOLKIEN's fantasy novels *The Hobbit* and *Lord of the Rings*. Hobbits are small creatures with many human characteristics, but are hairier, longer-lived and have a liking for good food and living underground. Hobbits are not normally adventurous, but Bilbo allows himself to be sucked into the role of burglar for some dwarfs trying to regain their lost gold. On this adventure he finds the magic ring, the disposal of which is the central theme of Frodo's adventures. See also GANDALF, GOLLUM, MORDOR.

BAGHEERA see MOWGLI

BAIRNSFATHER, BRUCE see OLD BILL

BAJORANS SEE KLINGONS

BAKER STREET IRREGULARS see SHERLOCK HOLMES

BALDRICK see BLACKADDER

BALDUR see LOKI

BALFOUR, DAVID see ALAN BRECK

BALOO see MOWGLI

BAMBI [*Film, Literature*]
The 1942 Disney film of *Bambi*, based on the book by Felix Salten, tells the story of how Bambi the deer develops from an adorable little fawn into a fine young stag, along with the experiences of his other friends, including the comic rabbit **Thumper**. Many a sensitive young child has been traumatised by the scene where Bambi's mother is shot by hunters. Bambi has been given as a nickname to the Prime Minister, Tony Blair, because of his supposed fawn-like looks.

BANKS, ROSIE M. see BINGO LITTLE

BANNISTER, MINNIE see GOONS

BARABBAS see PONTIUS PILATE

BARDELL, MRS see PICKWICK

BARKIS [*Literature*]
In Charles Dickens' *David Copperfield* (1850), Barkis is a haulier whose chief characteristic is his ability to drive his horse and cart while apparently asleep. His name is used almost exclusively in the catch-phrase **'Barkis is willing'**, originally his expression of his determination to marry.

BARMECIDE'S BANQUET [*Fable*]
In the ARABIAN NIGHTS the story is told of how Barmecide, a prince, offers a beggar a banquet of imaginary dishes served on non-existent plates. The beggar gets his own back by pretending to get drunk on the imaginary wine and attacking his host. Hence 'a Barmecide's Banquet' is used of an illusory advantage or empty promise.

BARNEY see STIG OF THE DUMP

BARSETSHIRE [*Literature*]
An imaginary county which was the setting for Anthony Trollop's novels of ecclesiastical life. Life in Barsetshire is rural and generally pleasant, but feelings run high and church politics can be vicious. Among the most memorable characters in these novels are the repellent and hypocritical **Reverend Obadiah Slope**; the formal and worldly **Reverend Doctor Theophilus Grantly**, Archdeacon of Barsetshire and rector of Plumstead Episcopi; the weak and not too bright **Dr Proudie**, Bishop of Barsetshire, and his domineering wife **Mrs Proudie**.

BARSOOM [*Literature*]
A series of 11 novels by Edgar Rice Burroughs (1875–1950) telling of the adventures of **John Carter** on Mars. Barsoom is the name given to their planet by the red-skinned Martians. While these novels are now old-fashioned (the heroes strong and upright, always rescuing the high-spirited heroine from a fate worse than death of in the nick of time) as well as scientifically weak (famously, the Martian princesses lay eggs but can have children by humans) Burroughs tells a good story, and his novels were very influential on later writers. The heroine of the first group of novels is Carter's beloved princess **Dejah Thoris**, while *Thuvia, Maid of Mars* (1916) introduces another set of characters.

BARTON, DICK [*Radio, Film, Television*]
The thrilling adventures of Dick Barton, Special Agent first won fame as an immensely popular radio series which was broadcast between 1946 and 1951, then became a series of films and finally a TV series.

BASH STREET KIDS [*Popular Culture*]
The Bash Street Kids are the group of uncontrollable little brats who make Teacher's life hell in the long-running strip in the children's comic *The Beano*.

BASIL BRUSH [*Television*]
Basil Brush is a fox puppet whose booming laugh, posh voice and

catch-phrase 'boom boom' made him a great success from his first appearance in 1962.

BASSET, MADELEINE see BERTIE WOOSTER

BATEMAN [*Popular Culture*]
H. M. Bateman (1906–1970) was a cartoonist who specialised in social embarrassment. He is famous for a series of cartoons showing 'The man who ... ', which depicted the pompous outrage of onlookers as some poor innocent contravened a minor but socially important rule, such as passing the port in the wrong direction or smoking before the loyal toast.

BATES, NORMAN [*Film*]
Norman Bates was the murderous mother-fixated madman in ALFRED HITCHCOCK's famous 1960 film *Psycho*.

BATMAN AND ROBIN [*Popular Culture, Television, Film*]
Superheros who first appeared in a strip cartoon created by Bob Kane and Bill Finger in 1939. Since then they have appeared in just about every possible medium. In everyday life the main characters are philanthropist **Bruce Wayne** and his ward **Dick Grayson**, but when crime strikes GOTHAM CITY they become Batman, **the Caped Crusader** and his sidekick Robin **the Boy Wonder**. With the help of **Alfred**, his butler and assistant, the **Batmobile** and other Bat-technology they fight exotic villains such as **The Joker** and **The Penguin**. Since the 1960s some half-hearted attempts have been made to add female interest to the cast of characters, which led to the invention of **Batgirl** and **Catwoman**.

BAUHAUS [*Design*]
The Bauhaus was a school of design, founded by the architect Walter Gropius, which ran in Germany from 1919–1933. The aims of the school were to integrate beauty, craftsmanship and functionality, and it was one of the first places where students were made to master both the theory of design and the practical side of making their designs. Their products tended to be lean, modern but elegant designs, often more comfortable to use than they looked.

BAY OF PIGS [*History*]
A failed attempted invasion of Cuba in 1961 by a troop of anti-Castro Cubans backed by the USA. They invaded Cuba at the Bay of Pigs to try to overthrow Cuban leader Fidel Castro. The invasion was a shambolic disaster, and the Bay of Pigs has become proverbial as a major foul-up.

BEACHCOMBER [*Popular Culture*]
Offbeat humorous column in the *Daily Express*, mostly written by J. B. Morton (1893–1978). It introduced a whole cast of characters including **Mr Justice Cocklecarrot**, an erratic judge, **Dr Strabismus** (Whom God Preserve) of Utrecht, a mad scientist, and 12 **red-bearded dwarves**, generally a nuisance.

BEAM ME UP, SCOTTY see STAR TREK

BEAN, MR [*Television*]
A near-silent TV comedy series (1990–97) starring, and partly written by, Rowan Atkinson. Mr Bean is a solitary and gormless type with a disastrous gift for causing accidents and havoc.

BEAST, THE, BEAST OF THE APOCALYPSE see NUMBER OF THE BEAST

BEATRICE AND BENEDICK [*Literature*]
Two characters from William Shakespeare's *Much Ado About Nothing*. In the opening scenes, Beatrice and Benedick are seen to be two wits who heartily trade insults. Their friends decide to trick them by telling each of them the other secretly loves them, and by the end of the play the sparring partners have become marriage partners. (For Dante's Beatrice see under INFERNO.)

BEAUTY AND THE BEAST [*Folklore*]
This story of the enchanted beast restored to human form by love and understanding is generally used as a shorthand for a pair unequal in physical attractiveness.

BEAVIS AND BUTT-HEAD [*Television*]
Television cartoon series about two slobbish, sexist, American

teenagers who get into various forms of trouble when not lounging on a sofa watching rock-videos and eating junk food. Beavis is the madder one, Butthead the stupider, and between them they represent everything that is objectionable about teenage boys.

BECKETT, SAMUEL [*Literature*]
Samuel Beckett (1906–89) was an Irish writer known for his bleak, gloomy, existentialist and usually plotless plays, which include *Waiting for* GODOT.

BEDLAM [*History*]
Bedlam as a term for a place of noisy confusion, gets its name from the priory of St Mary of Bethlehem at Bishopsgate, which started caring for the insane in 1377. The name was shortened to 'Bethlem' and then became 'bedlam'. In the 17th and 18th centuries is was a fashionable entertainment to watch the antics of the lunatics, and this led to a more general use of the term bedlam.

BEECHING, DR [*History, Transport*]
Richard, Baron Beeching (1913–1985) was responsible for the 1963 Beeching Report which advocated closing many rural railway lines and branch lines in order to make British Rail more profitable. The cuts were vehemently opposed, as the closures effectively isolated many rural areas, and Beeching's name was vilified. Beeching's name has thus become symbolic of ruthless cuts which do not take the human factor into account.

The name of Sir Eric Geddes (1875–1937) has been used in the same way. He was chairman of the 1922 Geddes Committee which advocated drastic cuts in public expenditure, including pay cuts for those employed in the public sector, which became known as **Geddes Axe**.

BEETLE see STALKY AND CO

BEETON, MRS [*History, Popular Culture*]
Victorian domestic-science writer Mrs Isabella Beeton published her *Book of Household Management* in 1861. As it contained 4000 recipes, it is often known as 'Mrs Beeton's Cookbook', and Mrs Beeton's name has come to mean any efficient housekeeper or cook.

BEHEMOTH [*Religion*]
Behemoth occurs in the Bible (Job 40) as the name of a great beast. It is used in relation to anything exceptionally large.

BELCH, SIR TOBY see MALVOLIO

BELLAMY FAMILY see HUDSON

BELSHAZZAR'S FEAST see DANIEL

BEN HUR [*Literature, Film*]
A novel by Lew Wallace, published in 1880, but the story is better known as a film. Ben Hur is a Jew who suffers under the Roman occupation of Palestine, is betrayed by his best friend the Roman **Messala**, and is converted to Christianity after the miraculous curing of his family's leprosy. The 1959 film version, starring Charlton Heston, was a great spectacular, and at four million dollars cost twice as much as any film ever made before it. It features a famous chariot race, during the filming of which one man and numerous horses were killed. The 1925 silent film of the story is also famous for its chariot race. (While Governor of New Mexico, Wallace once issued a pardon for BILLY THE KID.)

BENEDICK see BEATRICE AND BENEDICK

BENNY see CROSSROADS

BEOWULF see GRENDEL

BERGMAN, INGMAR [*Film*]
A Swedish film director famous for his dark films – slow-moving, depressing, claustrophobic, psychological and mystic. Despite this reputation, he has also made a good number of comedies.

BERLIN WALL [*History*]
A wall which appeared around West Berlin on the night of 12–13 August 1961, cutting this isolated enclave of western democracy off from Communist East Germany in which it stood. It came to represent the divide between East and West during the Cold War.

At first built of breeze-block and barbed wire, it soon became an all-but-impenetrable, booby-trapped, concrete barrier. Its purpose was to prevent East Germans fleeing to the West but 191 East Germans were killed trying to cross it. The opening of the gates in the wall in November 1989 after the end of Communist rule in East Germany, and its later dismantling, were emotional events and scenes of great rejoicing, as well as a tangible expression of the liberation of the East. See also CHECKPOINT CHARLIE.

BERMUDA TRIANGLE [*Modern Mythology*]
An area of sea between the USA and Bermuda which has a reputation as being the scene of the mysterious disappearance of ships and planes; hence, a place where things get lost, as in 'The classroom is the Bermuda Triangle of careers' (*Evening Standard* 12.6.96).

BETAMAX [*Popular Culture, Technology*]
A commercially unsuccessful system for operating video cassette recorders. In the 1970s there were two different systems, VHS and Betamax. Since tapes recorded on one system could not be used for the other, it was almost inevitable that one would be superseded. Although in some ways superior to VHS, it was Betamax which lost the commercial battle, and the term is now used for a failed system or alternative that did not work out.

BFG see SNOZCUMBERS

BICKLE, TRAVIS [*Film*]
A character from the 1976 film *Taxi Driver*, Travis Bickle is a disturbed and inarticulate Vietnam War veteran ('between Charles Manson and St Paul', according to director Martin Scorcese) who becomes a national hero by slaughtering assorted low-lifes. His best-known line is: 'Some day a real rain will come and wash this scum off the streets'.

BIG BAD WOLF [*Folklore*]
The Big Bad Wolf from the children's story of *The Three Little Pigs* has come to be used to represent any kind of threat. The use had been reinforced by the memorable use of his traditional words, 'Little pig, little pig, let me come in', in the 1980 film *The Shining*.

Big Bad Wolf has also long been used as an emphatic version of 'wolf' for a man who chases women.

BIG BANG [*Astrophysics*]
The theory that the universe began as the result of the cataclysmic explosion of a small, superdense mass. It was born of the observation that the universe is expanding today. Used allusively, a Big Bang is a spectacular or explosive beginning.

BIG BIRD see MUPPETS

BIG BROTHER [*Literature*]
In George Orwell's 1948 novel *1984*, Big Brother is the dictator who controls every aspect of life. His picture is everywhere, along with the slogan 'Big Brother is Watching You'. Big Brother is used of any domineering or over-protective organization, or of circumstances where people cannot act without being watched.

BIG EARS see NODDY AND BIG EARS

BIGGLES [*Children's Literature*]
James Bigglesworth, DSO, DFC, MC – Biggles to his friends – is a fictional air ace whose thrilling adventures, with his pals **Algy** (The Hon Algy Lacy) and **Ginger** (Hebblethwaithe, a former lower-class tearaway, rescued from a life of crime by Biggles' influence and friendship), first appeared in short stories in the 1930s, and then in nearly 100 books of boy's adventures until the death of his creator, Captain W. E. Johns, in 1968. Biggles fought in both world wars, and in between solved many crimes. His name is associated with stiff-upper-lip, gung-ho, handle-bar moustached RAF heroism and derring-do.

BILL AND BEN [*Television*]
The Flowerpot Men was an enormously successful children's TV puppet series of the 1950s and 60s. Bill and Ben were two characters made of flowerpots who played in the garden while the gardener was away. Their friend **Little Weed** (a tall, skinny, sunflower- like plant) warned them to retreat into their flowerpot homes whenever a human was about. They talked in a distinctive,

'flub a dub' nonsense language which their creator said was based on the noises her little brothers made farting in the bath.

BILLY THE KID [*History*]
William H. Bonney Jr, known as Billy the Kid, was one of the most notorious American outlaws of his time. He is said to have killed at least 27 men by the time he was gunned down in 1881. He was then only about 21. He was literally a legend in his own short lifetime, as various popular tales of his life and deeds had already been published. Nowadays Billy the Kid tends simply to be used as a term for anyone who is rather young for what they are doing. See also BEN HUR.

BIONIC WOMAN [*Television, Technology*]
The 1970s TV series *The Six Million Dollar Man* told of the adventures of **Steve Austin**, a US astronaut who was rebuilt (at a cost of six million dollars) with artificial cybernetic parts after a horrendous crash. He then used his superhuman skills working for the secret service. His girlfriend also had an accident, while skydiving, and was rebuilt as the Bionic Woman, and later got her own series. The term bionic woman caught on, and sometimes changes sex as in 'We risk ending up with "lean machine" radio that is a bit like the bionic man: rather heartless' (*Guardian* 17.7.96).

BISMARCK [*History*]
The foremost German politician of the late-19th century, Otto von Bismarck (1815–1898) became prime minister of Prussia in 1862 and turned a comparatively minor power into a major force in European politics. He made the various German kingdoms into a unified country and was chancellor of the German Empire for 19 years. His nickname of **The Iron Chancellor** became the model for various other political nicknames, such as **The Iron Lady** for Margaret Thatcher. When he was unceremoniously ousted from office in 1890, *Punch* magazine ran a cartoon with the title *Dropping the Pilot*; this phrase entered the language and is still occasionally used.

Bismarck's name was given to a Second World War German battleship which, it was claimed, was unsinkable. In May 1941 it sank HMS *Hood*, the pride of the British fleet, and almost all other naval action was called off as the British navy concentrated its forces to destroy the *Bismarck*. After a chase of some 1750 miles around the Atlantic the Bismarck was finally destroyed. In 1960 a film, ***Sink the Bismarck***, was made based on these events, and which is itself alluded to, as in the report of a new beer called Bismarck Hock, which 'needs to be sunk often' (*Independent* 2.2.94).

BLACK AND TANS [*History*]
This was the name popularly given to an irregular police force used by the British against the Nationalist forces fighting in the Irish War of Independence of 1920–21. Many of them were former First World War soldiers, and since there was a shortage of the dark green, almost black, police uniforms, many were dressed in a mixture of their old khakis and the black uniform – hence their nickname, which was taken from a term describing the colouring of a famous pack of hunting hounds from Munster. They became notorious for the savagery of their reprisals on the civilian population after attacks by the IRA, and were ultimately withdrawn in 1921.

BLACK DEATH [*History*]
The name given to the recurrent waves of bubonic plague that swept Europe in the 14th century, killing about one third of its total population. It has become symbolic of any uncontrollable epidemic.

BLACK HOLE [*Astrophysics*]
In theory, according to some astrophysicists, a burnt-out star should collapse in on itself, creating a gravitational pull so great that not even light could escape. This is a black hole. Not surprisingly, the term has become widely used for any place where things get lost, especially if irretrievably.

BLACK HOLE OF CALCUTTA [*History*]
In 1756 the Nawab of Bengal is said to have thrown over 100 British soldiers into prison overnight in a cell only 18 ft by 15 ft. Only about 25 men survived, and there was an enormous scandal once the news reached Britain. The term is now used for any cramped place.

BLACK PANTHERS [*History*]
The Black Panthers were a Marxist Black American Party founded
in California by Huey Newton and Bobby Seale in 1966. The party
advocated violent revolution and the arming of blacks and there
were a number of gunfights between party members and the
police, some caused by aggressive police behaviour. The Black
Panthers effectively died out in the early 1980s, but their name
lives as an example of this type of 60s and 70s revolutionary
behaviour: 'A panther-like revolutionary ... who'd rather shoot a
cop than get rich quick' (*Guardian* 31.8.96).

BLACK SPOT, TO TIP THE [*Literature*]
In R. L. Stevenson's *Treasure Island* (1883) the Black Spot was a
piece of paper bearing a black disc and sometimes a message. Any
man who was 'tipped the black spot' was warned that his life was
forfeit to the pirates. See also BLIND PEW and LONG JOHN SILVER.

BLACKADDER [*Television*]
Blackadder was a set of four TV comedy series (1983–89) which
showed the adventures in various incarnations of the nefarious
Edmund Blackadder at times ranging from the Middle Ages to
World War I. Other characters also appear in each era. The most
popular of these was Blackadder's dumb but willing servant
Baldrick, with his catch phrase of 'I have a cunning plan'.

BLACKBEARD see HANDS, ISRAEL

BLADE RUNNER [*Film*]
The nightmare future world convincingly shown in this 1982 cult
film (loosely based on Philip K. Dick's novel, *Do Androids Dream
of Electronic Sheep*), has become a shorthand term for any bleak
modern landscape: 'To reach the car park in the futuristic, Blade-
Runner-meets-Neasden complex that is CANARY WHARF, you have
to negotiate a long raised walkway over a patch of wasteland'
(*Independent* 2.12.95).

BLAISE, MODESTY [*Popular Culture*]
First created for the *Evening Standard* in 1963, Peter O'Donnell's
strip cartoon is now syndicated around the world. A retired gang-

ster who abhors unnecessary cruelty and drug dealing, Modesty Blaise is resourceful, a genius at unarmed combat and a master of deception. She knows how to enjoy leisure and life's good things, and her character is reflected in the trust and loyalty of her friends, especially **Willie Garvin**, a cockney ex-tough, now her loyal lieutenant with whom she has a deep but platonic relationship.

BLAKE, SEXTON [*Literature*]

The tough detective Sexton Blake has been appearing in print since 1883. Over the years more than 200 writers have had a hand in writing his adventures, many of them glad of the anonymity when they later made their names as distinguished authors. The name was so well known that it even made its way into rhyming slang for 'a fake'. Compare NICK CARTER.

BLAKENEY, SIR PERCY see SCARLET PIMPERNEL

BLAVATSKY, MADAM [*Mysticism*]

Madam Blavatsky (1831–91) was an enormously influential medium and one of the founders of the Theosophical Society. Her claim to have been instructed in mystic wisdom in India and Tibet has been very influential on both the modern Western interest in eastern philosophy and religion and on the development of fictional mystic realms such as SHANGRI-LA. The London Society for Psychical research declared her a fraud in 1885.

BLIGH, CAPTAIN WILLIAM see THE BOUNTY

BLIMP, COLONEL [*Popular Culture, Film*]

The original Colonel Blimp was the creation of the cartoonist David Lowe. He was fat and pompous, the ultimate reactionary for whom the younger generation could do no right. This clear and simple image was somewhat confused by the 1943 film *The Life and Death of Colonel Blimp* which is a sympathetic picture of the confused emotional life bubbling under the surface of a conventional military man.

BLOFELD, ERNST [*Film*]

Blofeld is the cat-loving arch-enemy of JAMES BOND.

BLONDIN [*Popular Culture*]
Charles Blondin (1824–1897) was a tightrope walker, famous for his act of crossing the Niagara Falls on a tightrope. He did this on several occasions, once blindfold and once pushing a wheelbarrow.

BLONDINI BROTHERS see BRISTOW

BLOODNOCK, MAJOR see GOONS

BLOODY ASSIZES [*History*]
In 1685 the Duke of Monmouth, illegitimate son of Charles II rebelled against his uncle, James II. His main following was in the West Country, and the trials held there by **Judge Jeffreys** after it was put down, while technically legal, were scandalous for the severity of the sentences. About 320 people were condemned to hang, over 800 transported to Barbados and hundreds more flogged.

BLOOM, MOLLY [*Literature*]
Molly Bloom is the wife of **Leopold Bloom** around whose day James Joyce's 1922 novel *Ulysses* revolves. Molly spends much of the book in bed with her lover, and is best known for her interior monologue at the end of the book where she muses on life in general, her sexuality and her feelings for her lover and her husband.

BLUE ANGEL [*Film*]
A highly influential film made in Germany in 1930 which made Marlene Dietrich an international star. She plays a shoddy night-club singer with whom a staid older professor falls in love. She despises him and humiliates him, but his love is grotesquely steadfast despite her evident inferiority to him. She enjoys her power over him and agrees to marry him, only to have him die of what seems to be a broken heart – although the film would not admit to anything so mawkish. The film is visually very powerful.

BLUEBEARD see GILLES DE RAIS

BLUEBOTTLE see GOONS

BLYTON, ENID [*Children's Literature*]
Enid Blyton (1897–1968) was a highly successful and prolific children's writer with over 600 books to her credit. As the creator of NODDY AND BIG EARS she gained a reputation for saccharine writing, as creator of the FAMOUS FIVE for stereotyping and representing mid-century, middle-class values. She has always been more popular with children than with parents and teachers. 'I longed for those simplistic Enid Blyton days, when all baddies had regulation cruel, thin lips and a single unbroken eyebrow' (*Evening Standard* 6.6.96).

BOBBIT, LORENA [*Popular Culture*]
Lorena Bobbit gained notoriety when, after a violent argument, she cut off her husband's penis. John Wayne Bobbit was rushed to hospital where surgeons successfully re-attached the severed member. She has become an symbol of a woman who will not be pushed too far, he has become a performer in pornographic films.

BOCCACCIO [*Literature*]
Giovanni Boccaccio (1348–75) was one of the great scholars of the Italian Renaissance, writing extensively in Latin and Italian. Unfortunately for him, he is best known for the collection of stories known as *The Decameron*. These cover a wide range of subjects, but since a small proportion of them deal with sexual adventures, Boccaccio's name has become identified with smut.

BOGART, HUMPHREY [*Film*]
Humphrey Bogart (1899–1957) was for a generation the symbol of dark, brooding manhood. At first cast as a gangster, he later moved on to playing the hero. He was always the romantic loner, a cynical tough guy, but deep down with a soft heart. He was probably the best cinema PHILIP MARLOWE and superb as Rick in CASABLANCA. Typical photographs of him show him in raincoat, homburg hat pulled down low, and always a cigarette.

BOLT, BEN [*Literature*]
Ben Bolt is the 'soldier bold' in Thomas Hood's comic but pointed poem, *Faithless Nelly Gray* (1826). Ben is crippled in action: 'A cannon-ball took off his legs, so he laid down his arms'; rejected by

his beloved, and when he dies 'They went and told the sexton, and the sexton tolled the bell'.

BOND, JAMES [Film, Literature]

Secret Agent Commander James Bond must be the most famous spy in the world. His code number, **007**, indicates by its first two digits that he is licensed to kill. He likes his martinis dry, shaken not stirred; his cars fast, his women many and nubile and his gadgets complicated. The original Ian Fleming books in which he appears have dated – not surprisingly as the first, *Casino Royale*, appeared in 1953 – but since Fleming's death Bond's adventures have been carried on in more modern hands, and his real life has been in his many film incarnations. Fleming's Bond was very much a product of the Cold War, with his main enemy being **SMERSH**, the Russian international terrorist organisation, with agents such as ROSA KREB, and backers such as **Auric Goldfinger**, but he also combated such super-villains as ERNST BLOFELD. His boss is **M**, ably served by the attractive super-secretary **Miss Moneypenny**.

BONNIE AND CLYDE [Crime, History, Film]

Bonnie Parker (1911–34) and Clyde Barrow (1900–34) were small-time bank robbers whose exploits between 1932 and 1934 when they were shot down in a police ambush, caught the attention of the US press. Much of their fame rests on the 1967 film romanticising their lives which 'busted the straitjacket of screen morality by showing that sex and violence could also be *fun*' (*Evening Standard* 19.12.91).

BOO BOO see YOGI BEAR

BOONE, DANIEL [History]

Boone (1734–1820) was an American frontiersman whose explorations in Virginia and Kentucky prepared the way for the first westward wave of settlers. In many ways a real-life HAWKEYE, his name is used to indicate a skilled woodsman. Compare DAVY CROCKETT.

BOOP, BETTY [Popular Culture]

The first cartoon character to have to deal with sexual harassment, and the first to be censored. She first appeared in 1930, but in appearance was essentially a '20s flapper with short curly hair, a short black strapless dress which showed one garter and a cutie-pie voice. Her figure was somewhat odd, with an outsized head with huge eyes, no neck and a tiny torso but voluptuous hips. In *Who Framed Roger Rabbit* (1988) she says 'I'm not bad, I'm just drawn that way'.

BOP see BOY'S OWN

BORDEN, LIZZIE [*History*]
In 1893 Lizzie Borden was cleared of charges of murdering both her father and step-mother the year before at Fall River, Massachusetts; but that did not stop her name being evermore associated with the anonymous rhyme 'Lizzie Borden took an axe / And gave her mother forty whacks; / When she saw what she had done / She gave her father forty-one'.

BORGIA, CESARE AND LUCREZIA [*History*]
Cesare (1476–1507) and Lucrezia (1480–1519) Borgia were the children of the ruthless Pope Alexander VI, who used them to further his ambitions. Cesare, who was made a cardinal at 17, was an unpleasant character. An effective but treacherous general, he arranged the murder of his sister's third husband. The case against Lucrezia is less clear. She was married off at 12 years of age and then again at 13, both marriages being annulled by her father. She was also accused of incest with both her brother and father. Like all the Borgias Cesare and Lucrezia were great patrons of the arts. Popular culture sees them as enthusiastic poisoners, hence such witticisms as Max Beerbohm's 'Though you would often in the 15th century have heard the snobbish Roman say, in a would-be off-hand tone, "I am dining with the Borgias tonight," no Roman ever was able to say, "I dined last night with the Borgias." '

BORROWERS, THE
The Borrowers are a race of tiny humans who live by scavenging (or as they call it, 'borrowing') from the normal-size humans, in a series of novels by Mary Norton which centre on the adventures of three Borrowers: Pod, Homily, and their daughter Arrietty. It is the activities of Borrowers that explains the disappearance of all

those little things around the house.

BOSCH, HIERONYMUS [Art]
Hieronymus Bosch (1460–1516) was a Low Countries painter, famous for his exquisitely detailed, nightmarish, surrealistic visions showing sin and corruption. He produced some well-known paintings of the punishments of Hell, while his best-known work is *The Garden of Earthly Delights*.
BOSEY see OSCAR WILDE

BOTT, VIOLET ELIZABETH [Children's Literature]
Ghastly spoilt brat in Richmal Crompton's *William* books (see WILLIAM BROWN). On the surface she is all sugar and spice but underneath she is highly manipulative, her ultimate threat being 'I'll thcream and thcream and thcream till I'm thick.'

BOUNTIFUL, LADY [Drama]
The character of Lady Bountiful appeared in the 1707 play *The Beaux Stratagem* by George Farquhar, and has entered the language for an ostentatiously charitable woman; 'You could say it was a nice gesture but it was over the top, like everything she does. She has to be Lady Bountiful.' (*Sun* 1.4.96).

BOUNTY, THE [History, Film]
In 1787 as HMS *Bounty*, captained by **William Bligh**, was on a voyage of scientific discovery in the Pacific, 25 seamen and petty officers, led by **Fletcher Christian**, mutinied. They claimed to have been incensed by Bligh's tyranny and insults, but were probably influenced by their long stay amid the pleasures of Tahiti. They cast Bligh and 18 men adrift in a small boat. The mutineers, with some Tahitians, then founded a colony on Pitcairn Island, where they fell out with each other and many were killed. Bligh, with no map and few provisions, managed to bring his boat and men to land 3618 miles away in Timor, an incredible feat of seamanship. Bligh experienced several more mutinies during his career, but nevertheless ended up Governor of New South Wales and an admiral. The image of these events has been greatly influenced by the two film versions of *The Mutiny on the Bounty* (1935 and 1962).

BOURBONS [*History*]
A large royal family, whose branches ruled at one time in many European kingdoms. References to the Bourbons usually mean the French royal family restored to the throne after the French Revolution, and the saying that they had learned nothing and forgotten nothing from their experiences – although this was in fact originally said of their courtiers.

BOY WONDER see BATMAN

BOY'S OWN [*Popular Culture*]
The Boy's Own Paper (1879–1912), also known as The **BOP**, was one of the first children's magazines to achieve mass popularity. Like the later **Magnet**, in which BILLY BUNTER first appeared, it told tales of high and highly unlikely adventure as experienced by stoutly middle-class schoolboys.

BRACKNELL, LADY [*Drama, Film*]
The character of Lady Bracknell is the terrifyingly intimidating aunt in OSCAR WILDE's comedy of manners, *The Importance of Being Earnest* (1895). She is famous for the lines 'To lose one parent, Mr Worthington, may be regarded as a misfortune ... to lose both looks like carelessness' and, after Charles Worthington has explained how he was a foundling and was discovered in a handbag, for her repeating '**A handbag**' – particularly in the utterly crushing way delivered by Edith Evans in the 1952 film of the play.

BRANESTAWM, PROFESSOR [*Children's Literature*]
Professor Branestawm is the crack-pot inventor in a series of children's books by Norman Hunter.

BRAVE NEW WORLD [*Literature*]
In William Shakespeare's *The Tempest*, the beautiful and innocent **Miranda**, brought up on an island with only her father PROSPERO for human company, exclaims 'O brave new world that has such people in it' when she sees the men who have been shipwrecked on the island. The irony of this wonder is seen by the audience, for they know that these are the very men who exiled Prospero to the island after he neglected his duty as Duke of Milan in favour of the study of magic. In 1932 this irony was extended even further

by Aldous Huxley in his novel *Brave New World*, which shows a distopia of the future where humans are mechanically produced, pre-programmed to a given level of ability, and manipulated throughout their ordered lives.

BRAY, VICAR OF [*Popular culture*]
In the 18th-century anonymous rhyme *The Vicar of Bray*, the vicar changes his politics and beliefs every time there is a change of official attitude, so that at all costs he does not lose his job. Thus a Vicar of Bray is a turncoat.

BRECHT, BERTOLT [*Literature*]
Bertolt Brecht (1898–1956) was a German playwright who worked part of his life in the USA. He had a distinctive dramatic style, developed through what he called his 'alienation effect'. He rejected realism, and his plays lack a simple narrative, but are more scenes from a life, using highly stylised acting, music-hall techniques and with a strong Marxist message.

BRECK, ALAN [*Literature*]
Alan Breck appears as a character in R. L. Stevenson's adventure novels *Kidnapped* (1886) and *Catriona* (1893), set in 18th-century Scotland. He is a Highland Jacobite rebel who befriends the highly conventional Lowlander **David Balfour** and rescues him when he is kidnapped by his wicked uncle. Breck is almost childishly vain and touchy and has a murky past, but he saves Balfour's life, and is a great man of action, cunning, astute, and skilled in the ways of the outlaw.

BRER FOX, BRER RABBIT see UNCLE REMUS

BRIDESHEAD [*Literature, Television*]
Evelyn Waugh's novel *Brideshead Revisited* (1945) was made into an internationally successful TV serial in 1981. The nostalgic evocation of the world of country houses and 1920s Oxford undergraduate japes so well created in this series that it is usually what is meant by the term Brideshead. Viewers, like so many readers and the story's narrator **Charles Ryder**, have been captivated by the charming but alcoholic **Sebastian Flyte** with his teddy bear

Aloysius, and usually miss the moral of what is actually a dark tale of the problems of Roman Catholicism. This aspect does occasionally surface, as in 'He is of the flighty Catholic reactionary generation of what I call "Brideshead Regurgitated".' (*Independent* 15.4.96).

BRIDGES, MRS see HUDSON

BRIEF ENCOUNTER [*Film*]

The 1945 film *Brief Encounter* was the tear-jerker of a generation. A superbly acted piece, it tells the story of an ordinary housewife who falls in love with the local doctor, but in a welter of stiff-upper-lipped passion they decide to do the decent thing and put their commitments before their love, despite the personal pain they feel. Significant portions of the action take place in grim railway stations, and these atmospheric scenes are often alluded to, as in 'Café Rouge-type High Street eateries that are replacing those moribund and depressing Brief Encounter-style tea shops' (*Sunday Times* 18.8.96).

BRING DOWN THE WRATH OF THE GODS see NIOBE

BRISTOW [*Popular Culture*]

Strip cartoon by Frank Dickens chronicling life at his firm **Chester-Perry's** and the small acts of rebellion against office life of Bristow, a buying clerk who otherwise spends his time avoiding work and calculating his place in line for the job of chief buyer. He is constantly in conflict with **Mr Fudge**, the chief buyer, and regularly featured are the **Blondini Brothers** (scaffolding to the gentry); a large pigeon that Bristow feeds on the office windowsill; and allusions to the **Great Tea-Trolly Disaster**, although one is never told what happened on this momentous occasion.

BROBDINGNAGIAN [*Literature*]

In Jonathan Swift's satire *Gulliver's Travels* (1726) **Lemuel Gulliver's** second set of adventures take place in **Brobdingnag**, where the inhabitants are as tall as steeples. Brobdingnagian therefore means gigantic. See also LILLIPUT, YAHOO.

BRODIE, MISS JEAN [*Literature*]

Muriel Spark's 1961 novel *The Prime of Miss Jean Brodie* tells the tale of an Edinburgh spinster school-teacher and her favourite six students in the 1930s. Although in her way a dedicated teacher, Miss Brodie admires fascism, and her political leanings are reflected in the way in which she thinks the rules do not apply to her and her chosen girls, whom she calls 'the **crème de la crème**'.

BRONOWSKI, JACOB [*Biology, Television*]

Jacob Bronowski (1902–1974) was a distinguished biologist who became an unlikely popular figure after his 1973 TV series *The Ascent of Man*. His evident enthusiasm and wide learning won him a much wider audience than might have been expected for the series and he became a symbol of learning.

BROOKSIDE [*Television*]

Long-running (1982–) TV soap opera set in Merseyside. The series broke new ground when a real Brookside Close in a real housing estate was bought to act as a set. Originally noted for its grim realism, the series has become increasingly sensational.

BROWN, CAPABILITY [*Horticulture*]

The landscape gardener Lancelot Brown (1715–83) earned the nickname 'Capability' because of his habit of talking about the 'capabilities' of a particular scene. He was notorious for being prepared to mould the landscape on a large scale, moving hills and creating vast lakes if necessary. One wit once remarked that he hoped he got to heaven before Brown had had a chance to improve it.

BROWN, FATHER [*Literature*]

Father Brown is a Catholic priest in a series of detective short stories by G. K. Chesterton, published in book form between 1911 and 1935. Father Brown seems a harmless, meek and innocent little priest, but in reality his work has left him with a deep and unshockable understanding of the dark side of human nature, which combines with a keen intelligence and sharp observation to allow him to understand the workings of the criminal mind. He had a special understanding of the flamboyant French master-thief **Flambeau**.

BROWN, JOHN see HARPER'S FERRY

BROWN, TOM see FLASHMAN

BROWN, WILLIAM [*Children's Literature*]
William Brown is the grubby schoolboy in Richmal Crompton's series of William books, the first of which *Just William* was published in 1922. William comes from a respectable middle-class background and lives in an idyllic country setting in which he and his friends – **Ginger**, Henry and Douglas, collectively known as the **Outlaws** – bring comic chaos, either through misunderstanding the adult world or through an imaginative determination to see and make the world as it ought to be rather than as it is. See also VIOLET ELIZABETH BOTT.

BRUCE, ROBERT [*History*]
Robert Bruce or Robert the Bruce (1274–1329), King of Scots, freed his country from English overlordship through a long and successful guerrilla war. There is a legend that at one time, with his fortunes at low ebb, he was in hiding in a cave and near giving up. He sat watching a spider trying to fix its web to the cave roof. It failed six times, but succeeded on the seventh attempt. Since Bruce himself had had six setbacks, he took this as an omen, and indeed his subsequent campaign led up the his great victory at Bannockburn (1314). Ever since, Bruce and his spider have become a symbol of the 'If at first you don't succeed ... ' maxim.

BRUTUS [*History*]
Marcus Junius Brutus (c. 78–42 BC) is the most famous of the conspirators who assassinated JULIUS CAESAR, and is described by his enemy, Mark Antony, in William Shakespeare's *Julius Caesar* as 'the noblest Roman of them all'. He seems to have been motivated by an idealistic attachment to republicanism. This may in part have been because one of his ancestors was supposed to have been **Lucius Junius Brutus**, who gained the nickname Brutus, 'stupid', by pretending to be dumb to escape death under the tyranny of TARQUIN, then led the rising against the Roman kings and became one of the first consuls in newly republican Rome.

There was a rumour at the time of Marcus Junius' birth that he was in fact Julius Caesar's son, Caesar having given his mother a remarkable pink pearl, in return, it was thought, for her favours; hence the added twist to Caesar's word's to Brutus when he was stabbed. These are usually given as 'Et tu, Brute?' ('You too, Brutus?'), but the earliest account has him speaking Greek to him, saying words that translate as 'You too, my child?' See also PORTIA.

BRYNNER, YUL [*Film*]
Despite a long and successful film career the actor Yul Brynner (1915–85) is best known for his trademark shaved head, and allusions to him usually refer to baldness.

BUBBLES [*Art*]
The title of a painting by the Pre-Rapaelite artist Sir John Millais (1829–96) which was bought by Pears' soap to use in its advertisements. Bubble shows a nauseatingly cute, blond, curly-haired, velvet-clad little boy using a bubble pipe to blow bubbles, and has become a term for a goody-goody; an alternative to ERIC or LITTLE LORD FAUNTLEROY. The poor five-year-old in the painting actually grew up to be Admiral Sir William James (1881–1973), inevitably known throughout his career as 'Bubbles James'.

BUCHAN, JOHN [*Literature*]
John Buchan (1875–1940), Scottish statesman and writer, is best remembered now for his adventure novels, particularly THE THIRTY-NINE STEPS (1915) and its hero RICHARD HANNAY. His fictional world is a very masculine one, with a regular cast of clubland heroes, takes place across a wide, international landscape although with a special place for his native Scotland, and is peopled with upright goodies and cunning spies.

BUCHANAN, DAISY see JAY GATSBY

BUCK, JOE see RATSO RIZZO

BUCKET, HYACINTH [*Television*]
Hyacinth Bucket – pronounced 'bouquet' – is the social-climbing suburban housewife in BBC TV's comedy *Keeping Up Appearances*.

She is quite ruthless in her drive for gentility, rejecting her own background as exemplified by the rest of her family which is always causing her acute embarrassment, and her social downfall is usually caused by this insensitivity and her own gaffes.

BUFFALO BILL [*History*]
Buffalo Bill Cody (1846–1917) got his nickname from the number of Buffalo – over 4000 in 18 months – he supplied as meat to railroad workers. He later became a showman, touring with a sort of circus recreating Indian attacks and life in the Wild West. Among his cast were the Sioux **Chief Sitting Bull** who had defeated General Custer (see CUSTER'S LAST STAND), and the sharpshooter ANNIE OAKLEY.

BUGGINS' TURN [*Popular Culture*]
Alas, there is no story behind this expression meaning promotion based only on seniority. No-one has yet come up with a reason why 'Buggins' is used rather than any other surname.

BUGS BUNNY see YOSEMITE SAM

BULGARIA, GREAT UNCLE see WOMBLES

BULL, JOHN [*Popular Culture*]
Supposed to represent the typical Englishman, John Bull is usually shown as a stout, florid man wearing a Union Jack waistcoat and accompanied by his British bulldog.

BULRUSHES see MOSES

BUMBLE, MR [*Literature*]
Mr Bumble is the cruel, hypocritical, inefficient and greedy beadle of the parish workhouse in Charles Dickens' OLIVER TWIST. It is he who refuses to give Oliver more gruel. His is best known for saying that 'the law is an ass'.

BUMPO, NATTY see HAWKEYE

BUNGO see WOMBLES

BUNKER, ARCHIE [*Television*]
Loud-mouthed bigot in the US TV comedy series *All in the Family* (1971–79), based on ALF GARNET and the British series *Till Death Do Us Part*.

BUNNY see RAFFLES

BUNTER, BILLY AND BESSIE [*Children's Literature*]
Billy Bunter is the **Fat Owl of the Remove** in Frank Richards' school stories written from 1908 onwards. Bunter is a pupil at **Greyfriars School** along with such other Richards creations as **Bob Cherry**, **Tom Merry** and **Harry Wharton**. They are fine upstanding example of British youth, unlike Bunter who as well as being fat and wearing glasses is greedy and devious, not above stealing another chap's food, always trying to borrow money until his postal order arrives and not in the least athletic. He is the butt of the other boys, frequently giving his distinctive cry of 'yaroooh!' as a result of their attentions. The only other comic character in this group is **Hurree Jamset Ram Singh**, Nabob of Bhanipur, who, while generally a good egg, does speak a comic, stereotyped form of Indian English. Bunter's nemesis is the dour schoolmaster MR QUELCH. **Bessie Bunter**, 'The Fatima of the Fourth' and Billy's sister, is his female equivalent in a separate set of stories.

BUNTER see LORD PETER WIMSEY

BUNTHORNE [*Music*]
Reginald Bunthorne is 'the Fleshly Poet ', the 'greenery-yallery … foot-in-the-grave young man' adored by all the women in Gilbert and Sullivan's 1881 operetta *Patience*. He is a parody of the aesthetes of the time, particularly OSCAR WILDE, and advises those who want to make a similar stir to 'walk down Piccadilly with a poppy or a lily in your medieval hand'.

BUNYAN, PAUL [*Folklore*]
Paul Bunyan is an American folk hero, a gigantic lumberjack of prodigious appetites and strength, to whom, for instance, the creation of the Grand Canyon is credited. Although a folk creation,

he was soon taken over by writers and publicity people.

BURKE AND HARE [*Crime, History*]
William Burke and William Hare were Edinburgh-based murderers in the early part of the 19th century. They started out as body snatchers, selling corpses to medical students for dissection, but when the supply of corpses dried up, moved on to creating their own, murdering at least 15 people. Burke was hanged in 1829 on Hare's evidence, and Hare is thought to have died in poverty in the 1860s.

BURNING BUSH see MOSES
BURNS, WALTER see HILDY JOHNSON

BURROUGHS, EDGAR RICE see BARSOOM, TARZAN

BUTLER, RHETT see SCARLETT O'HARA

BYZANTINE [*History*]
The highly formal and ritualised court life of the emperors at Byzantium, those bejewelled and in many ways decadent heirs of the Roman emperors who based their court in what is now Istanbul, has given us the term 'Byzantine' meaning inflexible or complicated.

C-3PO see LUKE SKYWALKER

C. J. see REGINALD PERRIN

CADMUS see DRAGON'S TEETH

CAESAR, JULIUS [*History*]
Before Julius Caesar crossed the RUBICON to seize power in Rome, he was governor of Gaul. During his time there he had gained power and prestige, as well as wealth, by conquering vast areas of the country that had previously been independent. Since he had no remit to do this, he wanted to make sure that his version of events was the one that got home, and so wrote his famous account of the Gallic Wars. This opens with the words 'Gaul as a whole is divided into three parts', and this has become proverbial, especially in forms such as 'divided into three parts, like Caesar's Gaul'. On another occasion a notorious young aristocrat called **Clodius** had scandalised Rome by attending a religious ceremony at Caesar's house which was for women only. He had been disguised as a woman, and Caesar accepted that his wife had known nothing about it, but nevertheless divorced her on the grounds that 'Caesar's wife must be above suspicion'.

CAIN AND ABEL [*Religion*]
Cain and Abel were the sons of Adam and Eve. The brothers quarrelled and Cain murdered Abel and hid the body. God forbade anyone to punish Cain, but instead put a mark upon him so that all might know who he was. Thus 'the mark of Cain' has come to mean anything that makes one an outcast in society.

CAIRO, JOE see MALTESE FALCON

CALAMITY JANE [*History*]
Although she has appeared so often in fiction that it is easy to imagine that Calamity Jane never existed, this was the nickname of Martha Hane Burke (c. 1852–1903) of Deadwood, South Dakota. She worked as a teamster supplying the mining camps, was an unusually accurate shot and is said to have cradled the dying WILD BILL HICKOK in her arms and vowed revenge. It was also said that although there was both good and bad in her she was as brave as a bull, tough as a harlot and that she never stole, or killed anyone.

CALCULUS, PROFESSOR [*Literature, Popular Culture*]
In the TIN-TIN books, Professor Calculus is the deaf, absent-minded scientist and inventor with a shock of white hair.

CALDWELL, MINNIE see ENA SHARPLES

CALIBAN [*Drama*]
In Shakespeare's *The Tempest* Caliban represents the darkest side of human nature. Misshapen and violent, he is more animal that human and incapable of finer feelings. When **Miranda** (see BRAVE NEW WORLD) teaches him to speak, the only good of it he can see is that he can now curse, and he repays her care by trying to rape her. He is the easy dupe of the less scrupulous characters in the play. His opposite is the spirit **Ariel**, who has no physical substance, and becomes PROSPERO'S servant in gratitude for having been released from imprisonment by him.

CALIGULA [*History*]
Caligula was Emperor of Rome from 31 AD until he was assassinated in 41 AD. Cruel and generally considered mad, he enjoyed seeing how far absolute power could be pushed. He is best known for his plans to make his favourite horse, **Incitatus**, a consul.

CALLAHAN, HARRY see DIRTY HARRY

CALLIOPE see MUSES

CALVARY [*Religion*]
Calvary is the name of the 'green hill far away' just outside the

walls of Jerusalem where Christ was crucified, hence it is used to mean an experience involving great suffering. Calvary is based on the Latin translation of the local Aramaic name **Golgotha**, both meaning 'place of the skull'.

CAMELOT [*Mythology, History, Business*]
Camelot is traditionally the name of the capital city of KING ARTHUR. It was also the name given to a musical based on the Arthurian stories which was a great hit in the early 60s, at the time of John F. Kennedy's presidency of the USA. Hence Camelot came to be used of the glittering 'court' which surrounded the Kennedys. It is now also the name of the company running the British National Lottery and renowned for the profits it makes in the process, but it is rather early to see if this is going to affect the use of the word.

CAMERON, DR see DR FINLAY

CAMLAN see AVALON

CAMPION, ALBERT [*Literature*]
Albert Campion is the rather effete-seeming but astute upper-class detective hero of a series of novels by Margery Allingham.

CANAAN [*Religion*]
Canaan is the PROMISED LAND of the Bible, so can be used for any ideal goal.

CANARY WHARF [*Architecture*]
The Canary Wharf Tower in London's Dockland is a vast, pyramid-topped office block which dominates the skyline and which has rapidly come to be used as a touchstone for size, as in 'She accepted a slab of cake they could have used for the cornerstone of Canary Wharf' (Martha Grimes *Rainbow's End* 1995).

CANDIDE [*Literature*]
In Voltaire's novel (1759) Candide is the young man whose essential innocence is no protection against his experiencing the basic evils of mankind. His tutor is Dr PANGLOSS.

CANUTE [*History*]
King Canute (c. 995–1035), King of England from 1016, and later king of Denmark and Norway, has had an undeservedly bad press. The story of his taking the court down to the sea, and his commanding the waves to go back is not an example of his own vainglory as is so often assumed, but was meant to be a lesson to his courtiers not to flatter him so much. Some of them had said that he was so great that he could even rule the waves, so he proved that he could not, to put them to shame.

CAPED CRUSADER see BATMAN

CAPONE, AL [*Crime, History*]
Al Capone (1898–1947) was the prominent Chicago gangster in the Prohibition period, and responsible for the infamous **St Valentine's Day Massacre** when seven members of a rival gang were gunned down in a garage. His character has been worked into many films, so that he is now used as the type of the tough gangster. See also ELIOT NESS.

CAPP, ANDY AND FLO [*Popular Culture*]
Andy Capp is the lazy, boozing, flat-capped layabout in Reg Smyth's long-running strip cartoon. His wife Flo alternates between waiting on him hand and foot while he lies on the sofa, and going for him hammer and tongs.

CAPRICORN see HORN OF PLENTY

CAPULETS AND MONTAGUES see ROMEO AND JULIET

CARDASSIANS see KLINGONS

CAREY STREET [*Finance, History*]
Carey Street used to be the address of the London bankruptcy court, so 'to be in Carey Street' came to mean to be bankrupt or just plain broke.

CARRINGTON, ALEXIS [*Television*]
Alexis Carrington (later both Colby and Dexter) was the scheming

bitch in massively shoulder-padded designer clothes in the TV soap *Dynasty* (1982–89). Played by Joan Collins, Alexis was so awful that she went full circle and won the admiration of the viewing public, as well as becoming a byword for those out for revenge.

CARRY ON FILMS [*Film*]
Starting with *Carry On, Sergeant* in 1958, the Carry On films are a long series of highly successful, low-budget comedy films, made with the same group of actors. Never aspiring to intellectual heights, the films were often gems of the genre, had only the flimsiest of plots, and depended on slapstick, double entendre, bad puns, and audience recognition of the types played by the familiar and much-loved actors.

CARTER, JOHN see BARSOOM

CARTER, NICK [*Literature*]
American detective Nick Carter has been appearing in print since 1886, making him three years younger than his English equivalent SEXTON BLAKE. Originally a clean-living all-American boy, he has since the 1960s been revamped into a tough 'Killmaster'.

CARTLAND, BARBARA [*Literature*]
Dame Barbara Cartland (1901–) is famous for the vast quantity of romantic novels she has produced, and for her pronouncements on modern behaviour and in praise of food supplements. The term Cartland pink – for a strong, sugary shade of this colour – comes from her habitual wearing of it.

CASABLANCA [*Film*]
Rick's Café in corrupt, Nazi-dominated Casablanca is run by a disenchanted American (HUMPHREY BOGART, playing his usual tough guy with a soft centre). Here, desperate refugees fleeing war-torn Europe try to get visas for the USA. Among these are Rick's lost love **Ilse** and her Resistance-hero husband. Rick loses all to give them a chance of freedom. This 1942 film caught the imagination of film-goers at the time and has been hailed as a masterpiece ever since. The many catch phrases from the film

include 'Here's looking at you kid', 'This could be the beginning of a beautiful friendship' and 'Round up the usual suspects'.

CASANOVA [*History*]
Giovanni Jacopo Casanova de Seingalt (1725–98) was an adventurer, a spy and a librarian (and founder of the French Lottery). He owes his reputation as the world's greatest lover to his own account of his affairs, his *Memoirs*, the full text of which was felt to be unpublishable until the 1960s.

CASAUBON [*Literature*]
In George Eliot's 1871 novel *Middlemarch* the Reverend Edward Casaubon is an unemotional, dry-as-dust scholar, confident of his own intellectual and moral superiority. After his death it turns out that his life's work is useless, and he has come to represent pointless research which cuts itself off from human contact, as in 'What makes it so terrible is that it is frosty and passionless, so obviously the work of some nocturnal Casaubon proud of his common sense' (*Independent* 28.1.94).

CASPER [*Popular Culture, Film*]
Casper is the name of a cartoon-strip ghost, made into a cute children's film in 1995.

CASPIAN see NARNIA

CASSANDRA [*Mythology*]
Cassandra is a term used of anyone who prophesies doom, especially one who is not believed. In Greek myth Cassandra is a beautiful princess to whom the god APOLLO offers the gift of true prophesy if she will sleep with him. When she reneges on the deal he punishes her by decreeing that although she will tell the truth of what is to happen no one will believe her. See also CLYTEMNESTRA.

CAT see RED DWARF

CATCH-22 [*Literature*]
Joseph Heller's 1962 novel *Catch-22* is set in a USA airforce base in Italy during the Second World War. Its anti-hero **Yossarian**, a

bomber pilot, sees the high death rate of those around him, and determines he will survive at all costs. He asks to be taken off pilot duties on the grounds of insanity. It is then he runs up against Catch-22. He cannot be taken off active service without a medical certificate, but the mere asking for one shows that you are concerned for your own safety which was taken as proof of basic sanity. Thus a Catch-22 situation is one in which the other side always wins. Yossarian finds that he can only survive in a world run mad by developing an insane logic of his own.

CATFISH ROW [*Opera, History*]
In the second half of the 19th century 'Catfish Row' was the slang term for any settlement of poor, black Americans. The term was used for the place where George Gershwin's opera *Porgy and Bess* (1935) takes place, and most people know it from there.

CATHY see HEATHCLIFFE AND CATHY

CATULLUS see LESBIA

CATWEAZLE [*Television, Children's Literature*]
The TV series *Catweazle* (1970–71), later a book, told the story of a Saxon wizard transported into modern times and fascinated by the 'magic' of modern technology. Catweazle is a bedraggled, smelly, ragged character, something of a WORZEL GUMMIDGE figure, and allusions to him are usually to this aspect. 'One fan describes Voyage clothes as "casual to a Catweazle degree ... designed to be dragged on in any order and absolutely never ironed".' (*Evening Standard* 12.12.96).

CATWOMAN see BATMAN

CAULFIELD, HOLDEN [*Literature*]
Holden Caulfield is the hero of J. D. Salinger's 1951 novel *The Catcher in the Rye*. He is a 16-year-old misfit, the despair of the adults who want to control him, who questions every convention and rails against what he calls the 'phoniness' of society. He won the hearts of adolescent readers and, although much of what he says now seems the standard stuff of teenage angst, at the time he

was seen as a potent symbol of the youth rebellion which was just getting under way.

CEMETERY RIDGE see ADDAMS FAMILY

CERBERUS [*Mythology*]
In Classical mythology Cerberus was the triple-headed hound who guarded the gates of the underworld. If you wanted to get past him in one piece the best ploy was to come armed with honey-cakes which would calm him and keep his mouths too busy to tear you to bits. From this comes the expression 'a sop to Cerberus' for a bribe, or at least something to sweeten the opposition and keep it quiet.

CERES see PERSEPHONE

CHAMBERLAIN, NEVILLE see MUNICH

CHANDLER, RAYMOND see PHILIP MARLOWE

CHANEY, LON [*Film*]
Lon Chaney (1883–1930) was a film actor famous for his skill at make up, often for grotesque figures such as QUASIMODO in *The Hunchback of Notre Dame* and for *The Phantom of the Opera*. He was given the nickname 'The Man of a Thousand Faces'. His son, Lon Chaney Jr (1906–1973) continued in his father's tradition and starred in many horror films, so that 'Lon Chaney' has come to be used as an alternative to 'monster, horror'.

CHAPLIN, CHARLIE [*Film*]
Charlie Chaplin (1889–1977) is best known for his silent films in which he played a comic tramp with baggy trousers, a bowler hat, a cane, a black, bristly moustache and a distinctive walk. His films combined comedy with pathos, particularly where the 'little man' is concerned, and **'Chaplinesque'** is often used to mean this combination.

CHARLIE'S ANGELS [*Television*]
Successful American TV show (1977–1982) in which three ex-

policewomen worked for a detective agency run by Charlie, who never appeared in person, but was only heard. The series was chiefly notable for the looks and immaculate turn-out of the women and their often revealing costumes.

CHATEAU D'IF see MONTE CRISTO

CHATTERLEY, LADY [*Literature*]
In the novel *Lady Chatterley's Lover* by D. H. Lawrence, Constance Chatterley is unhappily married to the effete and wheelchair-bound Sir Clifford Chatterley, but finds fulfilment in the arms of the gamekeeper **Mellors**. The novel contains lyrical, and for the time, graphic descriptions of sex and for a long time only an expurgated version was available in Britain. When the full text was published in 1960 the publishers were prosecuted under the then Obscene Publications Act. **The Lady Chatterley Trial** caused a great stir. Many prominent writers acted as witnesses giving their view that the work was not obscene, while the prosecution showed how cut off from everyday life the Establishment had become by asking a bemused jury if they would want their wife or servants to read such a book. When the publishers were acquitted the re-print sold three and a half million copies, a message not lost on later publishers of sex-as-art books.

CHAUVELIN see SCARLET PIMPERNEL

CHECKPOINT CHARLIE [*History*]
Checkpoint Charlie was the most famous of the heavily guarded crossing points in the BERLIN WALL, where many well-publicised attempts to escape East Berlin took place. Those crossing here were thoroughly searched and questioned, and Checkpoint Charlie has come to be used for any difficult place or point to negotiate.

CHEE CHEE THE MONKEY see DR DOLITTLE

CHEETA see TARZAN

CHEEVY, MINIVER [*Literature*]
Miniver Cheevy is a character in a 1907 poem by the American

writer E. A. Robinson. Cheevy is an aesthete who laments the death of art and is so wrapped up in this that he misses out on everything worth doing. Finally, having wasted his life, he takes to drink.

CHERRY, BOB see BILLY BUNTER

CHESHIRE CAT [*Literature*]
The Cheshire Cat is one of the characters which appears in Lewis Carrol's ALICE IN WONDERLAND. It is a chatty animal, but its chief characteristic is its big smile which, when the animal fades away, is the last thing to go.

CHESTER-PERRY'S see BRISTOW

CHEWBACCA see HAN SOLO

CHICO see MARX BROTHERS

CHINGACHGOOK [*Literature*]
In James Fenimore Cooper's series of novels about American frontier life Chingachgook is the friend and companion of HAWKEYE, and, after the death of his son UNCAS, the last of the Mohican chiefs. He is very much the noble savage – brave, resourceful and knowledgeable about the ways of the wild, controlled in everything he does, and showing no emotion.

CHIPPENDALES [*Popular Culture*]
The Chippendales are a male dance and strip group that have become a byword for tawdry muscle-bound narcissism.

CHIPS, MR [*Literature*]
James Hilton's 1934 novel *Goodbye Mr Chips* tells the story of Arthur Chipping, a devoted schoolmaster. His life is quiet and dedicated, but not without its own tragedy and romance, and Mr Chips has come to represent the heroically ordinary doer of good, as well as the idealised teacher.

CHOLET, MADAM see WOMBLES

CHOLMONDELEY-WARNER, MR [*Television*]
Mr Cholmondeley-Warner (pronounced 'Chumley-Warner') was a character created by the comedian Harry Enfield for a series of advertisements for Mercury telephones. Cholmondeley-Warner was from the 1940s and had a very old-fashioned accent, and the name has stuck for an old-fashioned, Establishment type.

CHRISTIAN [*Literature*]
Christian is the name of the pilgrim who must travel through the trials and temptations of life to reach the heavenly city in John Bunyan's *The Pilgrim's Progress* (1678).

CHRISTIAN see DE BERGERAC

CHRISTIAN, FLETCHER see BOUNTY

CHRISTIE, AGATHA [*Literature*]
The name of the prolific crime novelist Dame Agatha Christie (1890–1976) has become attached to the whole genre of the-butler-did-it murder-in-a country-house genre of crime fiction. See also HERCULE POIROT.

CHRISTIE, LINFORD [*Sport*]
The runner Linford Christie's name has become synonymous with speed and a quick reaction as in 'Brian Sewell, the Linford Christie of outrage and indignation, was quick off the blocks' (*Independent* 20.5.96).

CHRISTOPHER ROBIN [*Literature*]
Christopher Robin is the little-boy owner of WINNIE THE POOH. He also appears in various poems by A. A. Milne including *They're Changing Guard at Buckingham Palace*. His image is closely associated with the delightful illustrations of E. H. Shepard.

CHRONOS see APHRODITE

CICERO [*Literature, Oratory*]
Marcus Tullius Cicero (104–43 BC) was a Roman career politician famous for his oratory. His surviving speeches, letters and writ-

ings are still regarded as models of a certain measured and polished **Ciceronian** style.

CID, EL [*History*]
Rodrigo Díaz de Vivar (1040–99), known as El Cid ('The Lord') was a Spanish mercenary soldier who hired out his services to both the Christians and the Moors. However, he died fighting on the victorious Christian side, and many romances grew up around his name as he became the Spanish national hero. It is said that, wounded to the death, he had his body strapped to his horse, and his dead body led his troops into action against the Moorish Infidel.

CINDERELLA [*Folklore*]
The story of Cinderella, the despised step-sister made to sweep and clean while the UGLY SISTERS live it up; whose fairy godmother decrees she shall go to the ball, transforms a pumpkin into a coach and dresses her beautifully, but warns her to be back by midnight before the magic wears off; who runs from the ball on the stroke of midnight leaving her glass slipper behind and is finally married to Prince Charming after only her foot fits the glass slipper, is the ultimate rags-to-riches story. Curiously enough, though, it is used most often to mean a poor, neglected or unsuccessful person or thing, although it can be found used for a dramatic success.

CLANGERS see SOUP DRAGON

CLARENCE, GEORGE DUKE OF see MALMSEY

CLIO see MUSES

CLOCKWORK ORANGE [*Literature*]
Anthony Burgess's 1961 novel made a great stir when it was made into a much-banned, violent film. The story tells of a grim future Britain, where drug-crazed gangs of youths, called **Droogs**, run wild, murdering and raping, communicating in a slang which is almost a language of its own. The story is told by a former Droog who had been brainwashed into conformity. He is the one who is

'(queer as) a clockwork orange', an out-of-date slang expression for strangeness.

CLODIA see LESBIA

CLODIUS see JULIUS CAESAR, LESBIA

CLOUSEAU, INSPECTOR [*Film*]
Inspector Jacques Clouseau is the accident-prone, incompetent French policeman on the trail of the PINK PANTHER.

CLYTEMNESTRA [*Mythology*]
In Greek myth Clytemnestra is half-sister to HELEN OF TROY and wife to **Agamemnon** who led the Greeks to the TROJAN WAR. While he is away for ten years fighting she takes a lover. When Agamemnon returns, bringing the captive CASSANDRA whom he has made his mistress, Clytemnestra murders him in his bath.

COBBLEY/COBBLEIGH, UNCLE TOM [*Song, Folklore*]
The Devon folk song *Widecombe Fair* tells the story of the various adventures of seven men who borrow a grey mare to go to Widecombe fair. The chorus lists the names of these men and ends 'Old Uncle Tom Cobbley and all', and this has become a useful comic way of ending a list of people, or another way of saying 'and everyone else you can think of'.

COCKLECARROT, MR JUSTICE see BEACHCOMBER

COLD COMFORT FARM [*Literature*]
Stella Gibbon's 1932 novel *Cold Comfort Farm* is a brilliant parody of the then fashionable novel of primitive rustic passion. In it **Flora Poste**, a neat, rational, sensible orphan goes to live with her chaotic cousins the **Starkadders**. The father Amos is a lay preacher with an extreme sect, his son Reuben is passionate about the soil, his other son Seth is a **Lawrencian** figure (see D. H. LAWRENCE) who wreaks havoc among the local women but is only really passionate about the movies, and the daughter Elfine wants to be an ethereal child of nature but really doesn't have the build for it. Among other figures are the incredibly ancient cowherd **Adam**

Lambsbreath and **Miriam the hired hand** whose sexual urges get the better of her every time the **sukebind** blooms. The whole lot are dominated by **Aunt Ada Doom** who 'saw something nasty in the woodshed' when she was little and now rules the family with a rod of iron from her bedroom by threatening to throw a fit over her childhood trauma. By following the Higher Common Sense Flora soon has them all sorted out.

COLDITZ [*History, Television, Literature*]
During the Second World War the Germans turned the castle of Colditz into a highly secure prisoner of war camp where 'bad boys', officers who had already tried to escape from other camps, were sent. Pat Reid wrote two rather cheerful books telling of the various attempts made by the mainly public-schoolboy types to escape from the supposedly totally secure place, which were immensely successful, and later (1972–74) used as the basis of a widely shown TV series.

COLEMAN, DAVID [*Television, Sport*]
Veteran TV sports commentator David Coleman, now retired, gained a reputation for slips of the tongue during the heat of the moment. The satirical magazine *Private Eye* started publishing these and other commentators' similar errors under the name **'Colemanballs'** and the term has entered the language, as in 'Jameson ... even managed a classic piece of Colemanballs: "A new British record and I think that's the fastest swim we've ever done"' (*Evening Standard* 28.7.92).

COLMAN, RONALD [*Film*]
Ronald Colman (1891–1958) was a British actor the copying of whose smooth manner and distinctive thin moustache was the ambition of many a young man in the 1930s.

COLOSSUS [*History*]
The Colossus of Rhodes was a giant fourth-century BC statue. One of the seven wonders of the ancient world, it has come to mean something very big (it is the source of our word 'colossal'). It is sometimes used in the context of Shakespeare's words in *Julius Caesar*: 'He doth bestride the narrow world like a Colossus'.

CONAN THE BARBARIAN [*Literature, Film*]

Conan the Barbarian is a super-strong, inarticulate warrior in the sword and sorcery stories of Robert E. Howard, adventures later continued by other hands. Conan is a doer, not a thinker. The 1982 film *Conan the Barbarian* made a perfect vehicle for film star **Arnold Schwarzenegger** then making a transition from bodybuilder to film star and burdened with an impenetrable accent. Unfortunately for him he became strongly identified with the part, giving him a reputation that he has only shaken off with much effort.

COOKIE MONSTER see MUPPETS

COOPER, AGENT [*Television*]

Agent Dale Cooper is the strange FBI investigator (whose main goal in life seems to be finding a 'damn fine cup of coffee' and cherry pie) into the death of LAURA PALMER in David Lynch's TV series *Twin Peaks* (1990–91).

COOPER, GARY [*Film*]

One of the few actors to have been a real cowboy before becoming a screen one, Gary Cooper (1901–61) specialised in playing slow-spoken, upright men of integrity, often seen riding off into the sunset, duty done.

CORDELIA see GONERIL AND REGAN, LEAR

CORIOLANUS [*Drama, History*]

Coriolanus is one of the least likeable of Shakespeare's heroes. He is arrogant and selfish, despising the poor, but heroic in his own terms, those of the aristocratic warrior. Shakespeare's play is based on traditional Roman history. Coriolanus was a 5th-century BC Roman noble who defeated the Voluscians, but when threatened with prosecution for trying to become a tyrant, sided with the Voluscians against Rome. He was only deflected from destroying Rome by the pleas of the Roman women, including that formidable matron **Volumnia** (his mother in Shakespeare, his wife in Roman traditions).

CORLEONE FAMILY   [*Film, Literature*]
Mario Puzo's 1968 novel ***The Godfather*** is basically a family saga, with the difference that the family is a Mafia one. **Don Vito Corleone** is a prominent Mafia leader, but his son **Michael** rejects his ways, even becoming a war hero. However, after a failed assassination attempt on his father, events force him to assume his father's role, and he soon learns to be an even more ruthless killer. The immensely popular 1972 film of the book gave us the phrase 'I'll make him an offer he can't refuse' (in this case the coercion consisted of the decapitated head of his favourite horse being left in its owner's bed) as well as Marlon Brando's sinister, hoarse, widely imitated delivery as Don Vito. The name Corleone comes from a Sicilian village still notorious for its Mafia connections.

CORNUCOPIA see HORN OF PLENTY

CORONATION STREET   [*Television*]
Britain's longest-running TV soap opera, Coronation Street charts the daily lives, revolving round the ROVERS RETURN and the local shop, in a working-class backstreet in Manchester. Starting in 1960, early episodes showed the toughness of a grim and grimy life in what was still an industrial city, but the tone of the series has got steadily lighter. See also ENA SHARPLES.

CORTEZ   [*History, Literature*]
Hernán Cortez (1485–1547) conquered Mexico for Spain, crossing from the Atlantic coast to the Pacific. His name is almost invariably used in English with reference to Keats' poem *On First Looking into Chapman's Homer* (1817) in which he compares his experience of reading this book with various forms of astonished wonder, including 'Like stout Cortez when with eagle eyes / He stared at the Pacific – and all his men / Looked at each other with a wild surmise– / Silent upon a peak in Darien.'

COW PIE see DESPERATE DAN

COWARD, NOËL   [*Drama, Music*]
Known fondly as 'The Master', the play- and songwriter Sir Noël

Coward (1899–1973) was known for his elegance and wit and his distinctive clipped way of speaking. Typical publicity shots show him sitting at a piano in brocade dressing-gown holding a cigarette in a long holder.

COWARDLY LION see WIZARD OF OZ

CRATCHIT, BOB [*Literature*]
Bob Cratchit is the exploited clerk to SCROOGE in Charles Dickens' 1843 novella *A Christmas Carol*. Despite being poorly paid and over-worked he is rich in human kindness, in his loving family and in his ability to enjoy life; in effect he is the opposite of Scrooge. He is also the father of five children, one of whom is **Tiny Tim**, a tiny cripple who does not allow his misfortunes of weigh on him. Tiny Tim will die if not given help we are told by the Ghost of Christmas Yet to Come, and Tim's role in the book is very much that of the tear-jerker. It is Tiny Tim who delivers the line 'God bless us, every one'.

CRÈME DE LA CRÈME see JEAN BRODIE

CRESSIDA see PANDARUS, TROILUS

CRICHTON, THE ADMIRABLE [*History, Drama*]
James Crichton (1560–82) was a Scottish scholar and athlete given the nickname 'the admirable Crichton' because of his extraordinary gifts. The name was taken up by J. M. Barrie for his 1902 play *The Admirable Crichton* which tells a story of a shipwrecked group of aristocrats who find that Crichton, the butler, turns out to be the natural leader in what is forced to be a classless society. From there the name was taken up for two televised science fiction series, firstly as the snooty robot in the second series of BUCK ROGERS *in the 25th Century* (1981) and more recently (1988–) in the form **Kryten** for the android in the series RED DWARF.

CRIPPEN, DR [*Crime, History*]
Dr Crippen (1862–1910), an American living in England, murdered his wife and fled across the Atlantic with his mistress. But the ship's captain was suspicious of his passengers and using the

newly invented radiotelegraphy communicated his suspicions to the authorities and Crippen was arrested on landing, the first person to have been caught by the use of radio. He was later hanged. His name has come to be used for any wife-murderer.

CRISP, QUENTIN [*Popular Culture*]
Quentin Crisp, writer, raconteur and icon, has devoted a lifetime to just being himself. Always immaculately turned out and made up, his style is perhaps summed up in the story that when called up for conscription during the Second World War and asked what he did, he is said to have answered, 'Do? But it takes me all my time to look like this.' Among other things he is famous for never dusting his room, on the grounds that once it reaches a certain dustiness it never gets any worse.

CROCKETT, DAVY [*History*]
Davy Crockett (1786–1836) was an American frontiersman, politician and soldier. His status as a folkhero was not hindered by a series of romantic books about him of which he may well have been part author – he certainly had a talent for self publicity. He died in the battle of the **Alamo**, a Texan mission building where a small group fighting for Texan independence from Mexico made a heroic last stand. The **Davy Crockett hat** – a racoon-skin hat with the tail hanging down behind – became a must-have for small boys on both sides of the Atlantic from 1956 with the success of a TV series loosely based on Crockett. A few years later there must have been a certain amount of confusion among these children when the same actor, wearing the same hat, appeared in a series named after that other legendary frontiersman, DANIEL BOONE.

CROCODILE see CAPTAIN HOOK, PUNCH AND JUDY

CRO-MAGNON [*Pre-History*]
Cro-Magnon Man is the technical term for a type of early man who lived in the Stone Age in France. The term is used as an insult in the same way as NEANDERTHAL.

CROSSROADS [*Television*]
Crossroads (1964–88) was a TV soap opera based on the goings-on

in a Midlands motel. It was a popular show which ran five nights a week at one time, but also much mocked, being notorious for being under-rehearsed and above all for the wobbling of the shaky sets. One of its more enduring characters was that of **Benny Hawkins**, tongue-tied, slow-witted but sweet, in his trade-mark woolly hat, who became so well known that to describe someone as 'a real Benny' became a way of saying 'thick'.

CROUCHBACK, GUY [*Literature*]
Guy Crouchback is the hero of Evelyn Waugh's *Sword of Honour* trilogy about the Second World War. Guy hopes to find a purpose in life through enlisting to fight for a just cause, but finds only dis-organisation – often comic – and disillusion. Crouchback was also a nickname given in Shakespeare's play to Richard III (see PRINCES IN THE TOWER) because of his hunchback.

CROW, JIM see JIM CROW

CRUN, HENRY see GOONS

CULLODEN [*History*]
The battle of Culloden Moor in northern Scotland in 1746 was the last battle fought on British soil. At it the troops of George III under the **Butcher Cumberland** massacred the supporters of Prince Charles Edward Stuart or Bonnie Prince Charlie, the Young Pretender, and destroyed Jacobite hopes of restoring the Stuarts to the throne.

CUNCTATOR see FABIUS CUNCTATOR

CUPID [*Mythology*]
Cupid is the Roman god of love, shown as a winged boy with a bow and arrow with which he shoots people with love's darts. Thus he is used to mean love in general. See also EROS.

CURATE'S EGG [*Popular Culture*]
In 1895 *Punch* published a cartoon showing a nervous curate breakfasting with a bishop. The bishop says 'I'm afraid you've got a bad egg, Mr Jones', to which the curate replies 'Oh no, My Lord,

I assure you! Parts of it are excellent!' Since then the term 'a curate's egg' has been used for something that is good in parts.

CURTIS, SIR HENRY see ALLAN QUARTERMAIN

CUSTER'S LAST STAND [*History*]
The battle of **Little Bighorn**, or Custer's last stand (25 June 1876) was a battle between the troops of General George Custer and a group of Sioux and Cheyenne Indians led by Chief SITTING BULL, in which Custer and all his men were killed. The rights and wrongs of the battle have been much discussed, but there does seems to have been disastrous confusion on the part of Custer's men. See also BUFFALO BILL.

CYCLOPS [*Mythology*]
In Greek myth the Cyclopses were a race of giants with only one eye in the middle of their forehead. The term is usually used to mean one-eyed, but since the Greeks believed that the walls of early buildings made from gigantic stones could only have been built by the Cyclops, who had a reputation as craftsmen, **Cyclopean** is sometimes used for something built on a gigantic scale.

CYRANO DE BERGERAC see DE BERGERAC

D'ARTAGNAN [*Literature*]

D'Artagnan is the hero of Alexandre Dumas' novel of the 17th century *The Three Musketeers* (1844). A brash young Gascon, with all the touchiness of his race, he comes to Paris determined to make a name for himself in the brigade of musketeers. There he meets the three musketeers of the title: the religious **Aramis**, large, jolly **Porthos** and romantic **Athos**, and after initial conflict with them, and many exciting adventures, D'Artagnan becomes a fast friend of the three, included in their motto of 'All for one and one for all'.

DAD'S ARMY [*Television*]

The much-loved TV comedy *Dad's Army* (1968–77) showed the antics of the Home Guard of a small sea-side town during the Second World War. The home guard was, of course, made up of those not suitable for the forces – those too young, too weak and particularly too old to be able to fight, and this was exploited to its comic full. Led by the local bank manager, the pompous **Captain Mainwaring** (pronounced 'Mannering') the troop tried their best to be prepared to defend the homeland against attack. The series gave rise to catch-phrases such as 'Stupid boy', 'They don't like it up them' and 'Doomed ... we're all doomed'. Nowadays 'Dad's Army' tends to be a disparaging term for any group of older people actively involved in some field.

DAEDALUS see ICARUS AND DAEDALUS, MINOTAUR

DAHLIA, AUNT see BERTIE WOOSTER

DAKOTA, BLACK HILLS OF see WILD BILL HICKOK

DALEKS [*Television*]

The arch-enemies of DR WHO, the Daleks were sort of dome-topped, lumpy tapering tin cans containing the soft, vulnerable bodies of an aggressive alien race. They spoke in a tinny metallic voice, their favourite expression being 'Exterminate! Exterminate!' They tried repeatedly to conquer the world, but the best way to escape them was to run upstairs, for they had no legs and could only move on flat surfaces.

DALES, THE   [Radio]

Mrs Dale's Diary (later *The Dales*) was a radio soap opera running from 1948 to 1969. It told of the every-day life of Mary Dale and her doctor husband James in the country town of Exton, and had a vast following. The programme opened with a voice-over from Mrs Dale, as if writing her diary, before turning into dialogue, and the frequently used line 'I'm worried about Jim' became something of a catch-phrase.

DALEY, ARTHUR   [Television]

In the TV series *Minder* (1979–85, 1988–94) Arthur Daley was the fast-talking cockney con man, off-loading dodgy goods and second-hand cars on the gullible public. Originally meant as a vehicle for Dennis Waterman who played **Terry McCann**, the minder of the title, it was the character of Daley, a rogue who was always being tripped up by his own cunning, and willing to try to talk his way out of anything except a confrontation with **Her indoors** (his wife) that won the public's heart, to the extent that in the later series Arthur had a new minder.

DALI, SALVADOR   [Art]

The surrealist painter Salvador Dali (1904–89) is famous for his long, waxed moustache and for his exquisitely realised paintings of dream-like scenes, particularly those with melting watches in them.

DAMASCUS, ROAD TO   [Religion]

According to the Bible (Acts 9), Saul, 'breathing out threatenings and slaughter against the disciples of the Lord' and a noted persecuter of the early Christians was on the road to Damascus to deal with the Christians there when he was suddenly bathed in a bright light and had a vision of Christ. He was converted and changed his name to Paul, and became the great preacher we know from his epistles. Thus someone's road to Damascus is a sudden revelation or reversal of opinion.

DAMIEN [*Film*]
In the horror film *The Omen* (1976) and its sequels, Damien Thorn is an angelic-looking boy, the adopted son of the US ambassador to Great Britain; he murders his family and turns out to be the Antichrist. Thus Damien can be used of any really horrid boy.

DAMOCLES, SWORD OF [*History*]
Dionysius, tyrant of Syracuse in the 4th century BC was told by a certain Damocles that he was the happiest of men. Deciding to teach the flatterer a lesson, Dionysius gave him a luxurious banquet, telling him he was going to experience the joys of being a ruler. While enjoying the feast Damocles realised that there was a sword hanging over his head, suspended by a single hair, by which Dionysius meant to teach him the dangers that go with the pleasures of power. Thus a sword of Damocles is an ever-present threat.

DANAË [*Mythology*]
In Greek mythology Danaë is the mother of the hero PERSEUS. Her father had learnt that he would be killed by any son she had, so she had been locked up in a tower of brass. But ZEUS visited her in the form of a shower of gold, and Perseus was born. Uses of her name often relate to the connection between money and sex.

DANCE OF THE SEVEN VEILS see SALOME

DANGER MAN [*Television*]
Charles Drake, secret agent (played by Patrick McGoohan), was *Danger Man* in the TV series which ran from 1960 to 1961 and 1964 to 1967 (Shown as *Secret Agent* in the USA). He was a suave, intelligent and reticent man who disliked all violence, but often had to employ in it his mission to preserve world peace.

DANIEL [*Religion*]
The Bible's book of Daniel tells how Daniel, an influential counsellor and prophet among the Jews in captivity in BABYLON, made

enemies who plotted to have him thrown into a **lions' den**. God sealed up the mouths of the lions, and Daniel was found unhurt and restored to favour. On another occasion the wicked king Belshazzar had held a feast at which he used the sacred vessels which had been looted from the Temple of Jerusalem. During **Belshazzar's feast** a finger appeared writing the words '**Mene, mene, tekel, upharsin**'. This **writing on the wall** (the source of the expression) was interpreted by Daniel to mean 'God hath numbered thy kingdom, and finished it: thou art weighed in the balance and found wanting' (Daniel 5).

DANTE, DANTESQUE see INFERNO

DANTÈS, EDMOND see MONTE CRISTO

DANVERS, MRS [*Literature*]

Mrs Danvers is the chilling housekeeper in REBECCA. She worships the memory of the first Mrs de Winter, and does all she can to drive away the second. She had become a symbol of cruel hostility: 'She spits out her lines with a lofty contempt that would make Mrs Danvers seem like the last word in approachability' (*Independent* 30.3.94).

DARBY AND JOAN [*History, Popular Culture*]

In an 18th-century song Darby and Joan are an old couple who have been married since their youth and are still happily together; thus they represent happy old age: 'But [people with Alzheimer's] should be seen, as politicians talk of the very old as if they were rosy-cheeked Darby and Joans' (*Independent* 8.4.96).

DARE, DAN [*Popular Culture*]

Space Fleet Colonel Dan Dare was a spaceship pilot in the immensely successful Dan Dare cartoon strip which ran from 1950 to 1967 in *The Eagle* comic. Dan Dare was basically a Battle of Britain pilot down to the great-coat and bomber-jacket uniform, the pipe and the slang – enemies were 'bandits', and to give a futuristic note to things he would exclaim 'Suffering satellites!' Space Fleet was based at **Alphaville** and its great enemies were the **Treens** of Venus, under the command of the dreaded **Mekon**, a puny-bodied, dome-headed tyrant who travelled round on a floating disk. Dan Dare's sidekick was his batman **Digby** who, being fat, flustered and obsessed with food, provided comic relief. Female interest was provided by the nutritionist **Professor Jocelyn Peabody** who had beauty, brains and a neat line in not-too-revealing sweaters. The strip was set in the late 1990s (Dan Dare was supposed to have been born in 1967) and much of its power lay in the convincing visual creation of the future by the strips creator Frank Hampson and his fellow illustrators.

DARK, SATANIC MILLS [*Literature, Music*]
This expression comes from the hymn JERUSALEM, a setting of William Blake's vision of Christ's legendary trip to England 'And was Jerusalem builded here / Among these dark Satanic mills'. The work is generally regarded as an attack on both the industrial Revolution and Enlightenment 'rational' thought.

DARLING, WENDY, see PETER PAN, TINKER BELL, WENDY

DARLING, GRACE [*History*]
Grace Darling (1815–42) was the daughter of the lighthouse keeper on one of the Farne Islands who became a national heroine in 1838 after she rescued the survivors of a ship wrecked there.

DARTH VADER see VADER, DARTH

DASTARDLY, DICK [*Television*]
The sniggering villain of the Hanna–Barbera cartoon *Wacky Races* (1969–70) in which eleven highly assorted teams raced each other in the wackiest vehicles imaginable. Dick Dastardly, ineptly assisted by his sniggering dog side-kick **Muttley** would do anything to win, the more dastardly the better, particularly if it were against that fine girl-racer **Penelope Pitstop**. There were two later series involving the same characters: *The Perils of Penelope Pitstop* and *Dastardly and Muttley in their Flying Machines*.

DATA see STAR TREK

DAVID AND GOLIATH [*Religion*]

The Bible story (1 Samuel 17) of how, when still a shepherd boy, David used his sling to bring down the supposedly invincible Philistine giant Goliath has long been a popular image for the victory of the little men over those in power. Goliath's name is now used as a general term for a giant. David's name is also linked with that of **Jonathan** as a symbol of ultimate friendship, for the fact that Jonathan's father, King Saul, was doing all he could to kill David was not allowed to affect the love between them.

DE BERGERAC, CYRANO [*Drama*]

There was a real Cyrano de Bergerac (1619–1655), an important figure as both an intellectual, writer and soldier, as well as being famous for his grotesque appearance, especially his long nose; but he has been overshadowed by the character depicted in Rostand's 1897 play which uses his name and features. In this Cyrano is an intensely romantic Gascon of the D'ARTAGNAN type. Cyrano loves **Roxanne** but knows that his appearance tells against him, and when he finds Roxanne loves the dim but handsome **Christian**, so that she should not be disillusioned, he nobly puts his poetic talents to writing Christian's love letters for him and even stands in the dark feeding him lines as Christian woos Roxanne on her balcony. Christian is killed in battle and for fifteen years Cyrano helps Roxanne keep alive the memory of Christian and his wonderful words to her. Only on the point of death does Cyrano reveal his own love and the fact that the words were his. References to Cyrano are, however, often limited simply to the length of his nose.

DE MILLE, CECIL B. [*Film*]

Cecil B. de Mille (1881–1959) was one of the great producer-directors of early Hollywood. He made a wide range of films but his name is associated with grandiose epics, especially biblical ones (hence the clerihew 'Cecil B. de Mille / Rather against his will, / Was persuaded to leave Moses / Out of 'The Wars of the Roses'). In the famous quote from Billy Wilder's 1950 film *Sunset Boulevard* (in which de Mille played himself) NORMA DESMOND says 'All right, Mr de Mille, I'm ready for my close-up now', although this is often misquoted in forms such as 'I'm ready for you now, Mr de Mille'.

DE RAIS, GILLES [*Crime, History*]

Gilles de Rais (1404–40) was a wealthy Breton nobleman whose outstanding career as a soldier ended when he stood trial for Satanism, abduction, and child murder of the most horrible kind. His name is used as a symbol for such ritualised mass murder. The true facts are difficult to establish, particularly as his name has been linked with the story of **Bluebeard**. This is a story found throughout the world, but it is thought that the French version, which has become the best-known version for English speakers, of the husband who goes away telling his wife she must not look in a locked room, which when she opens it she finds full of the bodies of earlier wives, may have been based on de Rais.

DE SADE, MARQUIS [*Literature*]

The writings of the Marquis de Sade (1740–1814), combining physical cruelty and eroticism, gave rise to our term sadism.

DE VIL, CRUELLA [*Film, Children's Literature*]

Hair white on one side of her head and black on the other, Cruella De Vil is the villainess of Dodie Smith's novel *One Hundred and One Dalmatians* (1956). She is never warm enough, and her main interest is furs. She married her husband simply because he was a furrier, and when she sees some dalmations she thinks only that they would make nice spring coats and sets about buying or stealing enough puppies to go into business. The story became better-known after the Disney cartoon version (1961), and will be even more so after the 1996 live-action version.

DE WINTER, MAXIMILIAN see REBECCA

DEAD MAN'S HAND see WILD BILL HICKOK

DEAD PARROT see NORWEGIAN BLUE

DEAN, CHRISTOPHER see TORVILL AND DEAN

DEAN, JAMES [*Film*]

Film actor James Dean (1931–55) made his name playing HOLDEN CAULFIELD-like troubled adolescents, rebelling against anything and everything, as in REBEL WITHOUT A CAUSE. His cult status was assured by his death in a car crash just as his career was taking off.

DEEP THOUGHT see 42

DEFARGE, MADAME [*Literature*]
In Charles Dickens' *A Tale of Two Cities* (1859) Madame Defarge is a vindictive poor Parisian who spends her days knitting at the foot of the guillotine rejoicing at the death of each aristo, and working the number of that day's dead into the pattern of her knitting.

DEERING, WILMA see BUCK ROGERS

DEJAH THORIS see BARSOOM

DEL BOY see TROTTER

DELILAH see SAMSON AND DELILAH

DELPHI see APOLLO

DEMETER see PERSEPHONE

DEMON HEADMASTER [*Children's Literature, Television*]
The Demon Headmaster, whose motto is 'The man who can keep order can rule the world', is the villain in Gillian Cross's series of children's novels, three of which have been dramatised on BBC TV. The headmaster uses his piercing green eyes to hypnotise people, reducing them to helpless automatons completely under his control. His aim is to take over the world and abolish the messiness of personal choice, forcing people to lead ordered and efficient lives by his rules. Luckily, a girl called Dinah and her friends – Ingrid, Harvey, Lloyd and Mandy – can resist his powers and, forming themselves into a gang they call SPLAT (Society for the Protection of our Lives Against Them), repeatedly thwart his evil aims.

DEMOSTHENES [*Oratory*]
Demosthenes (383–322 BC) was a great Athenian orator, and is used, like CICERO, as a symbol of eloquence.

75

DENNIS THE MENACE [*Popular Culture*]
Dennis the Menace is the little horror with a shock of black hair, red and black striped jumper and hobnail boots who goes round terrorising the neighbourhood (particularly **Softy Walter**) in the children's comic the *Beano*. There is nothing good to be said of him, which is probably why he has been the magazine's most popular figure since his introduction in 1951. He has a dog, **Gnasher**, who is no better than he is. Gnasher looks like Dennis' hair on legs and is officially an **Afghan Tripehound**. In the past most episodes ended with a close encounter between Dennis and Dad's slipper, but he has not been given the slipper since the mid '80s.

DESERT STORM see HANNIBAL

DESMOND, NORMA [*Film*]
Norma Desmond is the faded silent-movie star in *Sunset Boulevard* (a 1950 Billy Wilder film, now a Lloyd-Webber musical) who takes up scriptwriter **Joe Gillis** and makes a tragic attempt at a comeback. The film includes the famous exchange where Gillis says 'You used to be in pictures. You used to be big.' and Desmond replies 'I am big. It's the pictures that got small.' See also DE MILLE.

DESPERATE DAN [*Popular Culture*]
Desperate Dan is the gigantic cowboy (created by Dudley D. Watkins), living in a world half-way between the Wild West and Dundee in the children's magazine *The Dandy*. Thick as two planks, he is a giant of a man with a vast stubbly chin which he shaves with a blow lamp (he has been known to cut his toe-nails with a lawn-mower). Despite his vast size he is completely under the thumb of his nagging **Aunt Aggie**, who does at least make him his favourite **cow pies** – vast pies containing a whole animal, as can be seen from the horns and tail which stick out from the pastry.

DICKENSIAN [*Literature*]
The term Dickensian is a slippery one, as Charles Dickens' work was so diverse. It is used in at least three different ways. If the scene is a jolly one, merry feasting and Christmas-card scenes, then Dickensian refers to works such as *The Pickwick Papers* which contain scenes of perfect conviviality and people enjoying the

snow. But Dickensian can also be used of the scenes of grim squalor and deprivation Dickens could describe so graphically, particularly in his later works. Finally, Dickens' comic characters were often very broadly drawn, so Dickensian can mean grotesquely comic or simply eccentric. See MR MICAWBER, OLIVER TWIST, PICKWICK.

DIDO AND AENEAS [*History, Mythology*]

Dido was queen of Carthage when the Trojan Aeneas, fleeing from Troy after it was sacked by the Greeks in the TROJAN WAR, was shipwrecked on her coast. Dido fell in love with him and would have made him her consort, but the gods ordered Aeneas to continue on his journey to found the Italian state which would eventually become Rome. When the heart-broken Dido found that Aeneas had deserted her she committed suicide. She had not always been so easily overcome, for years earlier she had herself landed on the coast of the country which was now Carthage at the head of a group of exiles from Tyre. The local king had told her he would give her as much land as could be encompassed by an ox hide, and Dido had taken the hide and skilfully cut it into a thin strip, long enough to enclose enough land to establish a flourishing kingdom.

DIGBY see DAN DARE

DIGBY GESTE see BEAU GESTE

DIONYSUS [*Mythology*]

Dionysus, also known as **Bacchus**, was the Greek god of wine. As such he represents the wilder side of life, the uninhibited and darker sides, the opposite of the god APOLLO. His followers – known as **Maenads** or **Bacchae** – were known to tear animals and even their own families to bits in their furious revels, and **Bacchanalia** – originally simply a feast in his honour – has become another term for 'orgy'. There was another side to his worship, but this is less well known. There were secret rites in which Dionysius was a suffering god and a god of resurrection. He was also associated with the literary arts, Greek drama having evolved from one of his feasts. Dionysus is often shown with his tutor, the

77

drunken **Silenus**, riding on his donkey, and accompanied by **satyrs**, spirits of the wild which were half-man, half-goat. See also ARIADNE.

DIRTY HARRY [*Film*]
Harry Callahan is the violent, unorthodox, San Francisco cop in the Dirty Harry series of films starring Clint Eastwood (*Dirty Harry* 1971, *Magnum Force* 1973, *The Enforcer* 1976 and *Sudden Impact* 1983). These gave the catch-phrases 'Go ahead, make my day' and 'Ask yourself one question: Do I feel lucky? Well, do ya, punk?'

DIVES AND LAZARUS see LAZARUS

DIVINE COMEDY, THE see INFERNO

DOE, JOHN [*Law*]
A name used for an unknown person, particularly in a law case.

DOG IN THE NIGHT TIME [*Literature*]
In Sir Arthur Conan Doyle's SHERLOCK HOLMES story *Silver Blaze* a famous racehorse is nobbled. Holmes' solution to the case turns on the fact that it must be an inside job, for on the night it happened the stable dog did not bark, indicating that the intruder was familiar, not a stranger. Thus 'a dog in the night time' can be used for something that should have happened, but did not.

DOGBERRY [*Literature*]
In Shakespeare's *Much Ado About Nothing* Constable Dogberry is the pompous and confused local law officer. In many ways a prototype of the flatfooted, plodding, comic, country policeman, he is also a prototype MRS MALAPROP, always trying to use words he doesn't understand and mispronouncing them.

DOLITTLE, DR [*Literature*]
Doctor John Dolittle is the hero of Hugh Lofting's series of Dr Dolittle books, published between 1920 and 1952. Dr Dolittle is too outspoken to be very successful as a human doctor, but after his parrot **Polynesia** helps him to learn the language of all the ani-

mals he become the world's greatest animal doctor, ably helped by his friends **Chee Chee the Monkey**, **Gub Gub the Pig** and **Matthew Mugg, the cat's-meat man**. The charm of these books owes no little to Lofting's illustrations, particularly of the **Push-Me-Pull-You**, a not surprisingly nervous beast, given that it has two heads and front halves, joined in the middle so it is always facing in two directions, never knows which half is in charge and is much hunted for its rarity value.

DONALD DUCK [*Film*]
Donald Duck, created by the Walt Disney studio, is the irascible duck who likes to dish it out but blows his top if he doesn't get his way. He has a distinctive quacking voice and it is this that is most frequently alluded to. His nephews are **Huey, Lewie and Dewey**.

DONNER see THOR

DOOLITTLE, ELIZA [*Drama, Film*]
In George Bernard Shaw's play PYGMALION, an attack on British class attitudes, Eliza Doolittle is the cockney flower girl who the phonetician Professor **Henry Higgins** decides to teach to speak standard English and introduce to polite society. Her father is the feckless dustman **Alfred Doolittle**, who, when asked if he has no moral standards replies 'Can't afford 'em, guv'nor'. The play was the source of the musical *My Fair Lady*.

DOOM, AUNT ADA see COLD COMFORT FARM

DOROTHY see WIZARD OF OZ

DOTHEBOYS HALL [*Literature*]
In Charles Dickens' novel *Nicholas Nickleby* (1839) Dotheboys Hall is the school run by **Wackford Squeers** and his wife, where the boys are beaten, starved and mistreated to the extent that **Smike** looses his wits. Thus Dotheboys can be used for any harsh school. Compare LLANABBA.

DOUBLE 'O' SEVEN (007) [*Film, Literature*]
The code designation of fictional spy JAMES BOND, the '00' prefix

indicating that he is licensed to kill.

DOUBLETHINK see 1948

DOUBTING THOMAS [*Religion*]
In the Bible (John 20) the disciple Thomas refused to accept the truth of the resurrected Christ until he had actually touched Christ's wounds. Thus a Doubting Thomas is anyone who will not believe without tangible proof.

DOUGAL [*Television*]
Dougal is the shaggy dog – rather like an elongated mop-head moving on castors – in the cult children's animated-puppet TV series *The Magic Roundabout* (1965–77). Other regulars in the series were the little girl **Florence**, the incredibly laid-back, spaced-out hippie rabbit **Dylan** and the strange creature on a spring called **Zebedee** who ended each series with 'Time for bed' followed by a loud 'boing' of his spring.

DRACONIAN [*Law, History*]
The seventh-century Athenian **Draco** was a legal reformer whose new laws were so harsh – enslavement for debt and death for most other crimes – that the term Draconian has been used to mean excessively hard rules ever since.

DRACULA [*Literature, Film*]
Dracula was originally created by Bram Stoker for his 1890 novel of that name, but the character has proved so popular that he has taken on a life of his own and many traditions have developed outside the book. Dracula is a Transylvanian vampire who can only be killed by a stake through the heart or exposure to sunlight, but has a disconcerting habit of coming back from the dead. He prefers to drink the blood of nubile young maidens, but can be held at bay using crucifixes, holy water and garlic. He is often shown living in a spooky castle and usually wears evening dress and a black cloak, a convenient garb for changing into a bat when he wants to fly around hunting for victims. Many elements in popular versions of the story have become blended with those of FRANKENSTEIN.

DRAGON'S TEETH [*Mythology*]
In Greek myth both the story of how **Jason** won THE GOLDEN FLEECE and of how **Cadmus** founded the city of Thebes tell of the heroes sowing dragon's teeth from which an squad of fully armed men sprung. The hero then throws a stone among the warriors which set them quarrelling until few or none were left. From this comes the expression 'to sow dragon's teeth' meaning to do something that leads to violent results.

DRAKE, CHARLES see DANGER MAN

DRAKE, SIR FRANCIS [*History*]
Sir Francis Drake (c. 1545–96) had a varied career, but allusions to him usually refer to either his sailing round the world in his ship, the *Golden Hind*; to the story of his being in the middle of a game of bowls on Plymouth Hoe when the Spanish Armada was sighted and insisting on finishing the game on the grounds that they had time to do that and beat the Spanish too; or to Drake's drum. This is the legend, made famous in the 1897 poem by Sir Henry Newbolt, that striking his drum can summon Drake back to defend his country if it is threatened.

DREW, NANCY [*Children's Literature*]
The girl detective in a series of children's adventures published since the 1930s under the name Carolyn Keene (actually a variety of different writers). She is the female equivalent of THE HARDY BOYS.

DREYFUS, ALFRED [*History*]
Alfred Dreyfus (1859–1935) was a Jewish French army officer who was accused of selling French military secrets to the Germans in 1894. Later evidence showed that much of the evidence against him was forged, but he was found guilty and sent to the notorious penal colony of Devil's Island, off the coast of French Guyana, a place of indescribable hardship from which it was said that no-one could escape. Despite mounting evidence for his innocence French anti-Semitism prevented the evidence being properly assessed, and the Dreyfus affair split France in two. Among those campaigning on Dreyfus' behalf were **Emile Zola**, whose famous 'J'Accuse' article revealing an army cover-up landed him with a

one-year jail sentence. Dreyfus was finally recalled and pardoned in 1899, but was not fully cleared of the accusations until 1906.

DRONES CLUB   [*Literature*]
The Drones is the club where **P. G. Wodehouse**'s BERTIE WOOSTER and his friends meet each other and indulge in all sorts of wild japes.

DROOGS see CLOCKWORK ORANGE

DROPPING THE PILOT see BISMARCK

DRUMMOND, BULLDOG   [*Literature*]
Hugh 'Bulldog' Drummond is the ex-army captain whose adventures feature in a series of novels by 'Sapper'. Drummond and a number of friends, finding life dull after the excitement of the First World War set up the Black Gang to right wrongs that need seeing to – mainly international plots which show Sapper's strong anti-Semitic streak – and combating the devilish plans of the master criminal **Carl Petersen** and his mistress **Irma**. By modern standards Drummond is nothing but a bullying, over-privileged thug, but even so the stories still have a certain power and were once enormously popular.

DULCINEA see DON QUIXOTE

DUNKIRK   [*History*]
In 1940 the British army in Europe had been defeated by Germany and was forced to make a hasty withdrawal. Troops piled up on the beaches at Dunkirk and were being strafed by the German airforce. The Navy could not muster enough ships to transport the men to safety, and an appeal went out for anyone who had a boat to go to Dunkirk to help. This fleet of **little ships** was blessed by an unusually calm sea and was able to get many more men back to England than would otherwise have been possible. This all-pulling-together became known as the **Dunkirk spirit**. This massive defeat was hailed as the country's finest hour.

DYALL, VALENTINE [*Radio*]
The deep, portentous tones of Valentine Dyall's voice became famous from 1943 onwards when he played **The Man in Black**, the narrator of the BBC radio's *Appointment With Fear* series of mystery and horror stories.

DYLAN see DOUGAL

E.T. [*Film*]
E.T. is the extraterrestrial left behind on Earth in Steven Spielberg's sentimental film *E.T.* (1992). Allusions to E.T. are usually to its appearance – great big, pitiful eyes in a large bony head, skeletal body with immensely long fingers; to the publicity slogan 'E.T. phone home', or, visually, to the scene in which the children cycle through the air with E.T. in a bicycle basket.

ECCLES see GOONS

ED, MR [*Television*]
Mr Ed is the name of a talking horse in a surprisingly successful American situation comedy that ran on TV from 1961 to 1966. The programme might have faded into obscurity but for the fact that the cartoonist GARY LARSON obviously has fond memories of Mr Ed as he appears in a number of his 'Far Side' cartoons.

EDEN, GARDEN OF [*Religion*]
In the Bible The Garden of Eden is the earthly paradise created for the first humans, **Adam** and **Eve**. There the **Serpent** tempted them to eat the forbidden apple and they were banished to the toils of this world. Thus Eden can be used for a paradise, a state of innocence or bliss, or simply a garden.

EDINA see ABSOLUTELY FABULOUS

EEYORE [*Literature*]
Eeyore is the gloomy, pessimistic donkey in A. A. Milne's WINNIE THE POOH stories. 'There is an "Eeyore" side to us that glumly enjoys mulling over these depressing facts' (*Radio Times* 13.7.96).

ELBA see NAPOLEON

ELECTRA see OEDIPUS

ELM STREET see FREDDIE KREUGER

ELYSIAN FIELDS [*Mythology*]
In Greek myth the Elysian Fields or **Elysium** (also called the **Islands of the Blessed**) is the place where the virtuous and the gods' favourites, such as heroes, go after death. As such it is the antithesis of HADES, and can be used as the equivalent of Paradise.

EMERALD CITY see WIZARD OF OZ

EMIL AND THE DETECTIVES [*Children's Literature, Film*]
Eric Kästner's children's novel *Emil and the Detectives* (1929) has long been popular in English translation and has been filmed a number of times. It tells the adventures of a group of children in central Berlin who track down a criminal.

EMMET [*Popular Culture*]
The cartoonist Rowland Emmet (1907–90) had a special fondness for cartoons involving trains, but is best-known for what he called his 'things', inventions of frivolous, useless machines, made from all sorts of oddments such a gramophones and broken umbrellas. These appeared both in drawings and in three-dimensional creations. His work is often compared with the cartoonist **William Heath Robinson** (1872–1944) but Heath Robinson's inventions, elaborate machines for performing simple tasks such as raising your hat, were theoretically practical and depended for their humour on their apparent seriousness and earnestness, while Emmet's creations were always purely for enjoyment.

ENTERPRISE, U.S.S. see STAR TREK

EPHESUS [*History, Mythology*]
The city of Ephesus, in what is now Turkey, was an important centre of early Christianity, as shown by the Bible's Epistles to the Ephesians. It was already a major religious centre famous for its temple to many-breasted Artemis ('Diana of the Ephesians' in the Bible). This temple was the site of the earliest recorded case of

someone committing a crime for the sake of the publicity it would bring, for in October 356 BC Herostratus set fire to the temple and destroyed it, simply to win eternal fame. Since this happened on the night that Alexander the Great was born, the story soon arose that Herostratus was only successful because the goddess herself was absent, helping at the god-king's birth. PETRONIUS linked the town's name with hanky-panky when he told the story of the Widow of Ephesus in the *Satyricon*, a story of a woman so famous for her fidelity to her husband that people would make journeys just to look at her. When her husband died, she joined him in the tomb to lament him. In the same graveyard a robber had been crucified, and a handsome young soldier set to guard the body so that his relatives did not take it to give it a decent funeral. The widow of Ephesus succumbs to the young man's charms, and when the robber's body is taken while they enjoy themselves, decided that she would rather have her beloved husband's body replace the robber on the cross, than lose two men in quick succession. Christian legend gave it a better name with the story of the **Seven Sleepers of Ephesus**, supposed to have been early Christians who took refuge in a cave in AD 250 during one of the regular persecutions of Christians, fell asleep and did not wake until the 6th century. They explained their miracle had happened to bear witness to the miracle of the Resurrection, and then died.

EPHIALTES see THERMOPYLAE

EPICURUS [*Philosophy*]
Although not an accurate reflection of his teaching, the Greek philosopher Epicurus (341–270 BC) is linked with the slogan 'Eat, drink and be merry, for tomorrow we die', and the following of pleasure.

ERATO see MUSES

ERIC OR LITTLE BY LITTLE [*Literature*]
Dean Farrar's children's novel of school life *Eric or Little by Little* (1858) is a moral and elevating tale of school life which would be unlikely to appeal to the modern child. Although the book is actually more racy that its reputation would give it credit for, Eric has come to be used for an over-virtuous school-boy in the same way

as LITTLE LORD FAUTLEROY. More readers are probably familiar with Eric from allusions to it in Kipling's STALKY AND CO, where 'beastly Ericing' means being a goody-goody, than from the original.

ERINYES see FURIES

EROS [*Mythology*]
Eros is the son of APHRODITE, the Greek equivalent of CUPID, the irresponsible boy who shoots at people with his arrows and makes them fall in love. A famous statue of Eros stands in the middle of Piccadilly Circus, so his name is sometimes linked to London's West End and its entertainments.

ERSKINE-BROWN see RUMPOLE OF THE BAILEY

ESAU [*Religion*]
The story of Esau and Jacob in the Bible (Genesis 25) is one of sibling rivalry and deceit. Esau and Jacob are twins who fought even in their mother's womb. Esau is the first born and loved by his father, but the mother, Rebecca, loves Jacob. They plot to get Jacob the privileges of the elder son. Esau was a great huntsman, and one day he returned from the hunt so hungry that he felt near death, to find Jacob, sitting at home in the tents, had made some food. Jacob will only give him some in return for the elder son's privileges. This is usually described as 'selling his birthright for a mess of pottage' although these words do not actually appear in the Bible. Later when Isaac, their father, has gone blind and feels near death he wants to give Esau his blessing. He asks Esau to find him some game and make him a tasty meal, and when he has done this he will get the blessing. Rebecca overhears this, and gets Jacob to kill two kids, cooks them up, and because Esau was a hairy man and Jacob a smooth one, uses the kid-skins to make Jacob's hands and neck feel like those of the hairy brother to the blind man, and thus Jacob steals his brother's blessing. Allusions to Esau are usually to selling something valuable for something trivial, as in the mess of pottage, or comparing a smooth and hairy man.

ESCHER [*Art*]
The Dutch graphic artist M. C. Escher (1896–1970) is famous for

drawings which trick the eye and distort perspective. Best known of these is one of interlocking staircases, each leading to the next, but all, impossibly, appearing to lead downwards.

ESTRAGON see GODOT

EUMENIDES see FURIES

EUREKA see ARCHIMEDES

EUTERPE see MUSES

EVE see EDEN

EVERYMAN [*Literature*]
The figure of Everyman, a representation of the common man, has been popular in English literature since at least the 15th century.

EVITA [*History, Music, Film*]
The life of the Argentinean actress and politician Evita Perón (1919–52) who inspired extremes of love and hate, was controversial and contained elements of legend even before her death. With the international success of the musical based on her life, the truth has probably been lost for ever.

EWING, J.R. SEE J.R.

EXXON VALDEZ see TORREY CANYON

EYRE, JANE [*Literature*]
The plot of Charlotte Brontë's *Jane Eyre* (1847) is the basic stuff of the romantic novel. Poor, downtrodden, plain Jane goes as a governess to the house of the mysterious, brooding, dark **Mr Rochester**, they fall in love and agree to marry but Jane finds at the altar that he is still married to his mad first wife. Jane runs away, the mad wife burns down the grand house and dies in the flames, and Jane returns to marry her man at last. 'Her mixture of ex-wife glamour and friendly grown-up charisma always makes me feel like Jane Eyre ... plain, poor and unentitled.' (*Independent* 30.10.95).

FAB FOUR [*Music*]
A nickname given to The Beatles.

FABERGÉ [*Design*]
Peter Carl Fabergé (1846–1920) was a Russian jeweller, famous for the enamelled and jewel-encrusted ornaments he created, particularly the golden Easter eggs he made each year for the Russian royal family.

FABIUS CUNCTATOR [*History*]
The Roman 3rd-century BC general Quintus Fabius Maximus won the nickname 'Cunctator' meaning 'the delayer' from his tactics against the brilliant general HANNIBAL. Knowing how difficult Hannibal was to defeat in battle Fabius instead chose to wear him down by following and harassing his forces rather than meet him in pitched battle. **The Fabian Society** took his name to show their more patient approach to reform, in contrast to the revolutionary socialism of other groups.

FAGAN, DR AUGUSTUS see LLANABBA

FAGIN [*Literature*]
Fagin is the evil dealer in stolen goods who trains little boys to be pickpockets in Charles Dickens' novel *Oliver Twist* (1838). The ARTFUL DODGER is the leader of Fagin's pickpockets. When Michael Heseltine said of John Smith 'He's like Fagin – "You gotta pick a pocket or two" – the battle hymn of any aspiring Labour Chancellor' he was quoting Fagin's best-known song in Lionel Bart's musical *Oliver!* based on the novel.

FAHRENHEIT 451 [*Literature*]
This is the temperature at which, according to Ray Bradbury's

1953 novel of that name, books burn. The novel tells of an ORWELLIAN future society where society is dominated by TV and books are seen as the cause of all unhappiness, and burnt. Just a few struggle to keep book-learning alive.

FALKENBERG see FLYING DUTCHMAN

FALL ON YOUR SWORD [*History, Folklore*]
In the Roman world suicide was seen as an honourable reaction to defeat, and generals were known to fall on their swords after a particularly bad battle, so to fall on your sword can be used for to meet your end or defeat as in 'IBM will fall on the sword of its sluggishness' (*Independent* 18.9.92).

FALLS ROAD [*Sociology*]
Western Belfast has two main roads running through it. The Falls Road and the surrounding area is almost exclusively Catholic, the **Shankill Road** almost exclusively Protestant. Both roads have seen much sectarian violence, and have become synonymous with such conflict.

FALSTAFF [*Literature*]
Sir John Falstaff is the fat knight of Shakespeare's *Henry IV* plays and *The Merry Wives of Windsor*. He is fun-loving and cheerful, but old and in refusing to take the responsibilities of his age, he behaves like a dissolute youth. His self-indulgence includes laziness, and laziness turns to dishonesty to avoid work. He is not at all a nice character underneath. However, **Falstaffian** is often used just to mean a fat, jolly type like Father Christmas, the dissolute element being ignored.

FAMOUS FIVE [*Children's Literature*]
ENID BLYTON's The Famous Five series of children's novels tell the adventures of the siblings **Julian** – the eldest and generally accepted leader – Dick and Anne, plus their tomboy cousin George (*never* Georgina which she hates) and her dog Timmy. Their adventures are wildly improbable involving such things as secret passages and stereotyped villains and have been generally sneered at by adults, but are greatly loved by children.

FAT BOY see PICKWICK

FAT CONTROLLER [*Children's Literature*]
The Fat Controller (originally the Fat Director) is the man in charge of **Thomas the Tank Engine**'s railway in the Reverend W. Awdry's long series of children's books about the adventures of various railway engines. He is very firm with the engines and does not let them get away with anything, but is generally well-meaning. His greatest compliment is to call them 'a really useful engine'.

FAT OWL OF THE REMOVE see BILLY BUNTER

FAUNTLEROY, LITTLE LORD [*Literature*]
Frances Hodgson Burnett's 1886 novel *Little Lord Fauntleroy* tells the story of Cedric Errol, a young, republican American boy who finds himself heir to an Earldom. He is an impressively self-reliant boy, more aware of the realities of poverty and social problems than his aristocratic grandfather. This reality of the book is totally in contrast with the image of Little Lord Fauntleroy, which belongs with that of BUBBLES and ERIC. This image arose because when the novel was turned into a highly successful play Fauntleroy was dressed in lace and velvet breeches and given long curling hair. The image was further re-inforced by the 1921 film, when the boy was played by Mary Pickford, 'the world's sweetheart'.

FAUSTUS [*Literature*]
The story of Doctor Faustus (**Faust** in German) tells of a 16th-century scholar, who sold his soul to the Devil in return for greater knowledge and power. Loosely based on a real person, the story is best known in English from Christopher Marlowe's play of the 1590s where he explores the relationship between Faustus and MEPHISTOPHELES, and shows Faustus summoning up the form of the dead HELEN OF TROY, this scene giving us the famous line 'Was this the face that launched a thousand ships'.

FAWLTY, BASIL [*Television*]
Basil Fawlty is the manic hotelier in the BBC TV comedy series

Fawlty Towers. (1975, 1979). Basil is rude, sarcastic and given to blind rages and unable to control anything, a state of mind not helped by his nagging wife **Sybil**. His Spanish waiter **Mañuel** is not much better, living in a constant state of bewildered panic. Fawlty Towers gave the language numerous catch-phrases, of which the most durable have proved to be Mañuel's bewildered 'Qué?' and 'Don't mention the war!', from the episode where Fawlty Towers had German visitors.

FEATHERSTONE, GUTHRIE see RUMPOLE OF THE BAILEY

FEEDING OF THE FIVE THOUSAND [*Religion*]
In the miracle of the Feeding of the Five Thousand (Matthew 14, John 6) the Bible tells us that a great crowd had followed Jesus to hear him preach, but found themselves without food. Jesus took five loaves and two fishes and blessed them, and ordered them distributed among the crowd 'and they took up of the fragments that remained twelve baskets full'. The Feeding of the Five Thousand is usually used allusively of any feat of mass catering.

FENRIR see LOKI

FERENGI see STAR TREK

FERIA, ABBÉ see COUNT OF MONTE CRISTO

FESTER, UNCLE see ADDAMS FAMILY

FEYDEAU [*Drama*]
The Frenchman Georges Feydeau (1862–1921) is widely considered the master of farce. His plays are built round set scenes involving mistaken identity; wives or husbands having to prevent their spouses finding out about their affairs; rooms with inter-connecting doors and handy cupboards to hide in; and wild excuses.

FIELD, W. C. [*Film*]
W. C. Field (1879–1946) played a cynical, hard-drinking ne'er-do-well in a series of films, mostly written by himself under such weird pen-names as Mahatma Kane Jeeves. He had a distinctive

drawled delivery of such famous lines as 'And it ain't a fit night out for man nor beast', 'Never give a sucker an even break' and 'Some weasel took the cork out of my lunch'. It was of him that Leo Rosten said 'Any man who hates dogs and babies can't be all bad'.

FIERY FURNACE see SHADRACH, MESHAK AND ABEDNIGO

FINK-NOTTLE, GUSSIE [*Literature*]
Gussie Fink-Nottle is BERTIE WOOSTER's shy, retiring, stammering and above all, newt-loving old school mate in **P. G. Wodehouse**'s books.

FINLAY, DR [*Television, Literature*]
The TV series *Dr Finlay's Casebook* (1962–71), based on the stories of A. J. Cronin, was set in the 1920s in the Scottish village of **Tannochbrae**. Finlay was the young doctor with the modern ideas, who did not always see eye to eye with his senior partner **Dr Cameron**. However, both were equally dedicated, and lived with the job, sharing a house and surgery and looked after by their housekeeper **Janet**, whose fey Highland accent was much imitated. Since 1993 there has been a revival of the series, this time set in the 1940s.

FINN, HUCKLEBERRY [*Literature*]
Mark Twain's great novel of American life and landscape, *The Adventures of Huckleberry Finn* (1884), tells of the adventures of Huck Finn as he tries to escape from his drunken father by sailing down the Mississippi on a raft with his friend the black slave Jim. See also TOM SAWYER.

FLAMBEAU see FATHER BROWN

FLASH GORDON see GORDON, FLASH

FLASH HARRY [*Film*]
Flash Harry, as a term for a poshly or over-smartly dressed man, has rather been overtaken by the character played by George Cole in the series of ST TRINIAN'S films. There Flash Harry is the name of

the cockney wide-boy or spiv who is always ready to place a bet for the schoolgirls or otherwise lead them astray.

FLASHMAN [*Literature*]

In *Tom Brown's Schooldays* (1857), Thomas Arnold's improving novel for children, Harry Flashman is the school bully who gets 'beastly drunk' and is expelled. This character was taken up by George Macdonald Fraser for his witty series of Flashman novels (1969–) in which he brilliantly recreates the events of Victorian empire, as seen through the eyes of Flashman, who despite his magnificent whiskers is an unmitigated coward, libertine and scoundrel. He nevertheless charms both the ladies and the reader, and finds himself involved in just about every major disaster of the time.

FLETCHER, NORMAN STANLEY [*Television*]

Fletcher is the old lag in the TV comedy series *Porridge* (1974–77) For him prison is a hazard of the job, and when he finds himself having to share a cell with the naive first-timer **Godber** he sets about showing him the ropes of how to survive prison; the attentions of the other inmates; and the bullying guard **Mr Mackay**. The series satirised both the hard and soft liners of prison reform, but did serve to make people think of the realities of prison life.

FLINT, CAPTAIN [*Literature*]

Captain Flint is the evil pirate whose treasure is being hunted in R. L. Stevenson's *Treasure Island* (1883). Although he died well before the story begins, his presence is always felt. It is also the name the LONG JOHN SILVER gave to his parrot. In Arthur Ransome's *Swallows and Amazons* books, Captain Flint is the nickname the children give their uncle.

FLINTSTONE, FRED AND WILMA [*Television*]

Fred and Wilma Flintstone are the Stone Age couple originally created for the Hanna–Barbera cartoon series *The Flintstones* (1960–66). Their neighbours are **Barney and Betty Rubble**. Fred has a distinctive exclamation of 'Yabba dabba do'. The humour of the series lies in the way that mid-20th-century suburban life has been translated into mock-Stone Age terms, with dinosaurs providing the amenities, such as using a pterodactyl's beak to provide the needle for a stone record player.

FLODDEN [*History*]
Flodden or **Flodden Field** in Northumberland was the site of a battle in 1513 where James IV of Scotland and most of the Scots nobility were killed after they had invaded England, in response to their alliance with France against Henry VIII of England.

FLORENCE see DOUGAL

FLOWERPOT MEN see BILL AND BEN

FLYING DUTCHMAN Folklore]
The Flying Dutchman is a Captain **Vanderdecken** who makes a pact with the Devil in order to get his ship round the Cape of Good Hope during a storm, and is condemned to roam the seas for ever, only landing once a century, unless he can be saved by the love of a woman. This is the version made famous by Wagner's opera, but there is another version of the story that gives the captain's name as **Falkenberg**, and has him sailing the North Sea forever, playing dice with the Devil.

FLYTE, SEBASTIAN see BRIDESHEAD

FOGG, PHILEAS [*Literature*]
Phileas Fogg is the eccentric Englishman who accepts and wins, with the help of his faithful servant **Passepartout**, a bet to circumnavigate the Earth in 80 days in Jules Verne's 1872 novel *Around the World in 80 Days*. The book is in part a celebration of all then-new forms of transport. In the 1956 film starring REX HARRISON there is a dramatic scene involving a hot air balloon, and Fogg is often invoked in the context of ballooning.

FOLIES-BERGÈRE see MOULIN ROUGE

FORCE, THE see DARTH VADER, OBI-WAN KENOBI

FORREST, DUKE see MASH

FORTY THIEVES see ALI BABA

42 [*Literature*]
42 is the answer to the ultimate question of 'life, the universe and everything', according to Douglas Adams' *The Hitch Hiker's Guide to the Galaxy* (1978–80). *The Hitch Hiker's Guide* has been presented on radio (its original form), as a TV series, and in book form. According to Adams, an incredibly advanced culture built a massive computer called **Deep Thought**, asked it the ultimate question, and after aeons of computation it came up with the answer '42'. A surprising number of people have since come up with evidence to support this.

FOTHERINGTON-THOMAS see NIGEL MOLESWORTH

FOUR HORSEMEN OF THE APOCALYPSE see APOCALYPSE

FOURTH ESTATE [*History, Government*]
The Fourth Estate is journalists, 'estate' here meaning force for government. The term comes from Macaulay's comment (1843) 'The gallery [in parliament] in which the reporters sit has become the fourth estate of the realm'.

FRANKENSTEIN [*Literature*]
In Mary Shelly's novel *Frankenstein, or the Modern Prometheus* (1818) Victor Frankenstein is the name of the scientist who creates a form of life by sewing bits of corpses together and galvanising them to life. However, many allusions to Frankenstein today treat it as the name of his monster. The standard appearance of the monster, with large head, bolt through the neck and sewing scars, owes much to film portrayals such as that of LON CHANEY, while elements such as the storm and lightening bolt which brings the creature to life, the scientist's maniacal laughter and the deformed assistant **Igor** have taken on a life of their own, totally unconnected with the novel. The element 'Franken-' seems also to be developing a life of its own, whether it be in such names as the ROCKY HORROR SHOW's Dr Frank N. Furter, or in such new words as the term 'Frankenfood' for genetically engineer food.

FRANKIE AND JOHNNY [*Song*]
In the old song Frankie and Johnny were lovers, who 'swore to be true to each other' but 'he done her wrong', so Frankie gets a gun and shoots Johnny as he sits drinking with his new girl. They are the opposite of DARBY AND JOAN.

FREUD, SIGMUND [*Psychoanalysis*]
The Austrian Sigmund Freud (1876–1939) was the father of psychoanalysis. He introduced many revolutionary ideas about the development of sexual identity, and inevitably these are the elements of his work that have caught the public's imagination. A Freudian slip is technically any action, such as a slip of the tongue which reveals an unconscious thought, but is often used merely for an unintentional sexual innuendo.

FU MANCHU [*Literature, Film*]
Doctor Fu Manchu is the archetypal cunning Oriental villain in a series of novels (1912–) by Sax Rhomer. There were also numerous films featuring the cruel doctor.

FUDGE, MR [*Literature, Popular Culture*]
Mr Fudge is a corrupt medium in Robert Browning's poem *Mr Fudge the Medium*. It is also the name of the Chief Buyer in the BRISTOW cartoon strip.

FURIES [*Mythology*]
The **Erinyes** or Furies, in Greek myth, had the job of avenging crime, especially those against the family. They were winged women, sometimes shown with snakes in their hair like MEDUSA, were called **Alecto**, **Megaera** and **Tisiphone**, and chased evil doers until their crimes were avenged. People were not surprisingly reluctant to call themselves to these beings' attention, and so if they had to name them might call them the **Eumenides**, or 'the kindly ones' in an attempt to placate them.

GADERENE SWINE [*Religion*]
In the Bible (Matthew 8), Jesus was preaching in the land of the Gadarenes when He was brought a man possessed by many devils. He cast them out of the man into a herd of pigs which thereupon rushed into the nearby lake and drowned themselves. Gadarene swine is thus used of people who rush headlong into things.

GAEA see TITAN

GAGOOL THE CRONE [*Literature*]
Gagool the Crone is the female witch-doctor in H. Rider Haggard's *King Solomon's Mines* (1885). See also ALLAN QUARTERMAIN.

GALAHAD [*Mythology*]
Sir Galahad was the noblest and purest of KING ARTHUR's knights, the only one pure enough fully to achieve the quest of the HOLY GRAIL. Strictly speaking, allusions to him should be to this nobility, but in practice his name is generally used for a rescuer, as an alternative for 'a knight in shining armour'.

GALATEA see PYGMALION

GALILEO [*Mathematics, Astronomy, Physics*]
The Italian Galileo Galilei (1564–1642) was a pioneering mathematician, astronomer and physicist. One of the things he is best remembered for is the perfection of the telescope and the number of new discoveries he made as a result, so allusions to Galileo sometime refer to the thrill and sense of wonder this must have caused. He is also remembered for being prosecuted by the INQUISITION for his belief that the earth moved round the sun, and not

the other way round as the Church believed. He was forced to renounce his view, but is said to have remarked 'Eppur si muove' ('Yet it does move') afterwards.

GALORE, PUSSY [Film]
Pussy Galore is the glamorous baddy who falls for JAMES BOND in *Goldfinger*.

GAMGEE, SAM see MORDOR

GANDALF [Literature]
Gandalf is the great White Wizard in J. R. R. TOLKIEN's *The Hobbit* and *Lord of the Rings*. It is he who first introduced BILBO BAGGINS to adventure and he plays a crucial part is guiding the participants in the fight against evil. In quieter times and places his is famous for his skill at making fireworks. See also GOLLUM, MORDOR.

GANDHI [History]
Mahatma Gandhi (1869–1948) was a major campaigner for Indian independence, but only through peaceful means, particularly passive resistance.

GANELON see ROLAND AND OLIVER

GANG OF FOUR [History]
In Chinese politics the Gang of Four were four politicians, including CHAIRMAN MAO's wife, who unsuccessfully tried to take power after Mao's death in 1976. From these the name was taken and applied to the four members of the Labour Party who broke away in 1981 to form the Social Democratic Party which later merged with the Liberals, and now the term can be found used of any group of four people operating together.

GANTRY, ELMER [Literature, Film]
In Sinclair Lewis's 1927 novel of that name, Elmer Gantry is a prototype televangelist. A handsome former professional footballer, he is a fiery evangelical preacher who turns his church into a profitable business, thanks to a large extent to the charms he has for his female parishioners.

GARBO, GRETA [*Film*]

The Swedish film actress Greta Garbo (1905–90) was famous for her austere beauty and for her reclusiveness. She probably never made her most famous declaration, 'I want to be alone', but rather that she wanted to be 'let alone' by the press; but nevertheless the image remains.

GARDEN OF EARTHLY DELIGHT see HIERONYMUS BOSCH

GARGANTUA, GARGANTUAN [*Literature*]

Gargantua is the giant king with the enormous appetite in RABELAIS' *Gargantua and Pantagruel* (1534). Thus **Gargantuan** means enormous.

GARNET, ALF [*Television*]

Alf Garnet is the small-minded, loud-mouthed, bigoted, racist, self-pitying East End docker in the TV comedy *Till Death US Do Part* (1966–68, 1972–75). Right-wing, easily enraged, sexist and politically incorrect, Alf was used to ridicule all he stood for and has become the symbol of his type. A great fan of the clean-up-TV campaigner **Mary Whitehouse**, it is said that, ironically, he was the character she made most complaints about. See ARCHIE BUNKER.

GARVIN, WILLIE see MODESTY BLAISE

GASCOIGNE, PAUL see GAZZA

GATSBY, JAY [*Literature*]

In F. Scott Fitzgerald's *The Great Gatsby* (1925), Jay Gatsby is a combination of the tough – he is an ex-bootlegger – and the innocent romantic. He has long loved **Daisy Buchanan**, and despite her marriage tries to break into her charmed social circle to win her heart, with tragic results.

GAUDI [*Architecture*]

The Spaniard Antonio Gaudi (1852–1925) was an architect of enormous originality. Starting where Art Nouveau left off, he created colourful buildings based on curves rather than lines, which look organic rather than built.

GAZZA [*Sport*]
Footballer Paul Gascoigne, 'Gazza', has won fame and notoriety for many things, but what perhaps remains most firmly fixed in the public mind is when he cried on the pitch at England's 1990 World Cup game with Germany. Thus 'to do a Gazza' is to burst into tears.

GEDDES AXE see DR BEECHING

GEHENNA [*Religion*]
In the Bible Gehenna is a place where the wicked are punished after death; thus the word can be used for an alternative to Hell.

GEKKO, GORDON [*Film*]
Gordon Gekko is the ruthless businessman in the trade-mark braces who believed greed is good in the 1987 film *Wall Street*.

GENGHIS KHAN [*History*]
Genghis Khan (c. 1162–1227) was the conquering Mongol leader who probably ruled a greater area of land than anyone else has ever done. His lands stretched from the Black Sea to the Pacific. He has a reputation for barbarity and cruelty. See also ATTILA THE HUN.

GEORGE see FAMOUS FIVE

GEPETTO see PINOCCHIO

GERONIMO [*History*]
Geronimo (1829–1909) was an Apache Indian chief who repeatedly led his people against the encroachment of the whites. For some reason – there is a story that one of the training grounds overlooks an bluff where is he said to have made a daring leap – 'Geronimo' was adopted by US paratroopers as a cry to give when they jumped, and from there it has spread into more general use.

GESSLER see WILLIAM TELL

GESTAPO [*History*]
The Gestapo were the secret state police (the meaning of their

name) of HITLER's Germany. They were notorious for their ruth-
lessness and the cruelty of their interrogation. Gestapo has come
to be used of any oppressive force.

GESTE, BEAU [*Literature*]
P. C. Wren's best-selling novel *Beau Geste* (1924) tells the story of
how the dazzling, romantic and quixotic Michael 'Beau' Geste
runs away to join the French Foreign Legion in order to draw
accusations of having stolen a priceless sapphire onto himself, to
save the real perpetrator from the consequences of their actions.
He is followed by his equally romantic (and equally snobbish)
brothers **Digby** and **John**, and they end up fighting Arabs in the
Sahara at **Fort Zinderneuf** in the charge of the sadistic **Sergeant
Lejaune**. The story is told in part by **Henri De Beaujolais**, a rather
comic, but brave and gentlemanly – he is, after all, half-English
and had been to Eton – French officer, and partly by John, the only
brother to survive the ordeal.

GETHSEMENE, GARDEN OF [*Religion*]
In the Bible the Garden of Gethsemene is the place where Jesus
went to pray on the night before His betrayal and where,
anguished and doubting His ability to face what was about to
happen, He prayed to 'let this cup pass from me' and found the
strength to go on.

GHENT TO AIX, HOW THEY BROUGHT THE GOOD NEWS FROM [*Literature*]
Robert Browning's *How They Brought the Good News From Ghent to
Aix* is an account of a mad ride, so bruising that the horses die
under them, of three messengers with the said news. It is told in a
rhythm that admirably imitates the galloping and is used as a
symbol of an epic, rushed journey.

GHOSTBUSTERS [*Film*]
Ghostbusters is a 1984 film in which a group of people set themselves up in business offering a supernatural cleaning service getting rid of spooks in New York. It had noted special effects,
including a device that vacuumed up the ghosts.

GIBSON GIRLS [*Popular Culture*]
The drawings of the American illustrator Charles Dana Gibson (1867–1944) defined the image of young American girlhood in the 1890s and 1900: junoesque, with big melting eyes, a tiny waist and usually dressed for sport. Important models for developing this image were three sisters, one of whom as Nancy Astor became the first woman to take her seat as a British Member of Parliament.

GILES [*Popular Culture*]
Giles was the name used by the cartoonist Carl Ronald Giles (1916–95). His famous cartoons featured a dysfunctional extended family full of horrible kids and which included skinny **Auntie Vera** with her permanent runny nose and the stout, formidable **Grandma**, with her black coat, Sunday hat and flailing umbrella.

GILLESPIE, DR see DR KILDARE

GILLIS, JOE see NORMA DESMOND

GINGER see BIGGLES, WILLIAM BROWN

GIOCONDA see MONA LISA

GIOVANNI, DON [*Opera*]
Don Giovanni is Mozart's form of the name of DON JUAN in his 1787 opera. He has a valet, **Leporello,** who keeps score of his master's conquests and whose role in the opera is to provide the wry comments of the common man on his master's doings.

GLINDA see WIZARD OF OZ

GLOSSOP, SIR RODERICK see BERTIE WOOSTER

GNASHER see DENNIS THE MENACE

GODBER see NORMAN STANLEY FLETCHER

GODFATHER, THE see CORLEONE FAMILY

GODOT [*Drama*]
Samuel Beckett's 1952 play *Waiting for Godot* features two tramps, **Vladimir** and **Estragon** sitting under a tree, arguing about many things, but mainly about Godot, who they are expecting any moment. Godot never turns up. Critics are still arguing about what the play means, but Godot, for someone who keeps you waiting has entered the language, as in 'Marilyn Monroe ... arriving on set with a lateness that would make Godot seem almost neurotically punctual' (*Independent* 11.5.96).

GODZILLA [*Film*]
Godzilla is a gigantic prehistoric monster wakened from the seabed by an atomic bomb test who threatens to overwhelm Tokyo in the 1955 Japanese film (originally called *Gojira*) which was the first of a series of Godzilla films. Although these are nominally horror films, they are so over the top that they are usually watched for laughs.

GOLCONDA [*History*]
Golconda is a ruined city in southern India which in the past was famous for the diamonds mined nearby. Thus Golconda became a term for a rich mine, and was often given to real (or fraudulent) mines in the USA gold rush.

GOLDEN AGE [*Mythology*]
In Classical myth the Golden Age was a time of innocent contentment, when humans did not fight, and did not have to work for their food; the equivalent of the GARDEN OF EDEN. From this it has come to mean an age when something had reached its most perfect form. See also ARCADIA.

GOLDEN APPLES [*Mythology*]
According to Greek myth, far away in the West in the garden of the **Hesperides** ('Daughters of Evening') stands a tree bearing golden apples. This is guarded by both the Hesperides and by a dragon. One of the labours of HERCULES was to pick some of these apples, but he needed the help of the giant ATLAS to get them, and had to take over his job of holding up the sky while Atlas got them for him. Apples are also important in Celtic mythology and the

poet W. B. Yeats develops this idea to write of picking 'The silver apples of the moon, / The golden apples of the sun.' (*Song of Wandering Aengus* 1899).

GOLDEN FLEECE [*Mythology*]
In Greek myth the task of **Jason** and the Argonauts (see ARGO) was to fetch the Golden Fleece kept by the king of Colchis (probably part of modern Georgia on the Black Sea). The fleece was well guarded by supernatural killing machines (see DRAGON'S TEETH) but Jason was helped by the king's witch-daughter **Medea**.

GOLDEN HIND see SIR FRANCIS DRAKE

GOLDFINGER, AURIC see JAMES BOND

GOLDILOCKS [*Folklore*]
The heroine of the story of *Goldilocks and the Three Bears*, despite the fact that she enters the bears' cottage and tests half their belongings to destruction, has come to represent any sweet little blond child, as in 'Cute little Goldilocks is patted and petted like a doll, while her dark little sister is treated more as a tomboy.' (*Mail on Sunday* 7.4.96).

GOLGOTHA see CALVARY

GOLIATH see DAVID AND GOLIATH

GOLLUM [*Literature*]
Gollum is a small, slimy creature in J. R. R. Tolkien's *Lord of the Rings*. We are repelled by him, but pity him at the same time. He found the ring of power, and has been utterly corrupted by it. Unable to be without it after BILBO BAGGINS finds it, he endures incredible hardships in his attempts to regain it, but its power over him is the ring's destruction, for while FRODO BAGGINS hesitates to destroy the ring, in a wild attempt to regain it Gollum grabs it and falls into the only fires that can end its power. See also GANDALF, MORDOR.

GOMEZ see ADDAMS FAMILY

GOMORRAH see SODOM AND GOMORRAH

GONERIL AND REGAN [*Literature*]
Goneril and Regan are the two ungrateful daughters of Shakespeare's KING LEAR, whose ill-treatment of their aged father brings on his final madness. They are alluded to far more frequently than their virtuous sister **Cordelia**.

GOOD SAMARITAN [*Religion*]
In the Bible (Luke 10) the Good Samaritan is the social outcast who looks after a man who has been mugged and beaten, and whose plight has been ignored by others. A Good Samaritan is therefore a person who comes to someone's help.

GOODY TWO SHOES [*Children's Literature*]
The History of Little Goody Two-Shoes, appeared in 1765 and is generally considered the first novel written for children. It tells the story of a poor orphan, Margery, who was persecuted by the local squire and who was so poor she had only one shoe, who got her name when she was given a pair, and went round showing everyone and saying 'Two shoes!' She was too poor to go to school, but got her learning by borrowing books from other children after school and became a school teacher, eventually marrying a lord and buying out the wicked squire. Nowadays 'a goody two-shoes' used for either sex is the equivalent of 'a goody-goody'.

GOONS [*Radio*]
The Goon Show was an enormously popular BBC radio comedy programme which ran from 1952 to 1960. The comedy was surreal and off-beat, with a regular cast of characters such as **Neddie Seagoon, Eccles, Bluebottle, Major Bloodnock, Minnie Bannister** and **Henry Crun**, voices all supplied by Spike Milligan, Harry Seacome and Peter Sellars. It spawned innumerable catchphrases including 'You've gone and deaded me, you dirty rotten swine, you!', 'He's fallen in the water!' and 'You can't get the wood, you know'.

GORDIAN KNOT [*History, Mythology*]
According to Greek legend, King Gordius had tied a knot so intri-

cate that no one could undo it, and it was said that if anyone could, they would rule all Asia. Alexander the Great is supposed to have solved the problem by taking his sword and cutting the knot in two.

GORDON, FLASH [*Film, Television, Popular Culture*]
Flash Gordon, American football star and space hero, started life as a strip cartoon in 1934, but since then has moved into other media including film and TV. Many of his adventures take place on the planet **Mongo**, where he and his girlfriend **Dale Arden**, aided by the eccentric **Dr Zarkov**, combat the evil **Ming the Merciless**.

GORGONS see MEDUSA

GORMENGHAST [*Literature*]
In the Gormenghast novels of Mervyn Peake (1911–68), Gormenghast is a vast Gothic castle – so vast you could wander in it for days, and it is all but a world of its own – where life is ruled by ritual, normal people are dehumanised and the wildest and most dangerous eccentricities can flourish. Life there has a nightmarish quality, (for instance one character disappears, believed eaten by owls), and events and emotions have a GARGANTUAN scale that matches the building. **Titus Groan** is the reluctant heir to the earldom, but yearns to learn of the outside world, a wish that is shockingly granted when the whole system is overturned by the sinister **Steerpike**.

GOTHAM, GOTHAM CITY [*History, Folklore*]
The village of Gotham in Lincolnshire was famous for its fools, referred to mockingly as the **Wise men of Gotham** (although there is a story that their foolishness was actually a clever way to get out of paying the medieval equivalent of taxes). The name Gotham was taken from here and applied ironically to New York, a use perhaps best known now from BATMAN's Gotham City.

GOTTERDÄMMERUNG [*Mythology*]
In German myth Gotterdämmerung, 'the twilight of the gods', is the time at the end of the world when there will be a mighty bat-

tle between the gods and their traditional enemies the forces of evil, and the world will end in flood and flames. In the related Norse myth this is called **Ragnarök**.

GRABBER see MRS JOYFUL, NIGEL MOLESWORTH

GRABLE, BETTY [*Film*]
The American singer, dancer and film actress Betty Grable (1916–73) was the most popular pin-up of the Second World War. Her legs were particularly admired, and were insured for one million dollars.

GRACELANDS [*Popular Culture*]
Gracelands was the home of the late, great **Elvis Presley**. Now open to the public, no money was spared on its lavish interior, and it has become a byword for vulgar, expensive bad taste.

GRACES [*Mythology*]
The Three Graces are variously named by different authorities, but are most commonly called Euphrosyne (Mirth), Aglaia (Splendour) and Thalia (Good Cheer). They represent the higher graces of life, but seem to have had little real function in classical myth other than as symbolic attendants. However, they have provided artists with a convenient subject for studies of scantily clad females.

GRACULUS see NOGGIN THE NOG

GRADGRIND [*Literature*]
Thomas Gradgrind is a soulless schoolmaster in Charles Dickens' *Hard Times* (1854). He believes only in hard scientific fact and discipline, and everything else is suppressed in his school. '[They] believed that all one needed in the national curriculum were English, maths and science. It was a sort of Gradgrind curriculum in my view, not a rounded one.' (Kenneth Baker, quoted *Evening Standard* 31.5.96).

GRAND GUIGNOL [*Drama]*]
Le Grand Guignol was originally the name of a theatre in Paris'

Montmartre. There they showed short, gruesome plays, designed to give their audience a thrill of horror. The name of the theatre became attached to this sort of play, and the term is now used to describe anything excessively gruesome.

GRANDMA see GILES

GRANGE HILL [Television]
Grange Hill is a hard-hitting children's soap opera shown on BBC TV since 1978. Set in Grange Hill Comprehensive school, this realistic series shows school life as it can really be (it is even filmed with the cameras at child height). It has been very controversial at times, but has a strong following among school-age children, many of whom find their own problems reflected in the series.

GRANTLY, REVEREND DOCTOR THEOPHILUS see BARSETSHIRE

GRAY, DORIAN [Literature]
In Oscar Wilde's The Picture of Dorian Gray (1891), Dorian Gray is an extraordinarily beautiful young man who gradually falls into a life of increasing corruption. His dissipation seems to have no effect on him, and he never seems to age. In the end it is revealed that he has a **portrait** or **picture in his attic** which changes, growing old and hideously revealing all his corruption, while Gray remains untouched.

GRAY, NELLY see BEN BOLT

GRAYSON, DICK see BATMAN

GREAT GATSBY see JAY GATSBY

GREAT LEAP FORWARD see MAO

GREAT TEA-TROLLEY DISASTER, THE see BRISTOW

GREEN-EYED MONSTER [Literature]
In Shakespeare's play Othello, Othello is warned 'Beware, my lord,

of jealousy; / It is the green-eyed monster which doth mock / The meat it feeds on', and from this the term has entered the language.

GREENSTREET, SIDNEY see MALTESE FALCON

GRENDEL [*Literature*]
In the great Anglo-Saxon epic *Beowulf* Grendel is a monstrous outcast of society, marked as a descendant of CAIN. The joy of feasting in King **Hrothgar's** hall is a torment to him, and while everyone is asleep he takes and eats Hrothgar's warriors. The hero **Beowulf** fights Grendel and tears off his arm. Grendel flees to the pool where he lives with his mother, and dies. The next night Grendel's mother comes to take revenge and kills another man. Beowulf tracks her down to her lair and kills her too after a mighty fight.

GREYFRIARS SCHOOL see BILLY BUNTER

GREYSTOKE, LORD see TARZAN

GRIM REAPER [*Folklore*]
In popular art Death is often shown as a skeleton in a black hooded cloak carrying a scythe with which he mows down the living. From this comes the term the Grim Reaper for Death.

GRIMES, CAPTAIN see LLANABBA

GRISELDA, PATIENT [*Literature*]
In the *Canterbury Tales* by Geoffrey Chaucer (c. 1340–1400), the story of Patient Griselda tells of a poor woman chosen as a wife by a duke, on condition she does not question anything he does. He tests her to the limit, even taking her children away and telling her (falsely) that they have been killed, but she keeps her promise. Thus a Patient Griselda is any long-suffering, uncomplaining wife.

GROAN, TITUS see GORMENGHAST

GROMIT see WALLACE

GROUCHO see MARX BROTHERS

GROUP 4 [*Business, Popular Culture*]
When the company Group 4 took over the running of some of Britain's prisons they were plagued by a series of escapes and similar problems, so that their name became synonymous in the public mind with inefficiency and the ability to lose things.

GRUB STREET [*History, Literature*]
At one time Grub Street in London was the chosen hang out of struggling writers and journalists, and the term has now come to mean a literary hack.

GRUNDY, MRS [*Drama*]
In Thomas Morton's play *Speed the Plough* (1798) the question 'What will Mrs Grundy say?' is always being raised. The play is now virtually unknown but the character of Mrs Grundy, for a small-minded person who likes to limit what other people can do, lives on.

GUB GUB THE PIG see DR DOLITTLE

GUINEVERE see ROUND TABLE

GULAG [*Literature, History*]
Strictly speaking 'Gulag' is the term for the administration of them, but it is generally used as a term for the Soviet Russian forced labour camps in which so many, particularly political, prisoners died. The word became widely known from Alexander Solzhenitsyn's 1974 work, *Gulag Archipelago*.

GULLIVER, LEMUEL see BROBDINGNAGIAN, LILLIPUT, YAHOO

GUMMIDGE, WORZEL [*Television, Children's Literature*]
Worzel Gummidge is the scarecrow of **Scatterbrook Farm** who comes to life and has comic adventures with **Susan and John Peters** in Barbara Euphan Todd's series of books about him. These were used as a basis for a very popular TV series (1979–81) using the comic talents of Jon Pertwee. Worzel Gummidge is chiefly known for his strong yokel accent and his wild straw hair.

GUMP, FORREST [*Film*]

This 1994 film tells the story of a very simple-minded man whose essential innocence carries him through all the horrors of 20th-century life, such as the Vietnam War, untouched, until he becomes a sort of reluctant guru. Forrest Gump is now used to indicate harmless idiocy.

GUNN, BEN [*Literature*]

In R. L. Stevenson's *Treasure Island* (1883), pathetic, wild-looking Ben Gunn is a former member of CAPTAIN FLINT's crew, marooned for years on Treasure Island. His isolation has affected his wits and his speech but this has not stopped him finding the buried treasure. The thing he has missed most is cheese: 'Many's the night I've dreamed of cheese – toasted, mostly'.

GUTENBURG [*History, Technology*]

Johann Gutenberg (c. 1400–68) was the inventor of movable type for printing, and set up the first printing press in his native Germany. In 1455 he produced the first printed Bible, know as the Gutenberg Bible. His invention made the wide ownership of books, and the spread of the information in them, possible, which introduced major social changes, and his name has come to represent the printed word. With the spread of other forms of communication, such as TV and the Internet, it has become common to talk in such terms as a pre- or post-Gutenberg society.

GUTMAN see MALTESE FALCON

GUYS AND DOLLS see RUNYON, DAMON

GWYN, NELL [*History*]

Nell Gwyn (1651–87) was the actress, and former orange-seller in theatres who became mistress of King Charles II. 'Don't let poor Nelly starve' is said to have been among the king's last words.

HACKER, JIM see SIR HUMPHREY

HADDOCK, CAPTAIN [*Literature, Popular Culture*]
Captain Haddock is the irascible, blustering sea-captain in the adventures of TIN-TIN. He is given to extraordinary exclamations such as 'Great blistering bashi-bazouks!'

HADES [*Mythology*]
Hades is the classical underworld, the land of the dead. In the past it was frequently used as a polite term for Hell.

HAIGHT-ASHBURY [*History*]
The Haight-Ashbury district of San Francisco became a centre of the Hippie life-style in the 1960s, but soon degenerated into the centre for the drug trade.

HAL [*Literature, Film*]
HAL 9000 is the talking computer running the space-ship in Arthur C. Clark's book *2001: A Space Odyssey* and the spectacular film made of it (both 1968). The space-ship is on a voyage to find the origins of a large, tomb-stone-like monolith that seems to have had a major influence on mankind's development, but HAL misfunctions, and after killing two of the crew has to be dismantled by the sole survivor.

HALL, ANNIE [*Film*]
This 1977 Woody Allen film about the difficulties of developing a relationship was a great box-office hit. The heroine's rather scatty, thrown-together style of dressing was also influential on fashions.

HAMLET [*Literature*]
Shakespeare's *Hamlet, Prince of Denmark* is usually referred to as

113

an example of hesitation and self-doubt, of a person who cannot make up his mind. Alternatively, since the plot of the play is kicked into action by the Ghost of Hamlet's Father, who tells his son how he has been murdered, he is used as an example of someone who had seen a ghost.

HAMMER, MIKE [*Literature*]
Mike Hammer is the 'one-man police force' private eye in Mickey Spillane's thrillers. He first appeared in 1947, and is a tough, bigoted sexist who seems to prefer violence to any other method. There have been several films featuring this unpleasant character, and a number of TV spin-offs.

HAMPDEN, JOHN [*History*]
John Hampden was a major player on the parliamentary side in the English Civil War. Hampden was a respected lawyer and Member of Parliament who opposed Charles I's attempts to rule without parliament, and when the king tried to levy 'shipmoney' refused to pay what he considered an illegal tax. This was one of the events which led directly to the outbreak of civil war. At one time Hampden was considered a national hero and a great defender of liberty, but nowadays his name is largely kept alive through the lines in Thomas Gray's *Elegy Written in a Country Churchyard* (1751), where he writes 'Full many a flower is born to blush unsees, / And waste its sweetness on the desert air. / Some village-Hampden, that with dauntless breast / The little tyrant of his fields withstood; / Some mute inglorious Milton here may rest, / Some Cromwell guiltless of his country's blood.'

HANDBAG see LADY BRACKNELL

HANDS, ISRAEL [*Literature*]
Although Israel Hands, first mate on the *Hispaniola*, is a comparatively minor character in R. L. Stevenson's *Treasure Island* (1883), his name crops up in allusion surprisingly often. This may be because, after LONG JOHN SILVER, he is the pirate that we see most of, and therefore the one in which we see the most evil; or it may be because Stevenson took the name Israel Hands from the real-life second mate of the notorious 18th-century pirate **Blackbeard**.

HANGING GARDENS OF BABYLON see BABYLON

HANNAY, RICHARD [*Literature*]

Richard Hannay is the hero of a series of JOHN BUCHAN adventure novels. He has made his pile in South Africa and retired while still in his prime to England, where he finds himself bored. However his life become much more exciting and he finds himself needing all his old bush-craft when he gets himself involved in murder and espionage in Scotland in *The Thirty-Nine Steps*. In subsequent books his patriotism and determination are put to good use countering other threats to his country.

HANNIBAL [*History, Military*]

The great Carthaginian general Hannibal (247–182 BC) is best known for taking elephants across the Alps, when he decided to take the Romans by surprise and invade from the north. No less a feat was the fact that he campaigned in Italy, cut off from his supply lines the other side of the Mediterranean, for 11 years, during which he ravaged Italy and inflicted several severe defeats on the Romans. Hannibal was a brilliant general whose tactics are still studied, and US General Norman Schwatzkopf says that he based his **Desert Storm** campaign against Iraq in the 1991 Gulf War on Hannibal's tactics.

HARDY BOYS [*Children' Literature*]

The Hardy Boys, Frank and Joe, are American teenage super-detectives. The male equivalents of NANCY DREW, their adventures, written by various hands, have been appearing since the 1920s. They should not be confused with the insufferably nice **Hardy Family**, inhabitants of a small midwestern town who appeared in 15 films made between 1937 and 1947.

HARDY, OLIVER see LAUREL AND HARDY

HARE see TORTOISE AND THE HARE

HARI, MATA [*History*]

The Dutch exotic dancer Mata Hari (1876–1917) was shot by the French on charges of spying for the Germans and using her relationships with various officers to extract information. Her name is thus used to indicate a seductive female spy.

HARPER'S FERRY [History]
In 1859 the Virginian town of Harper's Ferry was the site of one of the events which led up to the American Civil War, when **John Brown** and a group of anti-slavery followers tried to seize the government arsenal there, intending to use it for setting up a state for freed slaves. It took two days for Brown and his 21 followers to be defeated. Brown and the six survivors were hanged, but John Brown's name lives on in the song *John Brown's Body*.

HARPO see MARX BROTHERS

HARRISON, REX [Film]
The British actor Rex Harrison (1908–1990) was famous for his social polish, although his best-known part was that of the eccentric Professor Higgins in *My Fair Lady* (See ELIZA DOOLITTLE).

HARVEY [Film, Drama]
Harvey is a six-foot tall rabbit who can only be seen by the drunken Elwood P. Dowd. He comes from the 1944 comedy *Harvey* by Mary C. Chase, but is best known from the 1950 film of the play starring James Stewart. Harvey is therefore an imaginary friend, or anything other people cannot see.

HAW-HAW, LORD [History]
Lord Haw-Haw was the name, based on his posh voice, taken by William Joyce for the broadcasts he made to Britain during the Second World War from HITLER's Germany, urging the country to surrender and undermining morale.

HAWKEYE [Literature]
Hawkeye is the Indian name given to the backwoodsman **Natty Bumpo** in James Fennimore Cooper's 'Leatherstocking' series of stories. Hawkeye is intensely proud of his white blood, but has nevertheless adopted many of the ways of the red man and is more at home in the great American forest than among civilized people. The name comes from his unerring skill as a shot, using

the rifle he calls 'deer killer' but the Indians call 'la longue cara-
bine'. See also CHINGACHGOOK, UNCAS. For 'Hawkeye' Pierce see
MASH.

HAWKINS, JIM [*Literature*]
Jim Hawkins is the cabin-boy hero of R. S. Stevenson's *Treasure
Island* (1883). It is he who is given the treasure map that shows
where CAPTAIN FLINT's treasure is buried, and the story is told by
him. See also LONG JOHN SILVER.

HAYS CITY see WILD BILL HICKOK

HEARST, WILLIAM RANDOLPH [*History, Business*]
William Randolph Hearst (1863–1951) was a powerful newspaper
proprietor who used his wealth and influence to enter politics. He
was enormously wealthy and used some of this wealth to build
himself a fabulous castle home at San Simeon. Orson Welles'
much admired 1941 film **Citizen Kane** is based on Hearst.

HEATH ROBINSON see EMMET

HEATHCLIFF AND CATHY [*Literature*]
In Emily Brontë's highly romantic novel *Wuthering Heights*,
Heathcliff is the gypsy foundling adopted into the Earnshaw fam-
ily, whose dark, brooding presence dominates the novel.
Although he and the daughter of the house, Cathy, fall madly in
love, they never marry but, the novel implies, are united after
death. The 1939 film of the book has a memorable scene in which
Cathy and Heathcliff run from different direction across the
Yorkshire moors, calling to each other before embracing, which is
much alluded to.

HEEP, URIAH [*Literature*]
Uriah Heep is the ever-so-humble villain in Charles Dickens'
David Copperfield (1850). Physically repellent, he is an arch hyp-
ocrite and deceiver, who is always stressing his false humility.

HEIDI [*Children's Literature*]
In Johanna Spyri's 1881 children's novel which bears her name,

Heidi is a little orphan girl who comes to love the mountain life she leads in her grandfather's shepherd's hut where she plays with **Peter the goatherd**. Allusions to her are usually in the context of goats, mountains and all that is Alpine.

HELEN OF TROY [*Mythology*]
Helen of Troy was the most beautiful woman in the world, and her abduction from her husband **Menelaus** by the Trojan prince **Paris** was the cause of the TROJAN WAR. See also FAUSTUS.

HELICON [*Mythology*]
For the ancient world, Mount Helicon was the home of the MUSES, on which were found the two springs **Aganippe** and the better-known **Hippocrene**, drinking from which gave poetic inspiration. So to climb Helicon meant to aspire to write literature.

HELLFIRE CLUB [*History*]
The notorious Hellfire Club, which reputedly indulged in orgies and unspeakable rites at **Medmenham Abbey** was founded by Sir Francis Dashwood (1708–81) and included the radical politician John Wilkes among its members. It is used to indicate debauchery and indulgence as in 'You might therefore expect the followers of Arise to be some kind of latter-day Hellfire Club, made up of floppy-haired libertines and goblet-smashing sons of the stinking rich.' (*Evening Standard* 10.6.96).

HELMSLEY, LEONA [*Business, Crime*]
Leona Helmsley was a New York hotel owner famous for her meanness in running her organisations and the unreasonable demands she made of her staff. She is reputed to have said 'Only the little people pay tax', which caught up with her in 1989 when she was sentenced to four years in prison for tax evasion.

HÉLOISE see ABELARD

HELOTS see SPARTA

HEMINGWAY, ERNEST [*Literature*]
The American novelist Ernest Hemingway (1898–1961) wrote

admiringly of laconic, tough, macho men, and tried to live the life of those he admired. Thus his name has become a byword for this type, as in 'Rugged, hunter-gatherer, Hemingway men take huge risks and sacrifices in pursuit of their savage god.' (*Independent* 15.4.96).

HEPHAESTUS see ACHILLES, APHRODITE

HER INDOORS see ARTHUR DALEY

HERA [*Mythology*]
In Greek myth Hera is the Queen of the Gods. Plagued by the infidelities of her husband ZEUS, she has a tendency to turn his latest mistress into something unpleasant and to persecute the heroes who are his illegitimate sons. See also JUNO.

HERBERT, A. P. [*Literature*]
The English writer and politician A. P. Herbert (1890–1971) is best known for his comic and satirical writings presented in the form of legal reports.

HERCULES, HERACLES [*Mythology*]
Hercules to the Romans, Heracles to the Greeks, was one of the many sons of the god ZEUS by mortal women. He is famous for his strength and for performing twelve labours, imposed on him through the malevolence of HERA, such as the slaying of the **Nemean Lion,** whose skin he afterwards wore, and the killing of the **Lernaen Hydra.** The term **Herculean**, usually attached to such terms as 'strength' of 'effort', means 'mighty'. See also AUGEAN STABLES, GOLDEN APPLES, PROMETHEUS.

HERMES [*Mythology*]
Hermes was the Greek god of merchants and thieves, and also the messenger of the gods. He is shown wearing a hat and winged sandals and carries the caduceus, a rod with serpents twined round it. He also conducts the dead to HADES. The Romans called him **Mercury**.

HERMINIUS, TITUS see HORATIUS

HEROD [*Religion, History*]
Herod, King of Judea appears in the Bible nativity story as the king visited by the Three Wise Men. When they did not return to tell him where he could find the baby whom he regarded as a rival to his throne, he tried to make sure the infant Jesus was killed by ordering the **Slaughter of the Innocents** – the execution of all male children under two. His punishment was supposed to have been to die by being eaten alive by maggots which burst from his insides. Allusions to Herod are usually in the context of children, as in 'Jimmy Hill is to football what King Herod was to babysitting' (Tommy Docherty, June 1992) or Anthony Hope's comment after the first night of PETER PAN: 'Oh for an hour of Herod!'

HERODOTUS [*History*]
The Greek writer Herodotus (c. 484–424 BC) is known as 'The Father of History' as he was the first writer to try to asses the value of his sources, rather than to tell an uncritical story.

HESPERIDES see GOLDEN APPLES

HICKOK, WILD BILL [*History*]
The American James Butler Hickok (1837–1876), known as Wild Bill Hickok, led a varied life. As a young man he was involved in the anti-slavery movement and helped escaping slaves; in the Civil War he was a spy and scout. He even spent a couple of years appearing in BUFFALO BILL's Wild West Show. But he is most famous for his legendary marksmanship and as a lawman. In Kansas he was sheriff of **Hays City** and then Marshall of **Abilene**, two of the wildest frontier towns of the time; both became noticeably tamer for his work. Later he moved on to the **Black Hills of Dakota**, and became Marshall of Deadwood where his name was romantically linked with CALAMITY JANE. Soon after he was appointed Marshall he was playing poker and was shot through the back of the head by a stranger, Jack McCall, whose motives were never established. Hickok was holding aces and eights at the time, and this hand is said still to be known as the **Dead Man's Hand**, a tradition alluded to at the end of the 1939 classic cowboy film *Stagecoach*.

HIGGINS, HENRY see ELIZA DOOLITTLE

HIPPOCRATES [*Medicine*]
Hipporates of Cos (c. 460–377 BC) was famed throughout Greece in his lifetime for his skills as a physician and is known as the father of medicine. Sixty works attributed to him still survive. The Hippocratic oath, although probably not formulated by him, is an ancient oath, versions of which some medical schools still require their students to take. It sets out the duties of a doctor to the profession and to the patients – to prescribe only beneficial treatments to the best of their abilities and judgement; not to cause harm or hurt; and to live an exemplary personal and professional life.

HIPPOCRENE see HELICON

HIROSHIMA [*History*]
On 6 August 1945 the first atomic bomb to be used in war was dropped on the Japanese city of Hiroshima and 75,000 people were killed, with many more dying later from the radiation. **Nagasaki** later received the same treatment. Hiroshima has come to represent all the horrors of nuclear war.

HISPANIOLA see LONG JOHN SILVER

HITCHCOCK, ALFRED [*Film*]
The British film director Alfred Hitchcock (1899–1980) is regarded as the master of stylish thrillers, and is famous for his handling of terror and suspense and for his ability to surprise the audience by the twists of his plots.

HITLER, ADOLF [*History*]
The horrific career of Adolf Hitler (1889–1945) is too well known to need describing here. Allusions to him are usually to his melodramatic delivery of speeches (and their accompanying showmanship), his toothbrush moustache, or simply as another term for 'tyrant'. See also MEIN KAMPF.

HOBBITS see BAGGINS, BILBO AND FRODO

HOGARTH [*Art*]
The English painter and engraver William Hogarth (1697–1764) is

121

particularly noted for his engravings satirising social corruption –
as in *The Rake's Progress* or *Marriage à la Mode* – and for his depictions of the corruption of the poor as in *Gin Lane*.

HOLMES, SHERLOCK [*Literature*]
The great detective Sherlock Holmes first appeared in print in
1887 in Sir Arthur Conan Doyle's novel *A Study in Scarlet*. He lives
as **221B Baker Street** with his friend **Dr Watson** who is the narrator of the stories and something of a butt for Holmes. They are
looked after by their landlady **Mrs Hudson**. When he needs information Holmes calls on the **Baker Street Irregulars** – small boys
whom he pays to follow suspects and assist in other ways. During
the Second World War the Special Operations Executive, a branch
of the secret services which was based in Baker Street, took this
name for themselves, and it is also used by the US Holmes fan
club. Holmes often comes into conflict with **Inspector Lestrade**, a
policeman with not a fraction of Holmes' intelligence, although he
also helps Lestrade at other times. The only woman Holmes
admired was **Irene Adler**, a beautiful adversary who eluded him,
but his main antagonist is the fiendishly cunning **Professor
Moriarty**. Holmes has a brother, **Mycroft**, who is even more intelligent than he is. Holmes is a master of disguise, but his real skill
lies in his deductive abilities and his skill at interpreting evidence.
While capable of being very active, he is as likely to solve problems by sitting and thinking – a tough case may be described as 'a
three pipe problem'. Holmes' real enemy is boredom; at first this
may be helped by playing the violin, but if no cases come, then he
may take refuge in a **seven-per-cent solution** of cocaine –
although it should be remembered that such drugs were not illegal when Doyle was writing, and people had a very different attitude to them. The innumerable film and TV adaptation of the
Sherlock Holmes stories have played a large part in fixing his
image – the deerstalker hat and cape, curved pipe and the
swirling London fogs in which he operates.

HOLY GRAIL [*Mythology*]
In the legends of KING ARTHUR the Holy Grail is a dish or bowl
used by Christ and his apostles at the Last Supper. The search for
it becomes the last great quest of the ROUND TABLE, and ultimately

breaks up the group of knights, for only GALAHAD is pure enough to attain it. In modern times it is usually shown as a chalice of the sort used for Holy Communion, but in the earliest texts it is a dish, and it may originally have been something more like a cauldron, the Welsh equivalent of the HORN OF PLENTY. The term has come increasingly into use as an ultimate goal, of something every one aspires to, as in 'But the Holy Grail [of the media] is interactive TV' (*Evening Standard* 31.10.96).

HOMER [*Literature, Mythology*]

Homer was a Greek poet who lived around 800 BC and whose name is attached to the great Greek epics of the TROJAN WAR, *The Iliad* and *The* ODYSSEY. Little is known of him, but by tradition he was blind. His poems tell of the great deeds of heroes, and the term **Homeric** is used to mean imposing or heroic, and in the case of **Homeric laughter**, refers to unrestrained laughter such as he shows the Greek gods indulging in, particularly when watching the goings on of mere mortals or enjoying their feasts on OLYMPUS. Homer has long been regarded as one of the great masters of literature, but the Latin poet Horace (65–8 BC) wrote that 'even Homer nods' that is, makes mistakes, and this has become proverbial. So admired was Homer by the ancient Greeks that several cities disputed the honour of claiming to be his birth place and his burial place.

HOOD, ROBIN [*Folklore*]

Robin Hood is one of the great folk-heroes of England. An outlaw, deprived of his lands by the Norman overlord, Robin of Locksley became Robin Hood, and set himself up in **Sherwood Forest** to rob the rich – particularly the **Sheriff of Nottingham** – to give to the poor. With **Maid Marion** by his side, and with the help of his Merry Men including the gigantic **Little John**, the greedy **Friar Tuck** and the elegant **Will Scarlett**, he becomes a champion of the oppressed.

HOOK, CAPTAIN [*Drama, Film*]

Captain Hook is the Old Etonian pirate captain in PETER PAN. Peter and the **crocodile** have already disposed of his right hand, and the crocodile is out to get the rest of him. Luckily for Hook the crocodile has swallowed a clock, and for the moment its ticking warns him of the beast's approach. But he knows one day the clock will run down. A veneer of politeness hide's Hook's cruelty, and other than the crocodile the only thing he is afraid of is the sight of his own blood. See also TINKER BELL.

HORATIUS [*Literature, History*]

The story of how Horatius kept the bridge has become well known to English speakers through Lord Macaulay's stirring poem in his *Lays of Ancient Rome* (1842). After the TARQUINS had been expelled by BRUTUS, Tarquin turned to the Etruscans for help to regain his throne, and a large force under **Lars Porsena of Clusium** marched on Rome. The only hope for Rome was to chop down the bridge across the **Tiber** that gave access to the city and retreat behind the walls, but the enemy would be upon them before the bridge would fall. Horatius (Publius Horatius Cocles) volunteers to hold the head of the bridge against all comers, if two more will volunteer to help. **Spurius Larcius** and **Titus Herminius** volunteer, and the three are able to hold the narrow bride-head against the whole of Porsena's army. As the bridge starts to go Horatius send the other two back and holds it alone until it falls. Then praying to Father Tiber for help he plunges fully armed into the river, and against all the odds gains the bank of Rome in safety.

HORN OF PLENTY [*Mythology*]

The Horn of Plenty or **Cornucopia** was, in Greek myth, the horn of **Amalthea**, which provides its owner with whatever they desire in the way of food or drink. Authorities vary as to whether Amalthea is the name of the goat that suckled Zeus as an infant and which was rewarded by being turned into the star sign **Capricorn**, or the name of the goat's owner. Whichever, the goat's horn was turned into the cornucopia, which became a symbol of plenty, especially in art.

HORSEMEN, FOUR see APOCALYPSE

HOTEL CALIFORNIA [*Song*]

This is the title of a 1977 hit song by The Eagles. Allusions to it usually refer to the lines 'You can check out any time you like, / But you can never leave'.

HOUDINI [*History, Popular Culture*]
Harry Houdini (1874–1926) was an American magician and escapolgist whose death-defying feats caused his name to be used for someone who can get out of anything.

HOULIHAN, HOTLIPS see MASH

HOUYHNHNMS see YAHOOS

HOVIS BOY [*Advertising, Television*]
For many years Hovis bread was advertised on TV by a series of advertisements showing nostalgic scenes, purporting to be from the early part of this century, of a boy going through considerable physical effort to obtain his loaf of Hovis. The term Hovis boy had come to be used of this poor-but-honest image.

HOYLE, ACCORDING TO [*History, Popular Culture*]
Sir Edmund Hoyle (1672–1769) produced a book of rules for card games, which became the authority on how they should be played. From this the expression 'according to Hoyle' meaning 'by the book' or 'just as it should be' arose.

HROTHGAR see GRENDEL

HUDSON [*Television*]
In the hugely successful TV series *Upstairs, Downstairs* (1971–75) showed life in an upper-class London home between 1903 and 1930 through the eyes of those above stairs – the **Bellamy Family** -and through the eyes of the servants below stairs. The affairs of the Bellamy household were controlled by the quiet but firm butler Hudson, and his has become the name referred to most often, although the name of the cook, **Mrs Bridges** lives on as a brand name for food products. For the unrelated Mrs Hudson see SHERLOCK HOLMES.

HUER, DR see BUCK ROGERS

HUEY, LEWIE AND DEWEY see DONALD DUCK

HUGGY BEAR see STARSKY AND HUTCH

HUGHES, YOSSER [*Television*]
When Alan Bleasdale's hard-hitting series of TV plays *Boys from the Blackstuff* was shown in 1982 the character of Yosser Hughes struck the conscience of the nation. The plays showed the lives of a group of Liverpool tarmac-layers facing a bleak and hopeless future in the face of mass unemployment. Yosser Hughes goes round everywhere desperately searching for work to support his family, and his cries of 'Gissa job' and 'I can do that' after he has met with no success lead to violence and despair.

HUGO, VICTOR see QUASIMODO

HUMBERT HUMBERT see LOLITA

HUMPHREY, SIR [*Television*]
Sir Humphrey Appleby is the smooth-talking Permanent Under-Secretary who thwarts his supposed political master, **Jim Hacker**, at every turn in the TV series *Yes Minister* and *Yes Prime Minister* (1980–82, 1986–88). Unbending in his determination to have the country run the way he likes it – generally in the interests of the other Whitehall mandarins – he uses every means at his disposal. This often means going behind Hacker's back and using the contacts made at his club to pull strings. But Sir Humphrey's greatest weapon is his ability to produce jargon and statements that appear logical but distort meaning and are expressed so confusingly that they are impossible to argue against. Hence 'Both ["safe" and "good"] have now been redefined to suit the needs of the rule-makers, though with none of the eloquence and little of the style of Sir Humphrey, their fictional counterpart.' (*Independent* 26.9.96).

HUNCHBACK OF NOTRE DAME see QUASIMODO

HUNTER DUNN, MISS JOAN [*Literature*]
Miss Joan Hunter Dunn is a name taken from a poem by John

Betjamen, and used to describe an athletic young woman. See further ALDERSHOT.

HURREE JAMSET RAM SINGH see BILLY BUNTER

HYDE, MR see JEKYLL AND HYDE

ICARUS AND DAEDALUS   [*Mythology*]
In Greek myth Daedalus, the great inventor and creator of the labyrinth, and his son Icarus were imprisoned by Minos (see MINOTAUR). To escape, Daedalus made wings of feathers fixed with wax so that they could fly to safety. He warned his son not to fly too near to the sun or the wax would melt, but once he experienced the joys of flight Icarus forgot his father's warning and soared too high. His wings did indeed melt and Icarus fell and drowned in the area of see off Asia Minor still called the Icarian Sea after him. Thus Icarus has come to stand for over-confidence or those who aim too high. 'Like Icarus they are too cocky about their place in the sun.' (*Guardian* 17.7.96).

IGOR see FRANKENSTEIN

ILSE see CASABLANCA

INCITATUS see CALIGULA

INCY WINCY SPIDER   [*Folklore*]
In the child's rhyme Incy Wincy is the spider who climbs a water spout only to be washed out by the rain and so has to start all over again. He or she can be used as a type of perseverance or determination, a nursery variant of BRUCE'S spider.

INFERNO   [*Literature*]
The poet **Dante** Allighieri (1265–1321) wrote **The Divine Comedy**, a description of a journey through Hell (The Inferno), Purgatory and Paradise in which he is guided by the great Roman poet **Virgil** and by the spirit of his idealised love **Beatrice**. However, when people use terms such as **Dantesque** they nearly always refer to the Inferno, his description of a journey through

the rings of hell, some burning, some freezing, where various sinners suffer punishment tailored to their transgressions. 'An artist condemned to the **Dantean** punishment of confinement within the small, small box he has made for himself' (*Independent* 25.1.94); 'The routes through town were more than the mind could stand even in off-peak hours. In peak hours the scene was Dantesque'. (Clive James *Unreliable Memoirs*).

INNOCENTS see HEROD

INQUISITION see SPANISH INQUISITION

INTERNATIONAL RESCUE see THUNDERBIRDS

INVISIBLE MAN [*Literature, Television*]
H. G. Wells' 1897 novel introduce *The Invisible Man*, in the person of an antisocial, albino chemist, Dr Griffin, who discovers how to make himself invisible. Indeed, he is only able to make himself visible by wearing clothing, and the stock image of the invisible man is of someone in a heavy overcoat, gloves and a bandaged face as the only way of making his presence visible. Griffin is an unpleasant character, who in the end goes mad and tries to take over the world. Other writers have found the idea of the invisible man too good to waste, and there have been two TV series where the invisible man has been a secret agent, as well as a number of versions and spin offs of Wells' original concept.

IPANEMA, THE GIRL FROM [*Song*]
The 1964 song *The Girl from Ipanema* tells of a Brazilian girl so lovely that every man she passes turns to watch, while the narrator can only despair of winning her. She has come to be used as a benchmark of feminine beauty.

IRON CHANCELLOR, IRON LADY see BISMARCK

IRON JOHN [*Literature*]
In the 1990 book by Robert Blye, Iron John represents the post feminist man who has got in touch with his true masculine nature and is at peace with himself and the male role. The rituals

espoused in the 'Iron John' philosophy involved much male bonding through ceremonies using drums, fire, and, according to some accounts, the smelling of each other's armpits.

ISCARIOT, JUDAS see JUDAS

ISEULT see TRISTAN AND ISOLDE

ISHMAEL [*Religion*]
In the Bible (Genesis 21 and 25) Ishmael is the son of Abraham by his slave Hagar the Egyptian. Sarah, wife of Abraham is jealous, and causes the mother and son to be thrown out of the household. Ishmael later became the ancestor of the Arabs. The name Ishmael came to be used for a term for an outcast, best known from the opening of Herman Melville's 1851 novel MOBY DICK: 'Call me Ishmael'.

ISLANDS OF THE BLESSED see ELYSIAN FIELDS

ISOLDE, ISOLDA see TRISTAN AND ISOLDE

ITT, COUSIN see ADDAMS FAMILY

J. R. [*Television*]
J. R. Ewing was the man viewers loved to hate in the TV oil saga *Dallas* (1978–91). He usually wore a large Texan hat and an evil grin, and was never happy unless he was doing someone down. He got his comeuppance when he was shot by an unknown hand, and so many were his enemies that the question **Who shot J. R.?** was unanswerable during wait for the new series after this cliff-hanger.

JABBA THE HUTT see STAR WARS

JABBERWOCKY [*Literature*]
The poem *Jabberwocky* is a piece of nonsense poetry that occurs in Lewis Carroll's *Through the Looking Glass* (see ALICE IN WONDER-LAND). Although many of the words in the poem are Carroll's invention, some, such as the creatures the **slithy toves**, have entered the language.

J'ACCUSE see ALFRED DREYFUS

JACK AND THE BEANSTALK [*Folklore*]
Jack and the Beanstalk, also known as *Jack the Giant Killer*, is the story of a boy who foolishly sells the family's only cow for some magic beans, but then is proved right when the beanstalk that grows from them is so high it can be climbed into a new world where a rich giant lives. Despite his detection of Jack – 'Fee, fie, fo, fum, I smell the blood of an English man' – Jack steals a fortune from him, and when the giant tries to follow Jack down the beanstalk he is killed when Jack chops it down.

JACK THE RIPPER [*Crime, History*]
Jack the Ripper was the name given to an unidentified murderer

who killed and horribly mutilated at least seven prostitutes in London's East End in 1888. Theories as to his identify have been rife, but nothing has ever been proved. His name is attached to any such serial killer.

JACOB see ESAU

JADIS see NARNIA

JAMES, JESSE [*Crime, History*]
Jesse James (1847–82) and his brother Frank were the core of the James Gang of bank and train robbers who even in their lifetimes were romanticised as the typical Wild West outlaw. This image may have been helped by the fact that the James brothers were ex-confederate soldiers and tried to justify their crimes as forced on them by persecution.

JANE see TARZAN

JANE, BABY [*Film*]
The film *Whatever Happened to Baby Jane* (1962) tells the story of a demented ex-child star, mentally stuck in her glamorous youth but now middle-aged, persecuting her wheelchair-bound invalid sister. The atmosphere of the film is gothic, with memorable scenes such as Baby Jane serving the sister a rat on silver salver, or the panicking sister spinning round and round in her wheelchair, screaming.

JANET see DR FINLAY

JANUS [*Mythology*]
Janus was the Roman god of endings and beginnings, hence the first month of the year, January, is named after him. He had two faces, looking in opposite directions, and thus looked to the future and the past. Allusions to him usually refer to this double aspect, either as a sign of complexity, or simply being 'two-faced'. 'He suggests the janus-like quality of a man whose lewd comedy conceals a bitter hatred of his aristocratic patrons' (*Guardian* 22.4.96).

JARNDYCE AND JARNDYCE [*Literature*]

In Charles Dickens' *Bleak House* (1892), the court case of Jarndyce and Jarndyce is a dispute over inheritance which has dragged on for years, and become a standing joke in Chancery. The whole dispute comes to a sudden end when it is announced in court that the costs of litigation have eaten up the whole of the estate and there is no money left to argue over. Dickens based this on a real court case, Jennens vs Jennens which took over 80 years to settle. Jarndyce and Jarndyce has come to represent both the law's delays and the wastefulness and expense of going to court to settle disputes.

JASON see ARGO, DRAGON'S TEETH, GOLDEN FLEECE

JAWS [*Film*]

The 1975 film *Jaws* tells of the attacks of a great white shark on a Long Island beach. It is best known for the shots of the shark's dorsal fin coming ever nearer an unsuspecting swimmer, which has been much parodied since, and for the publicity for the first of several sequels, *Jaws II* (1978): 'Just when you thought it was safe to go back in the water'.

JEDI KNIGHTS [*Film*]

The Jedi are an elite band of warriors, endowed with supernatural gifts thank to their ability to tap into the mystic **Force** in the STAR WARS series of films. LUKE SKYWALKER is the last of their line. During the 1991 Gulf War the group of young majors involved in planning at base were nicknamed 'the Jedi Knights' by the frontline troops.

JEEVES [*Literature*]

Jeeves is the inimitable gentleman's gentleman who looks after BERTIE WOOSTER in **P. G. Wodehouse**'s stories. Bertie refers to Jeeves as 'shimmering' into the room, he is always restrained and calm and has many times the brains of his employer. Much to Bertie's chagrin, it is Jeeves who is regarded by all Bertie's friends as the person to consult when in trouble, rather than Bertie. Jeeves has very high standards of dress for Bertie, and his reward for getting him out of yet another scrape is often for Bertie to give up some beloved but unsuitable garment. Jeeves also has the recipe for an infallible hangover cure.

JEFFREYS, JUDGE see BLOODY ASSIZES

JEHU see JEZEBEL

JEKYLL AND HYDE *[Literature]*
R. L. Stevenson's 1886 story of *The Strange Case of Dr Jekyll and Mr Hyde* tell the story of how Dr Jekyll, in the course of his researches, makes a potion which he tries on himself, and which transforms him into a villainous character who calls himself Mr Hyde. This wicked side of him gradually takes over his normal personality. Thus Jekyll and Hyde is used of someone with two sides to him, one good and one bad, or as a term for a split personality.

JELLYBY, MRS *[Literature]*
In Charles Dickens' *Bleak House* (1853) Mrs Jellyby is a woman obsessed with doing good works, and especially with the poor benighted heathen in Africa. Such is her concentration on doing good that everything else is left to descend into chaos, and her own children suffer cruel neglect, sacrificed to her useless projects.

JELLYSTONE PARK see YOGI BEAR

JENKINS' EAR, WAR OF *[History]*
The war of Jenkins' Ear, fought in 1739 between Britain and Spain, started after a Captain Robert Jenkins testified before the House of Commons and displayed what he said was his ear, cut off by Spanish coastguards who had boarded his ship in the West Indies. Relations were already poor between the two countries, and this incident escalated into warfare. This war is thus alluded to when one wants to describe serious conflict arising out of a trivial beginning.

JEREMIAH, JEREMIAD *[Religion]*
The Book of Jeremiah in the Bible is a long prophecy of the dire fate that lies in wait for the Israelites because of their sins. A Jeremiah is therefore someone who foretells things turning out

badly, and a Jeremiad is a lament or a railing against people's behaviour.

JERRY MOUSE see TOM AND JERRY

JERUSALEM [*Literature*]
Jerusalem's prominence in the Bible and as a sacred city has led to a range of allusive uses. It stands for the PROMISED LAND in general; because of the role of the New Jerusalem in the APOCALYPSE it can be used to mean 'heaven', and from this has come to mean any ideal city. The fighting over it in the 20th century has added a new set of associations. For the hymn see DARK SATANIC MILLS.

JEZEBEL [*Religion*]
Jezebel gets a very bad press in the Bible. She was a worshiper of Baal who persecuted the prophets of Israel and supported her own priests. In the end she is killed on the orders of **Jehu** by being thrown out of a window, trampled by Jehu's horses and then eaten by dogs (II Kings 9: 29–37). Jezebel's name has become used for a shameless or scheming woman, and often occurs in the form 'painted Jezebel' since among the faults the Bible finds is that she 'painted her face', that is, wore make-up. Jehu's name has also entered the language, as an old-fashioned term for a fast driver, because at one point (II Kings 9: 20), a sentry recognises Jehu from afar as he approaches in his chariot for 'the driving is like the driving of Jehu the son of Nimshi; for he driveth furiously'.

JIM CROW [*History*]
Jim Crow was the name of a song in the early part of the 19th century, which was adopted in the USA as a offensive term for a Black. From that it became a term for segregation, and is found in terms such as jim-crow laws, which enforced segregation.

JIM'LL FIX IT [*Television*]
The title of a long-running children's TV programme (1975–94) in which Jimmy Savile made viewers' unlikely dreams come true.

JIMINY CRICKET [*Film*]
Jiminy Cricket is the nauseatingly up-beat insect friend of PINOC-

CHIO in the 1940 Disney cartoon film. He is associated with the term 'Give a Little Whistle', the title of a song he sings in the film.

JIMSON, GULLY [*Literature*]
Gully Jimson is the self-indulgent, egocentric and amoral artist in a trilogy of novels by Joyce Carey which appeared between 1941 and 1944. He is an unrefined character, totally driven by his art and everyone and everything is sacrificed in the pursuit of his work and of enough money for him to be able to continue painting.

JINGLE, MR see PICKWICK

JOAN OF ARC [*History*]
St Joan of Arc, the Maid of Orleans, French patriot and heroine, who heard the bells of her village and the saints of whom she had visions telling her to sweep the invading English from her country, has had her name used for any woman with a strong sense of mission.

JOCASTA see OEDIPUS

JOE HAWKINS [*Literature*]
Joe Hawkins is a skinhead thug, the hero of Richard Allen's novel *Skinhead*.

JOHN GESTE see BEAU GESTE

JOHN THE BAPTIST [*Religion*]
St John the Baptist, whose ministry was to foretell the coming of Christ, is sometimes alluded to as one who goes before, with reference to the quote 'The voice of one crying in the wilderness, Prepare ye the way of the Lord' (Matthew 3.3), but is most often met with in connection with SALOME.

JOHN-BOY see THE WALTONS

JOHNSON, AMY [*History, Transport*]
Amy Johnson (1903–41) was a pioneering woman aviator, who

made record-breaking flights to Australia and to South Africa and back. Her plane disappeared over the English Channel in the Second World War while she was ferrying planes for the Air Transport Auxiliary.

JOHNSON, HILDY [*Drama, Film*]
In Ben Hecht and Charles MacArthur's 1928 play *The Front Page* (filmed at least twice), which is set in Chicago, Hildy Johnson is a newspaper reporter totally dedicated to getting his story. This is ruthlessly exploited by his editor **Walter Burns**, even to the extent of Burns' trying to prevent Hildy's marriage in the interests of the latest scoop. Johnson's name is thus used for the ultimate in determined reporter.

JOKER, THE see BATMAN AND ROBIN

JONATHAN see DAVID

JONES, INDIANA [*Film*]
Indiana John is the rogue archaeologist-adventurer in the film *Raiders of the Lost Ark* (1981) and sequels. At university a mild and timid scholar, let him once put on his trademark wide hat and whip and put him in the field, and he becomes the ultimate action man.

JONES, JIMMY [*Cults*]
The Reverend Jimmy Jones' name is linked with charisma turned to evil. Jones was a Methodist preacher who founded a cult called The People's Temple in California in 1957. In 1976 he and some one thousand followers founded **Jonestown** in the jungles of Guyana. In November 1978 US Congressman Leo Ryan went to investigate worrying reports of brainwashing and tyranny at the settlement, and he and five companions were shot. Jones then persuaded 913 of his followers to commit mass-suicide by drinking Kool-Aid mixed with cyanide.

JONES, 'SPEARCHUCKER' see MASH

JONES, TOM [*Literature*]
In Henry Fielding's novel *The History of Tom Jones, a Foundling*

(1749), Tom is a frank, lively young man, led astray through youthful exuberance rather than innate evil. Because he is no good at deception he falls into all sorts of scrapes and adventures, sometimes of a sexual nature, before the book ends happily.

JONESES, THE [*Popular Culture*]
The expression 'keeping up with the Jonses' comes from a comic strip of that name which appeared in the New York Globe between 1913 and 1931. It was drawn by Arthur 'Pop' Momand.

JÖRMUNGAND see LOKI

JOYCE, JAMES [*Literature*]
The Irish writer James Joyce is known for the skill of his writing and his use of experimental techniques such as stream of consciousness. The term **Joycean** most often refers to the style Joyce uses in his novel *Ulysses* (see MOLLY BLOOM), as in 'He would write a novel – a real novel from the heart. A long, Joycean monologue, brooding and profound, bitter maybe, but funny too.' (*Changing Babies*, Deborah Moggach 1995).

JOYFUL, MRS [*Literature*]
In Geoffrey Willans' MOLESWORTH books, **Grabber**, as the son of the school's richest parent, is head boy of St Custard's, captain of games and winner of all the prizes including the **Mrs Joyful Prize for Raffia Work**, hence 'One imagines that she [Virginia Bottomley] was ... head girl, lacrosse champion and winner of the Mrs Joyful Prize for raffia work' (*Independent* 11.11.95).

JUAN, DON [*Literature*]
The legendary Spanish seducer forms a trio of libertines alongside CASANOVA and LOTHARIO. The legend has always shown him as witty and brave, not least when defying Hell as he is dragged down to eternal damnation, and this has made him a popular figure with a wide range of writers. See also DON GIOVANNI.

JUDAS [*Religion*]
The name Judas is used to mean traitor, for **Judas Iscariot** was the disciple who betrayed Jesus for THIRTY PIECES OF SILVER. He identi-

fied Jesus to the arresting soldier by going up to him and kissing him, so a **Judas kiss** has come to mean an act of betrayal. A **Judas goat** (or other animal) is a decoy, an animal used to lure others to their fate. Two legends about Judas have also given rise further terms. The **Judas tree**, which produces its pink-purple blooms in spring, before its leaves, is supposed to be the tree that Judas hanged himself on in remorse for his betrayal; and **Judas-coloured** hair means red hair, for Judas traditionally had hair that colour, and is usually identifiable in paintings because of this.

JUDGEMENT OF SOLOMON see SOLOMON

JUDY see PUNCH AND JUDY

JULIAN see FAMOUS FIVE

JUNO [*Mythology*]
Juno was the Roman equivalent of HERA, queen of the gods. Statues of her tend to show her as a stately regal matron, and the term **Junoesque** is used to describe women with this sort of figure, or as a polite way of saying 'large'.

JURASSIC PARK [*Film, Literature*]
The Michael Crichton novel *Jurassic Park* and blockbuster film Steven Spielberg made of it in 1993 tell of a theme-park where dinosaurs, created by cloning fragments of dinosaur DNA found in the insects preserved in amber which had sucked their blood, run amok. It is used in reference to both cloning and dinosaurs.

K9 [*Television*]
K9 was the robot dog side-kick to the Tom Baker incarnation of DR WHO.

KAA see MOWGLI

KAFKA [*Literature*]
The Czech novelist Franz Kafka (1883–1924) is known for his writings that show the ordinary man bewildered by his inability to deal with a nightmare dehumanised world where the logic of those in power has nothing to do with common sense. 'He thought the terms of the Act were so plainly idiotic that it should be taken as a kind of **Kafkaesque** joke.' (*Independent* 30.7.91).

KAMA SUTRA [*Literature*]
Kama is the name of an Indian god of love, 'sutra' literally means 'thread' but is used to mean 'path, way', and the Kama Sutra (sometimes one word) is an ancient Hindu text on lovemaking and allied topics. In use, the term often means little more than exotic sex manual.

KAMIKAZE [*History*]
In the Second World War the Japanese kamikaze pilots were a group of dedicated young men who flew on suicidal missions crashing their explosive-laden planes into targets to try and ensure their destruction. Kamikaze is now used to mean anyone suicidally fool-hardy.

KANE, CITIZEN see WILLIAM RANDOLPH HEARST

KANGA see WINNIE THE POOH

KARENINA, ANNA [*Literature*]
In Tolstoy's *Anna Karenina* (1875–7) Anna leaves her husband and child to be with the man she loves, **Vronsky**. When Vronsky tires of her, she throws herself under a train. Her name is used to indicate tragic, doomed love.

KARLOFF, BORIS [*Film*]
The English film actor Boris Karloff (1887–1969) made his name in Hollywood horror films. He became famous after portraying FRANKENSTEIN's monster in 1931, which he played as both chilling and deserving of the audience's sympathy. He later went on to play the same character in sequels. He portrayed numerous, largely silent, monsters on both film and stage, including the role of the corpse in the film *The Mummy* (1931). He has been called the 'king of horror'. 'The bass notes stalk, the trombones hint at troubles – all together conjuring up a picture of Boris Karloff waiting fiendishly in the shadows to pounce.' (*Independent* 4.2.94).

KEATON, BUSTER [*Film*]
The American comedian Buster Keaton (1895–1966) is known for his silent films in which his amazing acrobatic skills were combined with a deadpan expression.

KELLY, NED [*History, Crime*]
Ned Kelly (1855–1880) is the most famous of the bushrangers – the Australian equivalent of the Wild West outlaw. Kelly's name first came to public notice when he shot a policeman who was trying to arrest his brother Dan for horse theft. They fled into the Bush and built up the Kelly gang whose exploits caught the imagination of the public in much the same way as BILLY THE KID's did. Finally, the gang were cornered by police in a big shoot up and, despite his famous home-made armour, Kelly was wounded. He was later hanged. Some people regard Kelly as a victim of the large landowners of the time who failed to protect the workers at a time of economic depression.

KEMO SABE see LONE RANGER

KENOBI, OBI-WAN [Film]
In the STAR WARS trilogy Obi-Wan Kenobi is the retired JEDI KNIGHT with supernatural powers who introduced LUKE SKYWALKER to the Jedi skills and the power of **The Force**.

KENT, CLARK see SUPERMAN

KERMIT THE FROG see MUPPETS

KETCH, JACK see PUNCH AND JUDY

KEYNSIAN [Economics]
The English economist John Maynard Keynes (1883–1946) taught that unemployment was a part of an unregulated market economy and advocated government control of monetary policy to control the economy. His followers are called Keynsians.

KEYSTONE KOPS [Film]
The silent comedy films featuring the Keystone Kops featured wild incompetence, slapstick and hectic chases.

KILDARE, DR [Television]
Although he first appeared in print, Dr James Kildare is best known from the TV series (1962–66) in which glamorous young heart-throb Dr Kildare battled heroically to care for his patients and meet the standards set by his fierce superior, **Dr Gillespie**. Much of the action consisted of either rushing down corridors or staring intensely at people, and allusions to the Dr Kildare school of acting refer to this and the woodenness of some of the actors. Blood and mess never intruded and 'Apart from his firm jaw-line and innocent eyes, Kildare's essential quality was the fact that he looked as if he was daily steam-cleaned, inside and out.' (*Evening Standard* 30.11.96).

KING see STALKY AND CO

KING KONG [Film]
In the 1933 film of this name, King Kong is the giant ape brought to New York as a side show who escapes and, falling in love with

the ethereal Fay Wray, climbs with her to the top of the Empire State Building. The scene where he swats at seemingly tiny aeroplanes while clinging to the top of this building is often alluded to.

KING SOLOMON'S MINES see ALLAN QUATERMAIN

KING, JASON [Television]
Jason King was a TV series (1971–72) whose hero was a crime writer and part-time special agent. The series featured an extravagant, highly fashionable life-style, exotic settings and lots of attractive women hanging about in the background. King had previously appeared in a series called *Department S* (1969–70) and his name is usually invoked to describe tasteless 70s fashions, as in 'platform shoes, hot pants, satin flares and jackets not unlike those modesty-endangering shortie dressing-gowns favoured by Jason King' (*Independent* 25.7.91).

KIPPS [Literature]
H. G. Wells' comic novel *Kipps* (1905) tells of the adventures of Arthur Kipps, a draper's assistant who inherits money and tries to enter polite society. The story was turned into the musical *Half a Sixpence*. 'Both stories referred to "a clerk", "a House of Commons clerk", as if the miscreant were a whey-faced cousin of H. G. Wells' Kipps the draper's assistant, with a jaunty bowler and the top button of his jacket done up.' (*Independent* 19.4.96).

KIRK, CAPTAIN see STAR TREK

KITCHENER, LORD [History]
Lord Kitchener of Khartoum (1850–1916), the hero of Omdurman, had a distinguished military career, but is best known popularly as a poster used for recruiting during the First World War, which shows a pointing hand and his large-moustached face over the slogan 'Your Country Needs You'.

KLINGER, CORPORAL see MASH

KLINGONS [Television]
In the original STAR TREK series the Klingons are a fiercely mili-

taristic race, understanding only honour and aggression, and the Klingon Empire is constantly in conflict with Starfleet and the United Federation of Planets. By the time of *Star Trek: The Next Generation* and later series, the depiction of the Klingons had softened, and one of them, **Lieutenant Worf**, was even on the bridge of the USS *Enterprise*. They are no longer simple black-and-while villains, but are still shown as a race of warriors bound by an exacting code of honour, althought the treatment of them is much more sympathetic, their culture seen as complex and interesting, with its own strengths and weaknesses. Their place as the villains has been taken by the **Romulan Empire**, a half-VULCAN race of aggressors, and the semi-reptilian **Cardassians**, a people dominated by a sinister secret police and ruthless in their exploitation of conquered races such as the **Bajorans**.

KNACKER, INSPECTOR   [*Popular Culture*]
Inspector Knacker of the Yard is a policeman invented by the satirical magazine *Private Eye* who has come to represent all that is wrong, ineffective and corrupt in the police force. 'He answers those government ministers who would secretly like all trials to be conducted by Inspector Knacker in the friendly nick by saying: "Delays and inconveniences in the law are the price that all free nations must pay for liberty".' (*Evening Standard* 25.4.96).

KNEE, RON   [*Popular Culture*]
Ron Knee is another invention of *Private Eye*, used to satirise football managers. 'John Major grins gamely on, almost heroic in his personal optimism. But in weeks like these he seems reminiscent of *Private Eye*'s famously disastrous football manager, "The ashen-faced Ron Knee".' (*Independent* 13.4.96).

KRAFT-EBING   [*Sexology*]
Richard, Baron von Kraft Ebing (1840–1902) was a German neurologist and psychiatrist who pioneered the study of human sexuality and wrote extensively on the subject. His name is therefore used to mean 'connected with sex'.

KRAKATOA   [*Volcanology*]
The explosion of the Indonesian island-volcano Krakatoa in 1883

is the most violent volcanic explosion in recorded history. Its effects were felt in various ways all round the world. Krakatoa has thus come to be used for any extremely violent explosion.

KRAMER VS KRAMER [*Film*]
This 1979 weepy film about a divorcing couple fighting over custody of their child has come to symbolise the problems of divorced parents and their children.

KREB, ROSA [*Film, Literature*]
Rosa Kreb has come to represent all that was repellent and masculinised in Soviet Russian womanhood. She features as an enemy of JAMES BOND in *From Russian With Love*, where she is a moustachioed agent of **SMERSH** with lesbian overtones, who manages almost to kill Bond with the poisoned blades concealed in her heavy toe-caps. 'Elegantly besuited women tended the desk and Rosa Kreb's cousin did not sit guard, hairy legged, on every floor' (of a new Russian hotel, *Independent* 26.3.90).

KREMMEN, CAPTAIN [*Television*]
Captain Kremmen was the invention of the comic and disc-jockey Kenny Everett (1944–1995). Kremmen was a sort of comic-strip space cowboy, very much inspired by characters such as DAN DARE, and became an ideal vehicle for Everett's zany and outrageous humour.

KREUGER, FREDDIE [*Film*]
Freddie Kreuger is the murderous horror with knives that spring out of his gloves in the *Nightmare on Elm Street* series of films.

KRYPTON see SUPERMAN

KRYTEN see CRICHTON, RED DWARF

KUBLA KHAN see XANADU

KURTZ, MR [*Literature*]
In Joseph Conrad's 1902 novel *The Heart of Darkness* Mr Kurtz is an ivory trader, originally a civilised and cultivated man, who sets

up in the depth of the Congolese jungle. There, in the heart of darkness, he becomes a corrupted god to the natives, at the same time running the most efficient trading post in the area, but only at the cost of unspeakable cruelty, including human sacrifice. His dying words are 'The horror! The horror!' T. S. Eliot took as his epigraph to *The Hollow Men* (1925) a line from the same chapter 'Mistah Kurtz – he dead'. Francis Ford Coppola's 1979 film *Apocalypse Now* was based on Conrad's book, with Kurtz becoming **General Kurtz**, and the darkness transferred to Vietnam.

KURYAKIN, ILLYA see MAN FROM UNCLE

LA RUE, DANNY [*Entertainment*]
Danny La Rue (1927–) is a female impersonator, well known for the lavishness of his costumes and sets. 'There was laughter in court when Vagg said Mr Levine reminded him of "Danny La Rue without drag – all extravagance without the props".' (*Evening Standard* 2.4.96).

LABYRINTH see MINOTAUR. ARIADNE

LADY WITH THE LAMP see FLORENCE NIGHTINGALE

LAMBSBREATH, ADAM see COLD COMFORT

LANCELOT see ROUND TABLE

LAND OF MILK AND HONEY see PROMISED LAND

LANE, LOIS see SUPERMAN

LARCIUS, SPURIUS see HORATIO

LARKINS [*Literature, Television*]
Ma and Pop Larkin are the happy-go-lucky couple with a large family in a series of books by H. E. Bates, the best-known of which is *The Darling Buds of May* (1958, used as the basis of a popular TV series 1991–93). Written when memories of war-time and post-war shortages were still strong, the Larkins' ability to conjure up and enjoy vast quantities of food was one of their chief features. Pop Larkin is able to turn his hand at anything from being a dealer in second-hand goods to running his small-holding and solving other people's problems, and above all avoiding income tax. Ma, vast and jovial, is the centre of the family, producing meals and

babies equally readily and generally enjoying life. For a while in the 1990s Pop's trademark 'Perfick' became a catch-phrase.

LARS PORSENA see HORATIUS

LARSON, GARY [*Popular Culture*]
The American cartoonist Gary Larson's *Far Side* cartoons have became a byword for an off-beat, fundamentally different way of looking at the world.

LASSIE [*Film, Literature*]
Eric Knight's novel *Lassie Come Home* (1940), originally set in Scotland, was made into a film in 1943, and Lassie has been saving injured or endangered Americans ever since on film, radio and TV (even in a cartoon series). As with that other canine superhero RIN TIN-TIN, those who come into contact with Lassie all seem to develop an uncanny ability to know when she wants them to follow her, or whatever else she wants them to do. Although officially a 'she', Lassie has always been played by a male collie.

LAUREL AND HARDY [*Film*]
The American comic-film duo Laurel and Hardy are known for their slapstick incompetence. The English-born Stanley (Stan) Laurel (1890–1965) was the thin, white-faced, vacantly bemused one, frequently driven to panic or tears by the fat, bossy Oliver (Ollie) Hardy (1892–1957), who was always accusing him with the catch phrase 'This is another fine mess you've gotten us into', even when the fault lay at his door.

LAWRENCE, D. H. [*Literature*]
The writings of D. H. Lawrence (1885–1930), regardless of their real content, are usually referred to in terms of his belief that man was losing touch with his true sexual nature and the need for him to return to it. The term **Lawrencian**, used of a hero, usually means broody and sexually active.

LAZARUS [*Religion*]
In the Bible (John 11) Lazarus is the man raised from the dead by Jesus. Thus the name is used of anything revived or given a new

lease of life. Elsewhere in the New Testament (Luke 16) Jesus uses the name when he tells the parable of **Dives and Lazarus**. This is the story, Dives (the word is the Latin for a rich man), a wealthy man and of Lazarus, a beggar who waited outside Dives' house, hoping to 'be fed with the crumbs which fell from the rich man's table'. When they both die Lazarus is carried by angels to the bosom of Abraham while Dives burns in Hell. Dives begs Abraham to send Lazarus with water to cool his torments, but is sternly told that just as a gulf existed between them in life, so it is in death. Lazarus suffered in life, but is now richly compensated; Dives was rich in life and now must suffer.

LEAR, KING [*Literature*]

In Shakespeare's *King Lear*, Lear is a foolish old king who loves to be flattered. His two eldest daughters GONERIL AND REGAN flatter him, but when **Cordelia**, his youngest, refuses to do more than tell the truth, she is banished. Lear selfishly wants to have his cake and eat it by retiring from actively being a king, but keep the benefits. He splits his kingdom between Regan and Goneril and their husbands, and becomes a permanent guest with one or the other. Like so many daughters with aged parents they get steadily more impatient with his presence and demands and ungratefully strip him of all the trappings of a king and his dignity. Lear goes mad, and in one memorable scene spends a night on 'a blasted heath' raging against a storm. Cordelia comes to his rescue but is killed, and Lear, realising how foolish he has been, dies lamenting her.

LECTER, HANNIBAL [*Film*]

In the film *The Silence of the Lambs* (1990) Hannibal Lecter (spelled 'Lector' in the original novel) – 'Hannibal the Cannibal' – is the psychiatrist and mass murderer who is interviewed by an FBI agent needing help to track down another serial killer. Lecter revels in his past and uses his psychiatrist's skills to attract and repel, playing on the fascination aroused by his habit of eating his victims.

LEEFE, LETTICE [*Popular Culture*]

Lettice Leefe, 'the greenest girl in school', was the heroine of a strip-cartoon in *Girl* magazine (published from 1951), at one time the dominant publication for girls. Lettice wore a white shirt, tie and gym-slip and enormous round glasses and attended St Addledegga's School where she was always getting into trouble.

LEESON, NICK [*Finance*]
In 1995 Nick Leeson's unauthorised dealings in futures bankrupted his employers, Barings Bank. Since then his activities have become a standard by which other financial scandals are judged.

LEGREE, SIMON [*Literature*]
In Harriet Beecher Stowe's UNCLE TOM's *Cabin* (1852) Simon Legree is the hideous, whip-wielding slave-dealer who has Uncle Tom beaten to death.

LEIA, PRINCESS see LUKE SKYWALKER, STAR WARS

LEJAUNE, SERGEANT see BEAU GESTE

LEONIDAS see THERMOPYLAE

LEPORELLO see DON GIOVANNI

LERNAEN HYDRA see HERCULES

LES-DEUX-ÉGLISES [*History*]
Twice in his long political career the French President Charles de Gaulle (1890–1970) resigned from office and retired to his home at Colombey-les-Deux-Églises. There he waited for his country to come to its senses and recall him to glory, and the first time it worked. The suffix 'les-deux-Églises' has therefore come to be used of the base of a man out of favour, but who feels his time is yet to come. When Michael Heseltine resigned from office he was described as the MP for 'Henley-les-deux-Églises', and it has been written of ex-cricketer and aspiring Pakistani politician Imran Khan, 'He passionately believes in reform, but for the moment he devotes himself to the hospital and waits in Lahore-les-deux-eglises' (*Independent* 1.3.96).

LESBIA [*Literature*]
In the poems of **Catullus** (c. 84–54 BC), some of the most accessi-

ble poetry in Latin, Lesbia is the name of the women to whom some of his tenderest love-poems are addressed, the most famous one of which is an envious lament for a pet sparrow that used to hide is her clothing. It is thought that 'Lesbia' was the name he used for **Clodia**, a rebellious aristocrat who scandalised Rome by her wild living and determination to get what she wanted out of life. Her brother was the **Clodius** who caused JULIUS CAESAR to divorce his wife.

LESTRADE, INSPECTOR see SHERLOCK HOLMES

LETHE [*Mythology*]

In Greek myth Lethe is one of the five rivers of HADES. The name means 'forgetfulness', and to drink its waters is to loose memories of the world above. See also STYX.

LET MY PEOPLE GO see MOSES

LEVELLERS [*History*]

The Levellers were a radical reforming movement active during the period of the English Civil War, particularly between 1647 and 1649. They wanted a written constitution (still under discussion), an increase in the numbers entitled to vote, the abolition of the monarchy, and got their name from their desire to abolish all social distinctions. As they drew most of their followers from the lower classes, they have been seen by many as proto-socialists or even communists, and have been figures of some romance to the English Left Wing. In the 1990s a rock band called itself after them.

LEVIATHAN [*Religion, Government*]

The name Leviathan occurs several times in the Bible as the name of a water monster. Modern scholars suggest the word means either 'whale' or 'crocodile', but the popular image of Leviathan is of something much larger than a crocodile, and the word has come to be used of any huge or powerful thing – thus Dr Johnson was nicknamed 'The Leviathan of Literature'. When Thomas Hobbes came to write his book on sovereign power, he chose to call this vast power Leviathan, and used it as the title of his 1651 book.

LIAR, BILLY [*Literature*]

Billy Fisher, the hero of Keith Waterhouse's 1959 novel *Billy Liar* (later turned into a play and filmed) is a day-dreamer, dreaming of better things than his working-class life as an undertaker's assistant. His absorption in his fantasies leads to his telling lies and to many comic adventures. Billy Liar has come to be used of any such dreamer ' ... a gaggle of latter-day Billy Liars, doing what teenage boys have always done – sitting alone in their bedrooms and dreaming about ruling the world.' (*Evening Standard* 3.2.94). Compare WALTER MITTY.

LIBERACE [*Entertainment*]

The American popular pianist Liberace (1919–1987) was famous for his glitzy lifestyle, for his incredibly be-rhinestoned and fabulously expensive stage costumes, his collection of vast diamond rings and his trade-mark candelabrum placed on his piano. Both his playing and his taste were roundly condemned by arbiters of taste, but his popular success allowed him to react to this by saying that he had cried all the way to the bank, thereby adding the coining of a new popular phrase to his other achievements.

LIGHT SABRE see LUKE SKYWALKER

LILITH [*Religion*]

In Jewish folklore Lilith is a female demon. In some versions of the stories she is Adam's second wife, and the mother of him by demons, but better-known is the version that makes her his first wife, before the creation of Eve. She is said to have left him because she would not submit to him. This makes her a popular figure with feminists. She is a threat to new-born babies, but her attacks can be kept at bay by wearing amulets inscribed with the names of angels.

LILLIPUT [*Literature*]

In Jonathan Swift's satire *Gulliver's Travels* (1726) Lemuel **Gulliver's** first set of adventures take place in the land of Lilliput, where the inhabitants are only six inches high, with everything else in proportion. **Lilliputian** therefore means tiny. See also BROB-DINGNAG, YAHOO.

LIME, HARRY [*Film, Literature*]
In the Graham Greene film (1949) and book (1950) *The Third Man*,
Harry Lime is the charming but cynical and utterly ruthless black-
marketeer, trading in dubious penicillin in the bleak world of
post-Second World War Vienna. A childhood friend of Lime,
Holly Martins (Rollo in the book) thinks he sees Lime killed in a
motor accident, but comes to suspect that all is not as it seems, and
determines to find out the truth. The film of *The Third Man* is
known for its atmospheric shots of war-torn Vienna – 'The outer
streets of the city, with their blackened, turn of the century apart-
ment blocks, have a Harry Lime feel to them' (*Times* 14.3.92)'; for
the haunting zither music it uses; for scenes shot in the sewers
under the city and on the giant Ferris wheel that miraculously survived the war, both of which have become visual clichés; and for
Orson Welles' remarkable performance as Harry Lime, particularly for his speech beginning 'In Italy for thirty years under the
Borgias they had warfare, terror, murder, bloodshed – they produced Michelangelo, Leonardo da Vinci and the Renaissance. In
Switzerland they had brotherly love, five hundred years of
democracy and peace and what did that produce ...? The cuckoo
clock.'

LION KING [*Film*]
The Disney cartoon film The *Lion King* (1994) tells the story of a
king of the beasts whose death is engineered by his wicked brother. His only son escapes, spends a time in exile finding himself,
and finally comes back to claim his rightful place. However, uses
of 'Lion King' seem only to use the familiar combination of words
as an extension of the usually symbolism of simple 'lion'; as in 'At
this rate the Tories' fabled Lion King will end his days as a
neutered pussy cat' (*Mail on Sunday* 7.4.96).

LIONS' DEN see DANIEL

LION, THE WITCH AND THE WARDROBE see NARNIA

LISTEN WITH MOTHER [*Radio*]
The children's radio programme *Listen with Mother* was a daily
fixture for generations of children from the 1950s to the 1970s. Its

catch-phrase, 'Are you sitting comfortably? Then I'll begin' before the regular story, and its totally outdated, bright and rather condescending tone of delivery, have been widely parodied.

LISTER, DAVID see RED DWARF

LITTLE BIGHORN see CUSTER'S LAST STAND

LITTLE JOHN see ROBIN HOOD

LITTLE LORD FAUNTLEROY see FAUNTLEROY

LITTLE RED BOOK see MAO

LITTLE SHIPS see DUNKIRK

LITTLE WEED see BILL AND BEN

LITTLE, BINGO [*Literature*]
In **P. G. Wodehouse**'s books, Bingo Little is even more of a chump than BERTIE WOOSTER. Many of the comic episodes he finds himself involved in arise from this relationship with his wife. He is married to the romantic novelist **Rosie M. Banks** who rules him with a rod of iron, and strongly disapproves of his liking for gambling and kicking up his heels.

LLANABBA [*Literature*]
In Evelyn Waugh's blackly comic novel *Decline and Fall* (1928) Llanabba Castle School is the chaotic, snobbish, harsh-disciplined school run by the penny-pinching **Dr Augustus Fagan** with the help of hard-hitting **Captain Grimes**, a firm believer in the public school ethos. **Paul Pennyfeather** goes there after being sent down from Oxford after being debagged ('I expect you'll be becoming a schoolmaster, sir,' says his scout. 'That's what most of the gentlemen does, sir, that gets sent down for indecent behaviour.'). When the agent he applies to sends him there, he is told 'We class schools, you see, into four grades: Leading School, First-rate School, Good School, and School. Frankly ... School is pretty bad.' Llanaba definitely belongs in the last category. Compare DOTHEBOYS HALL.

LOKI [*Mythology*]

Loki is the Norse god of mischief and destruction. A cunning trickster and shape-shifter, the son of a gian and the traditional enemy of the gods, his position is ambiguous. His malevolence brings about the death of the golden god **Baldur**, and he often works against the gods, but at other times he is on their side. Among his children are the world-serpent **Jörmungand** and the giant wolf **Fenrir**, both of whom will play a major part in **Ragnarök**, the downfall of the gods at the end of the world (see GOTTERDÄMMERUNG).

LOLITA [*Literature*]

In Vladimir Nabokov's 1955 novel, Dolorez Haze, pet name Lolita, is an unpleasant child, as ready to seduce **Humbert Humbert** as to be seduced. However, in general use Lolita is simply used to mean a nymphet, an attractive but under-age female.

LOMAN, WILLY [*Drama*]

Willy Loman is the central character in Arthur Miller's 1949 play *Death of a Salesman*. Loman spends his life working hard as a travelling salesman, chasing the materialistic American Dream, but the dream fades and Loman becomes depressed and commits suicide. As it says in the play 'A salesman's got to dream, boy. It goes with the territory.'

LONE RANGER AND TONTO [*Television, Radio*]

The Lone Ranger and Tonto have appeared in just about every possible medium since they first appeared as radio characters in 1933, but are probably best known from the often-repeated TV series (1956–62). The Lone Ranger is a white-hatted, masked hero who rides the Wild West righting wrongs and shooting evil-doers – only to wound – with special silver bullets which came from the mine that John Reid, the Lone Ranger's real name, had owned with his murdered brother. He started out to avenge his brother's murder, but soon became a ROBIN HOOD figure, leaving those he had helped to ask 'Who is that masked man?'. His trusty Indian friend Tonto had had his life saved by Reid, and had in turn nursed him back to health after the ambush which had killed the brother. Tonto always called the Lone Ranger '**Kemo Sabe**' said to mean 'trusty scout'. The Lone Ranger rode a pure white horse called **Silver**, and the cry of 'Hi-yo Silver, away!' was one of the show's catch-phrases.

LONG MARCH [*History*]
Chairman MAO's Long March was a journey of about 6000 miles made in 1934–35 when the Chinese Communists were ousted from their base in south-east China and marched to Shensi in the north-west. Some 100,000 set out, but only about 8000 made it to the end. Thus it is used to indicate any particularly rigorous journey: 'Diane Modahl's progress to the Atlanta Olympics has made Mao's Long March look like an uneventful stroll to the corner shop for a pint of milk.' (*Evening Standard* 2.5.96).

LONGHURST, MARTHA see ENA SHARPLES

LORD-HIGH-EVERYTHING-ELSE see POOH-BAH

LORELEI [*Mythology*]
The Lorelei was a sort of fresh-water mermaid. She sat on a certain rock in the Rhine, combing her long blond hair and luring sailors to their death with her fascinating singing.

LOST BOYS see PETER PAN

LOT'S WIFE see SODOM AND GOMMORRAH

LOTHARIO [*Drama*]
The term Lothario for a seducer comes from a character in the now-obscure 1703 play *The Fair Penitent* by Nicholas Rowe. See also CASANOVA, DON JUAN.

LOTUS EATERS [*Literature, Mythology*]
In HOMER'S ODYSSEY, the lotus (in Greek spelt *lotos*) is a fruit which, when it is eaten, induces a dreamy languor. Some of Odysseus' crew eat it and, forgetting about home, simply want to while away their days eating the fruit. Thus a lotus-eater is someone who is happy to spend their lives in nothing but mild self-indulgence.

LOWRY, L. S. [*Art*]
The English painter L. S. Lowry (1887–1976) is known for his paintings of bleak industrial scenes peopled by dark, matchstick-man figures.

LUBIANKA [*Architecture*]
Although this Moscow prison is notorious for a long history of torture and murder, allusions to it are usually to its blank-faced, grim architecture: 'The BBC's Lubianka-style underground viewing rooms' (*Independent* 8.11.96).

LUCAN, LORD [*Crime, History*]
The seventh Lord Lucan was a British aristocrat and professional gambler. He disappeared in 1974 on the night that his wife was attacked and his nanny was murdered. Speculation has abounded ever since and the tabloid papers frequently run stories of sightings, but the truth has never emerged.

LUCIFER [*Religion*]
Lucifer is another name for the Devil or Satan. He was the leader of the rebellion in heaven. His name means 'light bringer' and he is described in the Bible as 'son of the morning'.

LUCRETIA see TARQUIN

LUCULLUS [*History*]
Lucius Lucinius Lucullus (c. 140–57 BC) was a successful general and keen reader, always ready to lend books from his library; but what he is most famous for is his love of food and the extravagant meals he served. A **Lucullan** banquet is therefore one of great luxury.

LUCY, I LOVE [*Television*]
I Love Lucy, which was first broadcast in 1955, was the first of the TV domestic sit-coms. Lucy (played by Lucille Ball) was a scatter-brained red-head who wanted to follow her husband into show-business, or failing that was always hatching disastrous plans to improve herself. Liberated it was not. 'Our changing place in the job market notwithstanding, an awful lot of women are still

stuck in a domestic-centred, *I Love Lucy* world.' (*Evening Standard* 16.4.96).

LUDDITES [*History, Technology*]
The Luddites were groups of textile workers who opposed the introduction of machines to do the work of hand-loom weavers. They rioted and broke up the new machines between 1811 and 1816. **Luddism** is thus the opposition to any form of industrial change or innovation.

LURCH see ADDAMS FAMILY

LYNCH, BET see ROVERS RETURN

M see JAMES BOND

M'TURK see STALKY AND CO

MAC THE KNIFE [*Song, Dram*]
Mac the Knife is the name given in the song of that title to
Macheath, a character in Kurt Weill's *The Threepenny Opera* (1931).
This in its turn was based on John Gay's *The Beggar's Opera*, where
Macheath is a highwayman and leader of a gang of robbers and
muggers. He has a way with women, and after being false to **Polly
Peachum**, the daughter of a confederate, is betrayed by her father.
He is put in prison where he becomes involved with the jailer's
daughter and has to choose between the two women, but finally
ends up with Polly.

MAC, UNCLE [*Radio*]
Uncle Mac was a radio presenter who dominated British children's radio from the 1930s to 1960s.

MACAVITY [*Literature*]
In *Old Possum's Book of Practical Cats* (1939) by T. S. Eliot Macavity
is the mystery cat. A master of crime, Macavity may be responsible for all sorts of crimes such as the loss of a vase that was 'commonly thought to be Ming', 'But when the crime's discovered,
then Macavity's not there'.

MACBETH, LADY MACBETH [*Literature*]
In Shakespeare's play *Macbeth*, Macbeth is a fine warrior, led
astray by a combination of misleading prophesies by three witch-
es and his wife's ambition. He seizes the throne by murdering his
guest, the king, Duncan. This leads to further murders, but neither
Macbeth nor Lady Macbeth can cope with the psychological

effects of being murderers. Lady Macbeth is particularly reviled, and has come to stand for any ambitious or ruthless woman: 'Shakespeare's First Lady of Dunsinane is once again being invoked as a role model for a hard-driven female at the heights of power in Washington. This time it is Cora Masters, wife of Marion Barry, Mayor of Washington, who is typecast as Lady McBarry, the sinister genius behind his tailspin political decline.' (*Evening Standard* 9.5.96). As with Richard III (see PRINCES IN THE TOWER), there have been several attempts recently to rehabilitate Macbeth in fiction, and there is no doubt that Shakespeare's play is not historically accurate.

MACGREGOR, ROB ROY see ROB ROY

MACHEATH see MAC THE KNIFE

MACHIAVELLI [*History, Literature, Government*]

The Italian statesman and writer Nicolò Machiavelli (1469–1527) wrote in his book *The Prince* a handbook on how to conduct and manipulate government. Although his advice would now mostly be considered mere common-sense by a modern political party, some of it is ruthless, and he quickly gained a reputation as a scion of the Devil himself. Nowadays **Machiavellian** is used merely to mean scheming, cunning, amoral.

MACKAY, MR see NORMAN STANLEY FLETCHER

MAD HATTER [*Literature*]

In ALICE IN WONDERLAND the Mad Hatter is one of the participants in an eccentric tea party, along with the March Hare and the dormouse. The character comes from the expression 'mad as a hatter' which arose because in the past hat-making involved copious use of mercury, a poisonous chemical that can cause insanity.

MAD MAX [*Film*]

The 1979 Australian film *Mad Max* is set in a post-holocaust world where survivors and motor-cycle gangs fight it out for the few remaining sources of fuel. Mad Max, an ex-policeman driven crazy by grief for the loss of his family, finds some kind of redemption helping those trying to rebuild society. Mad Max, like BLADE RUN-NER, is mainly used to describe this nightmarish vision of the future.

MAENADS see DIONYSUS

MAGIC ROUNDABOUT see DOUGAL

MAGNET see BOY'S OWN

MAGOO, MR [*Television, Popular Culture*]
The 1940s cartoon character Mr Magoo is a bald-headed, bad-tempered old man whose extreme short-sightedness leads him into all sorts of trouble through mistaken interpretations of what he sees. 'I compared him [Tony Benn] to Mr Magoo yesterday, a myopic agent of catastrophe' (*Independent* 12.12.95).

MAGUA see UNCAS

MAID MARION see ROBIN HOOD

MAIGRET [*Literature, Television*]
Inspector Maigret (Commissaire is his title in the original French books) is the hero of a long series of detective stories by Georges Simenon, the first of which appeared in 1933. The inspector wears a trilby and raincoat and smokes a pipe, an image captured in the opening credits of the TV series which ran from 1960 to 1963, and starred Rupert Davies.

MAILLOT JAUNE see YELLOW JERSEY

MAINWARING, CAPTAIN see DAD'S ARMY

MAKE IT SO see STAR TREK

MALAPROP, MRS [*Drama*]
In R. B. Sheridan's 1775 play *The Rivals* Mrs Malaprop is one of the comic leads. She is a middle-aged woman reluctant to recognise the fact, and not nearly as clever as she thinks, a fact which is chiefly shown by her misuse of language. Like DOGBERRY she never

uses a simple word where a complicated one will serve, and her tendency to produce a similar word rather than the one she wants, or to jumble the syllables of a word has given us the term **malapropism**. Her own name comes from the French *malapropos*, 'not to the purpose'.

MALMSEY, BUTT OF [*History*]

According to tradition, and to William Shakespeare, **George, Duke of Clarence** (1449–78), brother to Edward IV and Richard III and second in line to the English throne, was murdered by being drowned in a butt of malmsey wine at the instigation of his wicked younger brother Richard. Modern historians are more likely to point the finger of guilt at his other brother. See PRINCES IN THE TOWER.

MALTESE FALCON [*Film*]

Dashiell Hammett's 1930 novel *The Maltese Falcon* has been filmed at least three times, but is best known from the great 1941 version where HUMPHREY BOGART played **Sam Spade**, Hammett's hard-boiled private eye. This was publicised with the slogan 'A guy without a conscience! A dame without a heart!' which is a pretty accurate description of the two lead characters. The story is one of multiple deceit and betrayal, as various ruthless villains struggle to obtain the supposedly priceless statue known as the Maltese Falcon, which turns out in the end to be worthless. **Sidney Greenstreet**'s name has become practically synonymous with that of the sinister, fat, creepy, softly-spoken villain **Gutman**, and Peter Lorre's performance as his effeminate, highly-strung side-kick **Joe Cairo** is also famous. The film has been enormously influential on the whole genre of detective films.

MALVOLIO [*Literature*]

Malvolio is a self-important, censorious Puritan. It is not surprising that the pleasure-loving **Sir Toby Belch** and his boon companion **Sir Andrew Aguecheek** decide, in Shakespeare's *Twelfth Night*, to get their revenge on Malvolio, who has so often curtailed their pleasures. This they do by tricking him into thinking that his employer, the retiring Olivia, has fallen in love with him, and has left him love letters telling him how to behave if he feels the same way. Malvolio's vanity makes him an easy victim, and he proceeds to smarm up to Olivia to such an extent, and obey even the most ludicrous instructions as to his behaviour, such as wearing yellow stockings cross-gartered, that he is finally locked up as mad.

MAME, AUNTIE [*Literature, Music*]
A flamboyant, eccentric woman who takes in her orphaned nephew Patrick in Patrick Dennis' 1955 novel *Auntie Mame*, better known from the musical version *Mame*.

MAMMON [*Religion*]
In the New Testament the name Mammon is used to mean wealth, riches which can become a false god, for 'the love of money is the root of all evil'.

MAMMY [*Film*]
In the past Mammy (or **Mammie**) was a standard term for a Black woman employed by Whites to care for their children, but the term is found now specifically referring to the character who raises SCARLETT O'HARA in *Gone With the Wind*, particularly as played by Hattie McDaniel in the 1939 film, with her constant cry of 'Lordy, Lordy Miss Scarlett!'.

MAN FOR ALL SEASONS [*History, Drama, Film*]
'A Man for All Seasons' was a contemporary description of **Sir Thomas More** (1478–1535), author of UTOPIA and Henry VIII's Chancellor, executed for refusing to recognise Henry as head of the Church in England, for which, among other things, he was declared a saint in 1935. This was used by the dramatist Robert Bolt for the title of his play about More, filmed in 1966.

MAN FROM UNCLE [*Television*]
The Man from UNCLE was a semi-spoof, sub-BOND, spy series which ran on TV from 1965 to 1968 with innumerable repeats and spin-off films. The American **Napoleon Solo**, a suave lady-killer, although not quite as much of one as he thought, and the Russian **Illya Kuryakin** wise-cracked their way though various assignments for an international agency called the United Network

Command for Law and Enforcement as it battled against the international crime syndicate **THRUSH**.

MAN IN BLACK see VALENTINE DYALL

MAN WITH NO NAME [*Film*]
In Sergio Leone's 'spaghetti westerns' (so called because Italians made them) the Man with No Name was the quiet, mysterious, violent character played by Clint Eastwood in *A Fistful of Dollars* (1964), *For A Few Dollars More* (1965) and *The Good, the Bad and the Ugly* (1966). He wears a poncho, a hat pulled over his eyes, habitually has a small cigar in his mouth, and is vaguely on the side of good.

MANDERLEY see REBECCA

MANFRED [*Literature*]
In Byron's 1817 verse-drama *Manfred*, strongly influenced by the FAUSTUS legend, Manfred is a NIETZSCHEAN superman, living alone in a castle in the Alps and tortured by the guilt of his love for his sister. The spirits of the universe offer him everything but what he wants; he tries to commit suicide, but is always saved; visits the underworld, and dies unable to repent. Since Byron was himself not only a tortured romantic figure, but also suspected of incest with his half-sister, it is not surprising that he has been identified with his hero.

MANNA [*Religion*]
In the Bible (Exodus 16) God sent manna from heaven to feed the Israelites in the wilderness when the were fleeing from Egypt. From this 'manna from heaven' has come to mean any unexpected benefit or gift.

MAÑUEL see FAWLTY TOWERS

MAO [*History*]
The name of Chairman Mao (**Mao Tse-tung** or **Zedong**; 1893–1976), long-time hard-line Communist leader of China, is associated with many things. The **Great Leap Forward** was his

attempt (1958–60) to improve the lot of the peasant. The *Thoughts of Chairman Mao*, also known as his *Little Red Book*, was waved as a sort of talisman by the young thugs who led the Cultural Revolution which destroyed so much of China's culture, and taken up by some of the Western student revolutionaries of the 1970s. He was also the leader of the LONG MARCH.

MARADONA AND THE 'HAND OF GOD' [*Sport*]
The career of the Argentine footballer Diego Maradona has been filled with controversy, but no incident has been as controversial as the 'handball' incident in the quarter finals of the World Cup in Mexico City in 1986, at least for England fans. They will swear that the winning goal went into the net off Maradona's hand; he denied it and said the goal was thanks to 'the hand of God'.

MARCOS, IMELDA [*History*]
Imelda Marcos is usually alluded to with reference to her time as a shopaholic First Lady of the Phillippines, in particular to the thousands of pairs of shoes which were found at the presidential palace when her husband was toppled from power in 1986. 'There are more Mac [computer] models than there are shoes in Imelda Marcos's wardrobe' (*Independent* 26.2.96).

MARCUS AURELIUS [*History, Philosophy*]
The Roman Emperor Marcus Aurelius (121–180 AD) was a keen philosopher as well as an efficient ruler, and wore a beard to prove it. His book *Meditations* is still widely read, and he is remembered in particular for a short, touching, poem addressed to his soul.

MARIE ANTOINETTE [*History*]
Marie Antoinette (1755–93), Queen of France, is notorious for saying 'Let them eat cake' ('Qu'ils mangent de la brioche') when told the poor of Paris had no bread to eat. In fact, if she did say this, she was merely quoting, for it was a well-known saying at the time. She is also famous for her luxurious life-style, and her liking for playing at being a milkmaid in a luxuriously fitted-out farm. 'To assume that we [older people] all have access to "a small income" displays a rather Marie-Antoinette attitude' (*Independent* 15.5.96).

MARIE CELESTE [*History*]
The *Marie Celeste* (strictly the name was *Mary Celeste*) was an American ship found in 1872 sailing the Atlantic with sails fully set, but no one on board. The ship had obviously been abandoned, as a boat with navigation tools was missing, but no one has ever been able to find out why, or what happened to her crew.

MARINA see STINGRAY

MARLBORO MAN [*Advertising*]
The American brand of Marlboro cigarettes has long been associated in its advertising with rugged Western manhood and landscape, so that Marlboro Man has come to stand for a certain type of tough manhood. 'Gauchos are Argentinean cowboys … Such is their machismo that they make the Marlboro man look like Julian Clary'. (*ES Magazine* 17.5.96).

MARLEY, JACOB see SCROOGE

MARLOWE, PHILIP [*Literature*]
Philip Marlowe is the tough but compassionate private eye with the soft inside in the novels of Raymond Chandler (1888–1959). He walks down the mean streets of the Los Angeles area infuriating both the police and his wealthy (and usually corrupt) clients by his refusal to show them the respect they feel is their due, or stop investigating when told to. The stories are told in the first person, in a distinctive voice – laconic, street-wise and cynical, interspersed with sudden flashes of startlingly poetic images, which have given rise to the term **Chandleresque**. See BOGART.

MARPLES, MISS [*Literature*]
Miss Marples is one of the detectives created by AGATHA CHRISTIE (the other famous one being HERCULE POIROT). Miss Marples is an elderly English spinster. She looks harmless and those who do not know her can dismiss her as a nonentity, but as murderers find to their cost, despite her quiet and genteel exterior she has an insatiable curiosity, a steely determination, a sharp eye for telling detail and a deep understanding of human nature.

MARQUEE CLUB [*Entertainment, Popular Culture*]
In the swinging London of the 1960s, the Marquee Club was *the* place to see and be seen and to catch such latest musical phenomena as The Beatles or The Rolling Stones.

MARS [*Mythology*]
Mars is the Roman god of war, the equivalent of the Greek **Ares**. He is the lover of VENUS, despite the attempts of her husband **Hephaestus** (or **Vulcan**) to end the affair. Because of the workings of Latin grammar, the adjective from Mars is the slightly confusing 'martial'. See also RED PLANET.

MARSHWIGGLES see NARNIA

MARSYAS [*Mythology*]
In Greek myth Marsyas was a satyr who challenged the god of music APOLLO to a contest – Marsyas' pipe playing against Apollo's lyre. Since Apollo's followers the MUSES were to be the judges it is not surprising that Marsyas lost. His penalty was to be flayed alive.

MARTINS, HOLLY see HARRY LIME

MARVEL, CAPTAIN [*Popular Culture*]
Captain Marvel was an immensely popular, red-suited SUPERMAN clone who appeared in American comic-books from the 1940s.

MARX BROTHERS [*Film*]
Groucho, Chico and Harpo Marx were the wise-cracking stars of a series of 1930s comedy films, written in part by the great American comic writer S. J. Perelman (1904–1979). Each brother had a distinctive image – the harp-playing **Harpo** dumb and expressing himself by means of an old-fashioned car horn, with a curly fright wig and old mackintosh, and always chasing the girls; fast-talking **Chico** in his strange hat, with a cod Italian accent, crooked schemes and comic piano-playing routine; and best-known of all, **Groucho** with his crouching walk, heavy black moustache and glasses, and cigar-chomping, rapid-fire delivery of the best lines.

MASH [*Television, Film, Literature*]
First appearing in 1968 as a novel by Richard Hooker *MASH* (the standard shortening in the US military for Mobile Army Surgical Hospital) was a satirical look at life in a field hospital during the Korean war. The novel was made into a highly successful film in 1970, where the anti-authoritarian irreverence of **Benjamin 'Hawkeye' Pearce**, **'Trapper' John McIntyre** and **Duke Forrest** from their base in their tent known as '**The Swamp**', together with the way the film showed up the pointlessness of combat, greatly appealed to the anti-Vietnam generation. Other characters were the mild and strangely gifted **Radar O'Reilly, Hotlips Houlihan** the dedicatedly militaristic nurse against whom the Swamp had a vendetta and '**Spearchucker' Oliver Wendel Jones**, a black surgeon and athlete. The influence of the film was greatly overshadowed by the TV series (1973–84) starring Alan Alda. This too started off as an anti-war series, but with the ending of the war in Vietnam and changing tastes moved on to be more concerned with psychological matters. This introduced another character in the person of **Corporal Klinger**, desperately cross-dressing in an attempt to be sent home as unfit for military service.

MATTHEWS, STANLEY [*Sport*]
Sir Stanley Matthews (b. 1915) is regarded as one of the greatest wingers of all time. His football career lasted 22 years, and for whole generations his name was used as a standard of excellence.

MAXWELL, ROBERT [*Business, Crime*]
When Robert Maxwell (1923–91) died after falling off his yacht, his remarkable business empire was in ruins. A Czech refugee and war hero, he had built up a multi-million-pound publishing business using his Eastern European contacts and had been a Labour Member of Parliament. But he had also been declared unfit to run a company by the Board of Trade, and when he died it was found that he had been illegally tapping his company's pensions funds to shore up his own affairs. This, and various other crooked deals, is what he is chiefly remembered for.

McAUSLAN [*Literature*]
Private McAuslan, the dirtiest soldier in the world, is a

Glaswegian walking disaster-area and anti-hero of a series of comic stories by George MacDonald Fraser.

McCANN, TERRY see ARTHUR DALEY

McCARTHYISM [*History*]
Senator Joseph McCarthy (1908–57) was the leading light of the American virulent and vicious anti-Communist witch-hunt in the early 1950s. Although he actually made very few of his accusations stick, merely to be called before his Senate committee and be accused of un-American activities could be enough to lose the accused their job, and the climate of fear he engendered has been held responsible for the conformity of public life at the time. He lost his power after his bullying tactics became widely known after the showing on TV of one of his investigations.

McENROE, JOHN [*Sport*]
The champion American tennis player John McEnroe (b. 1959) is widely known for his abusive, sometimes obscene language on court and in disputes with umpires, and is particularly associated with the expression 'You cannot be serious!'

McGILL, DONALD [*Popular Culture*]
The humour of the cartoonist Donald McGill (1875–1962) depended on double entendre. He is famous for his sea-side postcards of large, red-cheeked women and their often shrimpish husbands, one of whom is saying something essentially innocent – 'I can't see my little Willie'; 'I've never seen such a big one' – which can also be interpreted as being risqué.

McINTYRE, 'TRAPPER' JOHN see MASH

MEDEA see GOLDEN FLEECE

MEDMENHAM ABBEY see HELLFIRE CLUB

MEDUSA [*Mythology*]
Medusa was one of the three **Gorgons** in Greek mythology. She had snakes instead of hair and she was so terrifying that anyone

who looked at her turned to stone, a phenomenon made good use of by PERSEUS. The goddess ATHENE later placed the head in the centre of her shield to petrify her enemies. 'Jacqueline froze him with a look as devastating as Medusa's glare' (Elizabeth Peters *Die for Love* 1993). Medusa's name was given to a French frigate which foundered on the reefs by the island of Arguin off the West coast of Africa in 1816. The ship was carrying French officers on the way to take possession of Senegal for France, and the wreck caused a political scandal when it was revealed that sailors had been cut adrift and left to drown. The shipwreck claimed 350 lives, but 15 people survived for 13 days without food (there are stories of cannibalism) on a makeshift raft before they were rescued. Two years later these events were turned into the painting *The Raft of the Medusa* by the painter Théodore Géricault, much to the disgust of the government which did not want reminding of the events. This became a benchmark of the new realism in art of the time. The harrowing images of suffering and deprivation shown in the painting have often been reused.

MEGAERA see FURIES

MEIN KAMPF [*History*]
Mein Kampf ('My Struggle') was the book written by the German Nazi leader ADOLF HITLER in which he set out his philosophy.

MEKON see DAN DARE

MELLORS, OLIVER see LADY CHATTERLEY

MELPOMENE see MUSES

MEMNON see AURORA

MENE, MENE, TEKEL, UPHARSIN see DANIEL

MENELAUS see HELEN OF TROY

MEPHISTOPHELES [*Mythology*]
Mephistopheles (or **Mephisto**) is the name of one of the seven

major devils in medieval mythology. His name is best known from the FAUSTUS legend, where he persuades Faustus to sell his soul to the Devil with a mixture of reason, wit and poetry. Because of this the term **Mephistophelean** tends to imply a certain degree of devilish charm.

MERCURY see HERMES

MERRY, TOM see BILLY BUNTER

MESHAK see SHADRACH, MESHAK AND ABEDNIGO

MESSALA see BEN HUR

METIS see ATHENE

MICAWBER, MR [*Literature*]
In Charles Dickens' novel *David Copperfield* (1850) Mr Micawber is a feckless and idle man who is always hoping that 'something will turn up' to put right his dire financial position. 'A sentimental Micawberish refusal to do anything but talk about putting things right' (*Independent* 21.7.93). Micawber always means to do something about his situation, and is, ironically, best known for his wise financial sayings, particularly 'Annual income twenty pound, annual expenditure nineteen nineteen and six, result happiness. Annual income twenty pound, annual expenditure twenty pounds ought and six, result misery.'

MICKEY MOUSE [*Film*]
The name of Walt Disney's famous cartoon creation has come to mean trivial, amateurish, unimportant, mechanical, unchallenging. This is probably because of the simple outlines and toylike quality of the figures in the early Mickey Mouse cartoons and Mickey's simple-minded attitudes.

MIDAS [*Mythology*]
In Greek myth Midas is the subject of a number of stories. In the best-known one he is granted a wish by the god DIONYSUS, and asks that everything he touches turn to gold. However, he soon finds

that he cannot eat, drink, or even touch another living being, without turning them to gold, and begs to have the gift removed. Thus 'to have the Midas touch' means to have the gift of making money.

MIDIAN, HOST OF [*Religion*]
In the Bible the Midianites are a tribe in conflict with the great Israelite general Gideon. They are defeated after Gideon has a vision in which God tells him that 'the host of Midian' have been delivered to him. 'The host(s) of Midian' therefore became a general term for 'the enemy', a term reinforced in the mid-19th century by a popular hymn (translated by the Rev. J. M. Neale from a hymn of the early Greek church) which begins 'Christian, dost thou see them / On the holy ground / How the troops of Midian / Prowl and prowl around?' 'And me beside myself with fear, not knowing what the devil was up, except that the host of Midian were after me' (George MacDonald Fraser, *Flashman and the Mountain of Light* (1990).

MIDNIGHT COWBOY see RIZZO, RATSO

MIKE TV AND VERRUCA SALT [*Children's Literature*]
These are two of the children who get to be shown round the eccentric **Willie Wonka**'s sweet factory in Roald Dahl's *Charlie and the Chocolate Factory* (1964). Every child except Charlie is horrid and come to a sticky end. Mike TV is TV mad and ends up shrunk to the size of a TV picture when he tried to get himself transmitted into a TV set, and Verucca Salt is a spoilt brat who throws a tantrum if her rich Daddy doesn't immediately get her whatever she wants. She is last seen heading for the rubbish furnace. Charlie is the last remaining child on the tour, and he gets to be Willie Wonka's heir to the factory that makes the best sweets in the world.

MILLENIUM FALCON see HAN SOLO

MILLSTONE see ALBATROSS

MINERVA see ATHENE

MING THE MERCILESS see FLASH GORDON

MINIVER, MRS [*Film*]
The 1942 film of Mrs Miniver, based on the writings of Jan Struther, was the ultimate in Hollywood's contribution to the image of 'plucky little Britain' during the Second World War. In an upper middle-class, almost unrecognisable rural Britain, doughty Mrs Miniver manages to be the perfect wife, mother and patriot and tries to lead a normal life while suffering through the sorrows of war including sending her husband off on one of the **little ships** to DUNKIRK and such adventures as having a German fighter pilot come down near her house.

MINOTAUR [*Mythology*]
The Minotaur was, according to Greek legend, a creature with a bull's head and a human body. He was the result of an relationship between **Pasiphaë**, wife of **Minos** king of Crete, and a bull. This bull was one that Minos had failed to sacrifice to **Poseidon**, the god of the sea, and the angry god inflicted this unnatural passion on Minos' queen as a punishment. To hide his shame Minos got the great craftsman **Daedalus** to build the **labyrynth**, a maze so complex that no one could find their way out. There the Minotaur lived, receiving twelve Athenian youths and maids as an annual sacrifice, until the great Athenian hero **Theseus** came and killed him, escaping the Labyrinth with the help of ARIANDNE's thread.

MIRANDA see BRAVE NEW WORLD, CALIBAN, PROSPERO

MIRANDA, CARMEN [*Film*]
The Brazilian film star and singer Carmen Miranda (1909–1955) came to represent for Hollywood the image of fiery-tempered exotic South America. She is best remembered for her exotic costumes and trade-mark turban hats decorated with tropical fruit.

MIRIAM THE HIRED HAND see COLD COMFORT FARM

MISS PIGGY see MUPPETS

MISSING LINK see PILTDOWN MAN

MR TOAD see TOAD OF TOAD HALL

MITTY, WALTER *[Literature]*
James Thurber's 1939 short story *The Secret Life of Walter Mitty* tells of a henpecked man who escapes his wife's nagging by retreating into a world of daydreams in which he has heroic adventures. The name was quickly adopted to mean a fantasist or daydreamer. Compare BILLY LIAR.

MJOLLNIR see THOR

MÖBIUS STRIP *[Engineering]*
If you take a long thin strip of a material such as paper, twist it through 180° and joint the two ends you have created a three-dimentional shape with only one surface. To prove this, run your finger over the surface and you will find that you have covered both 'sides' of the paper before you get back to your starting point. This Möbius strip has become an image of something unending or infinite, so that Terry Pratchett and Neil Gaiman in *Good Omens* can talk of the 'Möbius bickering' of a group of four children who are close friends.

MOBY DICK *[Literature]*
Moby Dick is the name of the great white whale in Herman Melville's 1850 novel. In it **Captain Ahab** in his ship *Pequod* obsessively hunts the whale that bit off his leg. Among the crew are the 'soothing savage' **Queequeg** and the sole survivor after Moby Dick sinks the ship, **Ishmael**, whose memorable words 'Call me ISHMAEL' open the book.

MODESTINE *[Literature]*
Modestine is the name R. L. Stevenson gave to his not-always co-operative donkey in his delightful account of walking through the Cevennes, *Travels with a Donkey* (1879).

MOLE, MOLEY see TOAD OF TOAD HALL

MOLESWORTH, NIGEL [*Literature*]
Nigel Molesworth is the horrid little schoolboy in the *How to be Topp* series of books by Geoffrey Willans, with their vivid illustrations by Ronald Searle. Although the books reflect life in the 1950s when they were written, they have remained consistently popular. Molesworth, 'the curse of **St Custard**'s', is a cynical child with a vivid imagination and absolutely no sense of spelling, and the books are his comment on school (or as he has it 'skool') and life in general. His strongest term of condemnation is 'chiz' ('a chiz is a swiz or swindle as any fule kno'), with 'utterly wet and weedy' coming a close second. Things he approves of are 'whiz'. Others at school with him are the school sissy **Fotherington-Thomas** ('he sa Hullo clouds hullo sky he is a girlie and love the scents and sounds of nature'), **Grabber** (see MRS JOYFUL), his best friend **Peason**, his younger brother **Molesworth 2** and the **Mekon**-lookalike (see DAN DARE) mad maths master **Sigismund Arbuthnot**.

MOLOCH [*Religion*]
In the Old Testament of the Bible Moloch was a Semitic god to whom parents sacrificed their children. So the name has come to be used for anything that demands excessive sacrifice.

MONA LISA [*Art*]
Leonardo da Vinci's portrait known as Mona Lisa (Lady Lisa) or **La Gioconda** ('The Smiling Lady' or 'Mrs Giocondo') is traditionally supposed to be a portrait of the wife of the Florentine Francesco Giocondo, but there is no real evidence for this. The portrait, which is kept in the Louvre in Paris, is famous for the way in which its eyes seem to follow you round the room and above all for its enigmatic smile.

MONEYPENNY, MISS see JAMES BOND

MONGO see FLASH GORDON

MONROE, MARILYN [*Film*]
Born **Norma Jean** Baker, the American film actress Marilyn Monroe (1926–62) represents the ultimate in film-star feminine

allure and at the same time, because of her apparent suicide, the ultimate in Hollywood tragedy.

MONTAGUES AND CAPULETS see ROMEO AND JULIET

MONTE CRISTO, COUNT OF [*Literature*]
Alexandre Dumas' novel *The Count of Monte Cristo* (1844–45) is one of the great romantic adventure novels, and has come to represent the best of the genre. In it **Edmond Dantès**, a young French sea-captain, is unjustly imprisoned on trumped-up charges of treason on the fortress island of the **Chateau d'If** (off the French Mediterranean coast near Marseilles, and now a tourist attraction thanks to the novel). One of his fellow prisoners is the **Abbé Feria**, who passes on some of his vast learning to Dantès and also tells him the secret of a treasure buried on the island of Monte Cristo. When Feria dies Dantès manages to escape after 14 years of trying by taking the place of the corpse when it is thrown into the sea. Now a deeply embittered man, Dantès finds the treasure, assumes the name The Count of Monte Cristo and sets about taking terrible vengeance on the men who profited by his imprisonment, before sailing away for an unknown destination with a beautiful slave girl.

MONTEZUMA [*History*]
The Emperor Montezuma II was ruler of the Aztecs in Mexico from about 1502 until overthrown and killed by the Spanish conquistador Hernan Cortés. Nowadays tourists to Mexico are often struck down by violent diarrhoea, which has been nicknamed **Montezuma's Revenge**.

MONTY PYTHON [*Television*]
Monty Python's Flying Circus was a ground-breaking comedy show which ran on BBC TV from 1969 to 1974. The show, with its rapid series of sketches, ability to take logic to the illogical extreme and keen sense of the ridiculous owed something to earlier radio shows, but also had a large element that was uniquely its own, soon became a cult, and has since spawned numerous, largely unsuccessful imitators. It has become a standard for subsequent humour: 'The waste of money and talent, together with

the sub-Python japes, make this a uniquely depressing experience' (*Radio Times* 24.8.96); 'And so you get organisations like the Pythonesque Loyalists Against Thuggery – people who go around beating people up with baseball bats in the name of stopping violence' (*Guardian* 10.8.96). See also NORWEGIAN BLUE, SPANISH INQUISITION and further under DES O'CONNOR.

MOORE, HENRY [*Art*]

The British sculptor Henry Moore (1873–1958) is best known for his works which echo organic forms, usually recognisably human, but which are pierced with holes. Hence such comments as 'The Court of Appeal ruled that Polo mints had no monopoly of the Henry Moore school of confectionery' (*Times* 23.8.96).

MORDOR [*Literature*]

In J. R. R. TOLKIEN's *Lord of the Rings* Mordor is the grim, evil land ruled by **Sauron** the Black, the Dark Lord and evil creator of the rings of power. It is an ecologist's nightmare, a volcanic landscape further ruined by remorseless, polluting, heavy industry, an embodiment of William Blake's 'DARK, SATANIC MILLS', which are run by the black-hearted **Orcs**, creatures part-medieval devil, part-goblin, who are Sauron's servants. The land is guarded by such creatures as **Shelob**, the giant, ravenous spider. FRODO BAGGINS and his faithful companion **Sam Gamgee** have to journey there to destroy the ring. See also GANDALF, GOLLUM.

MORE, SIR THOMAS see MAN FOR ALL SEASONS

MORGIANA see ALI BABA

MORIARTY, PROFESSOR see SHERLOCK HOLMES

MORPHEUS, IN THE ARMS OF [*Mythology*]

In Greek myth Morpheus is the god of sleep and dreams, so to be in the arms of Morpheus is a rather pompous and old-fashioned way of saying 'asleep'.

MORSE, INSPECTOR [*Television, Literature*]

Colin Dexter's Inspector Morse books, turned into a very successful TV series (1987–96), depict a detective at the opposite extreme from the NICK CARTER school. Morse is a confirmed bachelor, cultured, cerebral, squeamish when it comes to dead bodies and anything but a man of action.

MORTICIA see ADDAMS FAMILY

MOSES [*Religion*]
The events from Moses' long and complex life that are most often alluded to are his being found as a baby in the **bulrushes** by **pharaoh's daughter**, after his mother had placed him in a floating cradle to avoid Pharaoh's orders that all male Jewish babies should be killed; his demanding of pharaoh to '**let my people go**' and leading them out of the land of Egypt; his **parting of the Red Sea waters** to let his people cross safely while the pursuing Egyptian army was drowned by the returning water; his interview with God in the form of a **burning bush**; and his descending from **Mount Sinai** bearing the two stone tablets on which were written the **Ten Commandments**.

MOULIN ROUGE [*History, Entertainment, Art*]
The Moulin Rouge was a famous Parisian caberet, which has come to represent the essence of the fun-loving, daring '**Naughty Nineties**' in France. Founded in 1889 as a dance-hall, it developed into a place of more passive entertainment, and was the first place that the cancan was performed. The posters made for it by the artist **Toulouse-Lautrec** added further to its fame. The name of the **Folies-Bergère** is used in the same way, but although founded earlier (1869), its heyday was in the twentieth century and its reputation based more on its lavish shows and use of nude females. It has a glitzier, less bohemian reputation than the Moulin Rouge.

MOUNT RUSHMORE [*Sculpture*]
Mount Rushmore in South Dakota, USA, is famous for the portrait heads of the US Presidents George Washington, Thomas Jefferson, Abraham Lincoln, and Theodore Roosevelt which have been carved out of its granite side. Allusions to Mount Rushmore are usually to the vast size of these heads, being stony or rugged faced

– 'Nimoy, now so nobly ravaged he could play a face on Mount Rushmore ... ' (*Guardian* 27.8.96) – or to the famous chase scene involving climbing over these faces in the HITCHCOCK film *North by Northwest* (1958).

MOUNT SINAI see MOSES

MOWGLI [*Literature, Film*]
Mowgli is the hero of a series of short stories by Rudyard Kipling. As a baby he is lost in the Indian jungle after his family is attacked by **Shere Khan** the cowardly tiger, and is raised, like ROMULUS AND REMUS, by wolves, who name him Mowgli 'the frog' because he seems so weak, even though he is unafraid. With **Baloo** the wise old bear (turned into a figure of fun in the 1967 Disney cartoon film, which has only a tenuous connection with the stories), **Bagheera** the black panther and **Kaa** the giant python as his instructors he grows up wise in the ways of the jungle, but finds that the wolf pack think of him as a man, and when he attempts to join the man pack, he is rejected as a wolf-child.

MUFFIN THE MULE [*Television*]
Muffin the Mule was one of the early favourites of children's TV. A string puppet, he appeared dancing on a piano accompanied by Annette Mills. The first show was a five-minute slot in 1946, and he appeared regularly until 1957. Not only was he immensely popular with children, but in 1950 he even won the Television Society Silver Medal for 'outstanding artistic achievement'.

MUGG, MATTHEW, THE CAT'S-MEAT MAN see DR DOLITTLE

MULDER AND SCULLY, AGENTS see X FILES

MULDOON, SPOTTY [*Television, Song*]
Spotty Muldoon, 'He's got spots all over his face', was an invention of the humorist Peter Cook (1937–95). One of many of Cook's inventions, Muldoon chiefly figured in the surprisingly popular 1965 song named after him. The name now crops up simply for anyone or thing spotty, usually without any further significance.

MÜNCHHAUSEN, BARON [*History, Medicine*]

Münchhausen's name has come to mean at best a teller of an exaggerated story (if not an outright liar), and has become attached to a syndrome where someone makes up medical symptoms in order to get hospital treatment. There was a real man, Karl Friedrich, Baron von Münchhausen, behind the legend. He was a German who lived between 1720 and 1797, served in the Crimea with the Russian army against the Turks, and who gained a reputation for telling tall stories on his return home. When his fellow German Rudolph Erich Raspe wrote his collection of wildly outrageous, exaggerated tales *The Adventures of Baron Münchhausen* in 1785 he borrowed Karl Friedrich's name and reputation.

MUNCHKINS [*Film, Children's Literature*]

Frank Baum's 1900 children's book *The Wonderful **Wizard of Oz*** features a race of little people called Munchkins. The word has been taken up for a wide range of uses. It can mean simply a little person, or be used as a term of endearment for a child, or to suggest sweetness in a child. It can also be used to mean a minor official or low-ranker in an organization, or be used as a rather condescending or camp term of address to a group of people.

MUNICH [*History*]

In 1938 ADOLF HITLER was claiming the **Sudetenland** area of Czechoslovakia, where many ethnic Germans lived, as part of greater Germany, and threatening armed invasion if the Czechs did not cede this land. Russia, France and Britain all had treaties with Czechoslovakia to protect it against invasion, but none of them actually wanted to go to war. Instead there were a series of meetings in Munich where one after another the major powers (but not Czechoslovakia, which was not consulted) gave in to Hitler's steadily increasing demands, a policy later vilified as **'appeasement'**. Finally the Munich agreement, giving Hitler all he wanted, was signed on 30 September. **Neville Chamberlain,** then British Prime Minister, flew home and announced that the treaty meant 'Peace in our time' and 'peace with honour'. Since he appeared in public waving a copy of the treaty it became known as Mr Chamberlain's **piece of paper**, the word 'worthless' being added when Hitler invaded Czechoslovakia after all the following

March, and made war unavoidable in September 1939 by invading Poland.

MUNSTERS [Television]
The Munsters is a TV comedy show, a less subtle version of the ADDAMS FAMILY, originally shown from 1965 to 1967 and repeated frequently since. **Herman** Munster is a FRANKENSTEIN lookalike, his wife **Lily** and **Grandpa** vampires and their son **Eddie** a werewolf. The humour rests on the fact that they consider themselves perfectly normal and the rest of the world weird, and cannot understand why everyone reacts to them with alarm.

MUPPETS [Television]
Muppets are the half string-puppet and half glove-puppet creations of Jim Henson. They have been appearing on children's TV since the 1950s. They are best known from two sources, *The Muppet Show* (1976–81, with revivals and films since) and those in the long-running pre-school education programme *Sesame Street*. **Kermit the Frog** and the would-be blond bombshell with the powerful punch **Miss Piggy** are found in both. Much-loved characters from *Sesame Street* include **Big Bird**, a rather gormless giant fluffy yellow creature, **Oscar the Grouch**, a bad-tempered creature who lives in a dustbin and loves mess, and the big blue **Cookie Monster**, a sweet-natured creature who can hardly string two words together but who has a vast appetite.

MUSES [Mythology]
In Greek myth the nine Muses, who attend the god APOLLO, are the daughters of ZEUS and Mnemosyne, the goddess of literature, and are the patronesses of the arts and sciences. They are **Calliope** (epic poetry), **Clio** (history), **Erato** (lyre playing), **Euterpe** (flute playing), **Melpomene** (tragedy), **Thalia** (comedy), **Urania** (astronomy), **Polyhymnia** (sacred song) and **Terpsichore** (dance). This last gives up the term Terpsichorean as a posh term for dance, and Terpsichorean ecdysiast as a term for a stripper. The Muses were said to live on MOUNT HELICON. They are also called the Pierians, hence Pope's 'A little learning is a dang'rous thing / Drink deep or taste not the **Pierian spring**', for their spring water was supposed to provide inspiration.

MUTTLEY see DICK DASTARDLY

MY FAIR LADY see ELIZA DOOLITTLE

MYCROFT see SHERLOCK HOLMES

MYSTERY MACHINE, THE see SCOOBY DOO AND SCRAPPY DOO

NAGASAKI see HIROSHIMA

NANCY see BILL SIKES

NAPOLEON [*History*]
The name of Napoleon Bonaparte (1769–1821), Emperor of the French, is used allusively in a wide number of ways. He was a brilliant general and leader and his name is used in this way 'Susan B. Anthony ... The Napoleon of the woman's rights movement' (*Guardian* 30.9.96). It is also used to mean a megalomaniac, for he was the man who was so keen on personal power that he turned the great experiment of the First French Republic into a personal empire and at his coronation seized the crown from the Pope and placed it on his own head. (The tradition that madmen think they are Napoleon is probably derived from this aspect of his character.) He is used as an example of the man who overstretched himself on his famous **retreat from Moscow**, when the Russian weather defeated him and led to his downfall. His return from exile in **Elba** and the support he got to try to return to power before his final defeat at **Waterloo** are also referred to, and finally he becomes the image of bitter defeat in his lonely exile on remote **St Helena**. (For Napoleon the pig see ANIMAL FARM.)

NARNIA [*Literature*]
C. S. Lewis's Narnia books are a series of children's religious allegories which are also fantasy novels. Narnia is a land in a parallel universe, reached most memorably in the first of the series, *The Lion, the Witch and the Wardrobe*, through a wardrobe in a spare room. There the four children involved find a world where, thanks to the machinations of **Jadis** the white witch, it is always winter but never Christmas. The inhabitants of Narnia include talking animals and creatures from fairy tale and Greek myth,

including centaurs and fauns such as **Mr Tumnus**. Once in Narnia the children help the great lion **Aslan** to break the power of the witch. Later stories in the cycle include characters such as **Prince Caspian** and **Puddleglum**, a member of a strange frog-like race called **Marshwiggles**. 'The explosive growth of the Internet ... has led to mounting fears that every child who goes to a darkened bedroom with a computer for company is somehow walking through a wardrobe into an evil Narnia where cyberperverts poison their minds with unbelievably gross pictures' (*Independent* 24.9.96).

NAUGHTY NINETIES see MOULIN ROUGE

NAUSICAÄ [*Literature*]
In HOMER'S *The ODYSSEY* Nausicaä is the daughter of the king on whose shores Odysseus is shipwrecked. She is playing ball on the beach with her maidens after completing the household washing, and when the naked, disreputable-looking Odysseus approaches the girls, the maidens run away. Nausicaä however is undaunted, takes pity on him and conducts him to her father's house where he is treated as an honoured guest. The character of Nausicaä has charmed many a generation of crusty scholars, to the extent that it has even been suggested that only a woman could have written her, so that the author of *The Odyssey* must have been female.

NEANDERTHAL [*Pre-History*]
Like PILTDOWN MAN, the term Neanderthal, originally used of a race of man which lived in Palaeolithic times, has come to mean 'primitive, uncouth'. It is also used to mean 'ultraconservative, reactionary'. The term Neanderthal comes from the name of the valley in Germany where their remains were first found.

NEBUCHADNEZZAR, NEBUCHADREZZAR [*History, Religion*]
King of BABYLON from 605 to 562 BC. He conquered Jerusalem and took the Jewish people into captivity in Babylon. There he was responsible for throwing SHADRACH, MESHAK AND ABEDNIGO into the fiery furnace. His pride was later punished by his being inflicted with insanity, and living like an ox eating grass until he acknowledged his sins against God. Nebuchadnezzar's name is

also used for a bottle of wine holding the equivalent of 20 ordinary bottles. This is part of a tradition of naming large wine bottle after characters in the Old Testament.

NELSON [*History*]
Admiral Horatio Nelson (1758–1805), who had already lost an arm and an eye before he died at the Battle of Trafalgar, has given his name to a number of terms. Navy slang for rum is **Nelson's Blood**. According to tradition, after Trafalgar Nelson's body was brought back to England for burial preserved in a cask of rum (in one version the rum had all been surreptitiously drunk by the time he body reached home), and this is how the daily rum rations got its name. Another tradition says that at the Battle of Copenhagen Nelson refused to acknowledge his orders, by putting his telescope to his blind eye and saying, 'I see no ships', allowing the navy to fight on and win. So 'to turn a **Nelson eye** to' something is the same as 'to turn a blind eye'. A **Nelson knife** is a combined knife and fork that can be used by a one-armed man, and 'to have the **Nelson touch**' refers to the inspiring leadership or a self-confident and daring approach associated with the man.

NEMEAN LION see HERCULES

NEMESIS [*Mythology*]
In Greek myth Nemesis is the goddess of retribution and vengeance, so she represents anything that is going to catch up with you in the end.

NERO [*History*]
The Roman Emperor Nero (37–68 AD) is famous for fiddling while Rome burned. In fact Nero's instrument was the lyre (the violin had not yet been invented). He did perform on this in public (as well as paint and write poetry) and he may indeed have sung to it during the great fire of Rome. He was, however, suspected of having started it, although there is not evidence to support this. The suggestion is that he was keen to rebuild Rome and his own palace on a grander scale (architecture being another of his interests), and fire was a good way to clear land. Nero found it useful to blame the Christians for starting the fire.

185

NESBITT, RAB C. [*Television*]
Rab C. Nesbitt is the Glaswegian, philosophising, hard-drinking hero of his own situation comedy (1990–). He wears a string vest and a bandage around his head, is extremely violent in his behaviour and specialises in bamboozling authority by spouting a stream of dialect so thick as to be incomprehensible.

NESS, ELIOT [*Crime, History, Television, Film*]
The real Eliot Ness (1903–1957) was an agent of the U.S. Department of Justice who headed the Prohibition bureau in Chicago and was charged with the job of bringing AL CAPONE to book. His nine-man team of law enforcers were given the nickname **The Untouchables** because they could not be bribed to turn a blind eye to Capone and other's criminal networks. Ness used the press to gain publicity for his successes by inviting reporters along to his raids on speakeasies, breweries and other dens of iniquity, and his men successfully went undercover in the underworld. Even so, in the end they could only convict Capone of income-tax evasion. With such a high profile it is not surprising that Ness's life was soon turned into fiction, with a police drama called *The Untouchables* running on TV from 1959 loosely based on his activities, and other appearances on film.

NEVER NEVER LAND see PETER PAN

NEW JERUSALEM see APOCALYPSE

NEWMAN, ALFRED E. [*Popular Culture*]
Alfred E. Newman is the bat-eared grinning idiot central to *MAD Magazine*. 'Scuttling into another corridor, I collided with a little man wandering along completely alone. It was Ross Perot, looking like the father of MAD magazine's prototype middle American, Alfred E. Newman.' (*Independent* 22.3.96).

NEWSPEAK see 1984

NIAGARA FALLS [*Popular Culture*]
The Niagara Falls on the border of the USA and Canada are famed for their beauty and as a popular honeymoon destination. Used

allusively the name is used to indicate a torrent of anything, or even just a large quantity. In the past Niagara Falls was a popular venue for stunts such as going over the falls in a barrel, which has become a commonplace of such things as cartoons, and was the site of some of BLONDIN's tightrope stunts.

NIETZSCHE, NIETZSCHEAN [*Philosophy*]
The German philosopher Friedrich Nietzsche (1844–1900) is best known for his declaration that 'God is dead' as well as for his concept of the 'superman' who would control the weak, and for the influence this idea had on the Nazis.

NIGHTINGALE, FLORENCE [*History, Medicine*]
Known popularly as **the Lady with the Lamp** from her habit of doing the rounds of hospital wards at night carrying a lamp to light her way, Florence Nightingale (1829–1910) was instrumental in saving many lives in the Crimean War by insisting on raising the standard of nursing of the wounded. Before she arrived the mortality rate on the wards was 42%. She got this down to only 2%. On her return she helped found a school for nurses in London, and her name became used for any good nurse or carer, although nowadays the name is more likely than not to be used ironically rather than sincerely.

1984 [*Literature*]
A novel by George Orwell showing a nightmare world where BIG BROTHER controls people's thoughts and actions. There is no privacy or independence of action, and the media are used to brainwash people into docile, unthinking co-operation. The use of **Newspeak** – a limited and simplified version of English – makes it impossible to express complex ideas or shades of meaning; history is rewritten to fit the current political aims of those in power; and **Doublethink** – the ability to hold two or more logically inconsistent beliefs at the same time – is the order of the day. The hero, **Winston Smith**, need only begin to question this way of life before he is brainwashed by the dreaded **Thought Police**.

NIOBE [*Mythology*]
In Greek myth Niobe was the daughter of TANTALUS who was

unfortunate enough to **bring down the wrath of the gods** on herself when she boasted of her seven sons and seven daughters. All
of them were killed to humble her pride, and she was over-
whelmed with grief. She was turned into a pillar of rock, but her
tears still flowed from the stone.

NIRVANA [*Religion*]
In the theology of Buddhism and Hinduism Nirvana is the final
release from the cycle of reincarnation through the extinction of all
desires. In English it tends to be used loosely to mean 'Paradise'
or a state of perfect contentment.

NOAH [*Religion*]
Noah is best known for the Old Testament story of how God
decided to punish mankind for their sins, but decided to save the
virtuous Noah. He therefore told Noah to build an **ark** in which
he was to take a male and female of every kind of animal in order
to repopulate the earth. After forty day and forty nights the flood
began to subside and the ark came to rest on Mount Ararat, where
the credulous can still find it. In the past Noah was also well
known as the first person to cultivate the vine to make wine, and
consequently as the first drunk. In Australian rhyming slang a
noah is a shark – Noah's Ark: shark.

NODDY AND BIG EARS [*Children's Literature, Television*]
The characters of the little nodding man Noddy and his friend Big
Ears in ENID BLYTON's books for small children are an inescapable
part of most British children's childhood. This has made them a
target for many parodies, and also made the name Noddy serve
much the same function as MICKEY MOUSE, in that it is used for
something toylike or insignificant. The place where they live,
Toytown, has also entered the language. Since the illustrations
used in the book show buildings made of children's wooden
bricks, the term has been applied to the style of architecture, often
found in out-of-town shopping centres, which is reminiscent of
such buildings.

NOGGIN THE NOG [*Television*]
Television's *The Saga of Noggin the Nog* (1959–65) was a series of

ten-minute animations about a Norse prince (later king) and his various adventures, and was enormously popular with children. Many of Noggin's adventures were helped along by a large, harsh-voiced bird called **Graculus**, which had been raised by **Nooka**, Princess of the **Nooks**, who became Noggin's queen. He was also helped, and often hindered, by the inventions of **Olaf the Lofty**. He needed to be constantly on the lookout for attempts to dethrone him by his wicked uncle **Nogbad the Bad**.

NORMA JEAN see MARILYN MONROE

NORWEGIAN BLUE [*Television*]
One of the most enduringly famous of all MONTY PYTHON sketches and also known as the **dead parrot** sketch, this was first shown in 1969 and involves a petshop where an irate customer brings back a parrot he has just bought, complaining that it is dead. The shop assistant identifies it as a Norwegian Blue and says it is either resting or pining for the fjords. A whole generation of fans can quote John Cleese's subsequent furious tirade: 'It's not pining – it's passed on! This parrot is no more! It has ceased to be! It's expired and gone to meet its maker! This is a late parrot! It's a stiff! Bereft of life it rests in peace – if you hadn't nailed it to the perch it would be pushing up the daisies! It's rung down the curtain and joined the choir invisible! This is an ex-parrot!'.

NOTTINGHAM, SHERIFF OF see ROBIN HOOD

NUMBER OF THE BEAST [*Religion*]
In the APOCALYPSE of St John, among many visions are those of ravening, vengeful beasts. The number of the second beast, we are told, is **666**. John probably meant the beast to represent the Emperor NERO, but as the Apocalypse is open to a wide range of interpretations, the number of the beast has been a source of fertile imaginings. Fairly typical is the case of Pierre Bezuhov in Tolstoy's *War and Peace*, where by fiddling about with the pseudo-science of numerology he manages to make the Emperor NAPOLEON'S name add up to 666 and identify him with the beast. Nowadays the Beast of the Apocalypse is often identified with the Devil.

NUREYEV, RUDOLPH [*Dance*]

The name of the great Russian ballet dancer and choreographer Rudolph Nureyev (1938–1993) has come to indicate any great dancer, as in 'The Spanish Nureyev, Antonio Gades, stars ... in Carlos Suara's film version of Carmen' (*Evening Standard* 1.5.96).

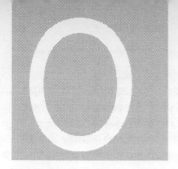

O'CONNOR, DES [*Entertainment*]
Although Des O'Connor has had a long and successful career as a singer and light entertainer, including eight hit singles over a twenty-year period, there is a media tradition of mocking him for his middle-of-the-road appeal. Perhaps this is best summed up in a long quote from a Kit Hesketh-Harvey review of the musical *Salad Days*: 'Truly this is the Des O'Conor of musicals. It is permatanned. Of gossamer substance. Lampooned from the day it appeared by the intimate reviews at the Gate Theatre and 20 years later, in MONTY PYTHON's memorable punk chainsaw version. And yet, like Des, Salad Days has proved bafflingly enduring. Like Des all those who have actually seen it in live performance agree it is hilarious.' (*Independent* 17.4.96).

O'HARA, SCARLETT [*Film, Literature*]
Strong-willed, brave, enchanting and totally selfish, Scarlett O'Hara is the heroine of Margaret Mitchell's 1936 novel of the American Civil War, *Gone with the Wind* and the immensely successful film of it made in 1939. It is ironic that Scarlett is often taken as the embodiment of the Southern Belle, as in the book her father is an Irish immigrant who has only won his plantation, TARA, though gambling, and she herself is always struggling to act like a lady, and, despite all MAMMY's coaching, always finding her strong will makes her fail. Her determination is summed up in her famous line 'Tomorrow is another day', while her ultimate failure as a person is summed up in her last husband, **Rhett Bulter**'s, dismissive view of what will become of her: 'Frankly, my dear, I don't give a damn'.

O'REILLY, RADAR see MASH

OAKLEY, ANNIE [*History*]
Phoebe Anne Oakley Moses (1860–1926) who performed under

the name of Annie Oakley was a renowned markswoman from an early age. She was the star of BUFFALO BILL'S Wild West Show where her act included firing through playing cards held edge-on, shooting coins from the air and shooting a cigarette from her husband's mouth. Such was her fame that for a time a complimentary theatre ticket, which was usually punched with a hole, was called an 'Annie Oakley', from her skill at shooting holes in cards.

OATES, TITUS [History]

The name of the priest Titus Oates (1649–1705) has long been symbolic of treachery and deceit. In 1678 he announced that he had evidence of a Popish Plot to kill the king, Charles II, burn London and massacre Protestants. In the ensuing panic many innocent Catholics were executed before it was realised that Oates 'evidence' was fabricated. He was publicly flogged and imprisoned, but later given a state pension.

ODIN [Mythology]

Odin is the one-eyed Norse ruler of the gods. He appears in Wager's operas in the German form of his name **Wotan** and was brought over to England by the invading Anglo-Saxons in the form **Woden**, where his name is preserved, amongst others, in the name of the town of Wednesbury which originally meant 'Stronghold of the god Woden'.

ODO see STAR TREK

ODYSSEY [Literature, Mythology]

An Odyssey, meaning a long and hard journey, comes from the title of HOMER'S epic poem *The Odyssey*, which tells of the ten years the hero **Odysseus (Ulysses** in Latin) took to get home from the TROJAN WAR. Odysseus had already played a major part in *The Iliad*, Homer's epic of the Trojan War, where he is show fully deserving his reputation for wisdom and cunning. *The Odyssey* deals much less with fighting, and more with Odysseus' encounters with magical or monstrous beings, his difficulties with his crew, the dangers of sea voyages and of his longing to return to his island home of Ithica and his faithful wife PENELOPE. Odysseus' reputation in later times has been varied. In medieval and

Renaissance times the main sources of information on these stories were Latin texts, and since the Latin-speaking Romans claimed descent from the defeated Trojans on whom Odysseus' cunning had been practised, he tended to be seen unfavourably. However, by the 19th century Homer's Greek version of the story was the dominant one, and Odysseus had become a goody. See also NAUSICAÄ, ARGUS.

OEDIPUS [*Mythology, Literature*]
According to Greek myth, when Oedipus was born to Laïus, King of Thebes and his wife **Jocasta** it was prophesied that he would kill his father and marry his mother. Horrified, the parents had the child exposed on a hillside to die, but he was found by shepherds and survived. When a young man, Oedipus met his father, whom he did not know, at a cross-roads and in a dispute over who had priority (in what was possibly the first recorded instance of road rage) Oedipus killed his father. Oedipus then journeyed to Thebes when he found that the throne and the hand of the now widowed queen were being offered to anyone who could rid the country of the sphinx which was terrifying it by waylaying people, asking them riddles and eating them when they failed to guess the answer. Oedipus was asked the famous riddle of the Sphinx – What goes on four legs in the morning, two legs at midday and three in the evening? – and produced the correct answer of a man, who crawls on all fours at the beginning of his life, then walks on two legs until the evening of his life when he needs the aid of a third leg in the form of a stick. The sphinx kills itself in annoyance at its defeat and Oedipus marries Jocasta and became king of Thebes. It is not until the unconsciously incestuous couple have had four children – two sons, Eteocles and Polynices, and two daughters, **Electra** and **Antigone** – that the horrific truth comes out, whereupon Jocasta kills herself and Oedipus blinds himself. This story gave us the term **Oedipus Complex** for the desire of a child for its parent of the opposite sex. Oedipus Complex is often restricted to the feelings of a son for his mother, with **Electra Complex** used for the feelings of a daughter for her father.

OLAF THE LOFTY see NOGGIN THE NOG

OLD BILL [*Popular Culture*]
Old Bill was a creation of cartoonist Bruce Bairnsfather (1888–1959). Bairnsfather became famous for his First World War cartoons featuring this large, walrus-moustachioed soldier. One which showed Old Bill and another soldier cowering in shell holes with the caption 'Well, if you knows a better 'ole, go to it', became proverbial.

OLIPHANT, OLIVER see ROLAND AND OLIVER

OLYMPUS [*Mythology*]
Mount Olympus is the highest mountain in Greece, and in Greek mythology the home of the major gods. Hence 'Olympian' came to mean first god-like, and from that superior to mundane considerations.

OPEN SESAME see ALI BABA

OPHELIA [*Literature*]
In Shakespeare's HAMLET Ophelia is a young girl in love with Hamlet. Before his 'madness' Hamlet appeared to love her, but he speaks harshly to her and rejects her. Hamlet then kills Ophelia's father by mistake and, distraught with grief, Ophelia runs mad. She takes to singing bawdy song in public and wandering off gathering flowers. While doing this she falls into a river and drowns, her death counting as suicide since she made no attempts to save herself. There is a famous painting of this scene by Millais.

ORCS see MORDOR

ORINOCO see WOMBLES

ORLANDO, THE MARMALADE CAT [*Children's Literature*]
The adventures of Orlando the marmalade cat are told in a series of books by Kathleen Hale, the first of which was published in 1938. They are mainly picture books, beautifully illustrated and full of detail, and place an emphasis on Orlando's happy home life with his wife Grace and their three kittens 'pansy the Tortoiseshell, white Blanche and coal-black Twinkle'.

ORWELLIAN [*Literature, Government*]
The term Orwellian nearly always refers to **George Orwell's** 1949 novel *1984*, with its horrible world dominated by the media controlled by BIG BROTHER. See also ANIMAL FARM.

OSCAR THE GROUCH see MUPPETS

OSMONDS [*Entertainment*]
The Mormon singing group the Osmond Brothers were enormously popular in the 1970s. Performing wholesome song and dance routines in white jump-suits, they are chiefly remembered for their wonderful dentistry and flashing white smiles.

OSSA see PELION

OUTLAWS, THE see WILLIAM BROWN

OVERALL, MRS [*Television*]
In Victoria Wood's spoof soap opera **Acorn Antiques** which sent up all that is worst in cut-price, under-rehearsed, cliché-ridden soaps, Mrs Overall was the 'help' who was always bringing in cups of tea and delivering the wrong lines at the wrong time and giving a virtuoso display of wooden acting.

OWL see WINNIE THE POOH

OZ see WIZARD OF OZ

OZYMANDIAS [*History, Literature*]
The Egyptian Pharaoh Ramses II (1279–13 BC), also known as Usermare Ramses, built himself a vast funeral temple which included a 57-foot-high statue of himself, which has survived only in fragments today. In the first century BC the Greek historian Diodorus Siculus described this as 'the Tomb of Osymandias', Osymandias being a corruption of 'Usermare Ramses'. In the 19th century AD the poet Percy Bysshe Shelley (1792–1822) was inspired by this to write his poem *Ozymandias*, in which he tells of 'a traveller from an antique land / Who said: Two vast and trunk-

less legs of stone / Stand in the desert' on this statue are written the words ' "My name is Ozymandias, king of kings: / Look on my works, ye Mighty and despair!" / Nothing beside remains. Round the decay / Of that colossal wreck, boundless and bare / The lone and level sands stretch far away.' Thus the name Ozymandias has come to represent overweening pride and boastfulness, and the impermanence of absolute power.

PAINE, TOM [*History*]

Tom Paine (1737–1809) was an English-born radical who fought on the American side in the War of Independence. He later become a member of the French Revolutionary Parliament. He published many influential books of which the most famous are *The Rights of Man* and *The Age of Reason*. His name is used to indicate those who struggle for liberty against unfair authority. Not surprisingly, it is more often used in the USA than in Great Britain.

PALMER, LAURA [*Television*]

Laura Palmer is the seemingly innocent victim whose death is being investigated by AGENT COOPER in David Lynch's surreal TV detective series *Twin Peaks*. While nothing in *Twin Peaks* is ever what it seems, the question 'Who killed Laura Palmer?' comes as near as anything to being the narrative centre of the series. See also J. R.

PAN, PETER [*Drama, Film*]

Peter Pan is the boy who never wants to grow up in J. M. Barrie's play of 1904 (published in book form in 1911 as *Peter and Wendy*). Peter lives with the **lost boys** in the fantasy world of **Never Never Land**, but visits the house of the **Darling** family where he loses his shadow. Surprised by the three Darling children (see WENDY) he teaches them to fly and takes them to live with him, where, along with the fairy TINKER BELL, they have various adventures with Tiger Lily and the Indians and CAPTAIN HOOK and his pirates. The original story has dark elements, but these have been greatly diluted by the various adaptations (including the Disney film of 1953). Peter Pan can be used loosely simply to indicate immaturity, but often allusions are linked more closely to the story. He is associated with the quotes 'To die will be an awfully big adventure' and 'Second [star] to the right and then straight on till morning'

PANDARUS [*Literature, Mythology*]
In HOMER's writings, Pandarus is a noble TROJAN warrior, but in medieval legend he is converted into the uncle of **Cressida** who actively encourages her love affair with TROILUS. He first appears in English in this role in Chaucer's *Troilus and Criseyde*, and 'Pandar', the form of the name used by Chaucer rapidly became the word 'pander', a pimp. In Shakespeare's play *Troilus and Cressida* his character is even more bawdy, and he spends much of his time passing cynical comment on the action.

PANDORA [*Mythology*]
In Greek myth, Pandora was a woman created by the gods. Life then was a GOLDEN AGE, for they gave Pandora a box in which all the troubles that afflict mankind were locked, with strict instructions to her not to open it. She did open it, which explains the woes of the world, but PROMETHEUS, who loved mankind, had also locked Hope in the box, to make life tolerable. 'A Pandora's box' is often used now simply as an alternative to 'a can of worms'. In the past the story was often used as anti-feminist propaganda, in the same way as the story of the Garden of EDEN, but few would use it like that now.

PANGLOSS [*Literature*]
In Voltaire's CANDIDE (1759) Pangloss is Candide's hapless tutor, whose philosophy is that 'all is for the best in the best of all possible worlds'. After many absurd and harrowing adventures they find the quiet life, following the view that 'We must cultivate our garden' and get on with the practical business of living rather than theorise.

PANTAGRUEL see RABELAIS

PANTHEON [*Religion*]
The Pantheon was a striking round temple in Rome dedicated to all the gods. It is still standing today and in use as the church of Santa Maria Rotonda, and great Italians are buried there. A similar building was build in Paris in the 18th century and used for the great of France. From this the word came to be used as a term for the great and the good. Since Pantheon means 'all the gods' it can

also be found used loosely to mean a complete set of something imposing.

PANTHER see BLACK PANTHERS, PINK PANTHER

PANZA, SANCHO [*Literature*]
Sancho Panza is the peasant chosen by DON QUIXOTE to be his squire. He is a mixture of shrewdness and gullibility, hard-headedness and compassion, and much given to quoting proverbs. The name is often used to indicate a comic sidekick to someone with rather batty ideas.

PARKER [*Television*]
Parker is the cockney butler and chauffeur to the glamorous LADY PENELOPE in THUNDERBIRDS.

PARKER, PETER see SPIDERMAN

PARKINSON'S LAW [*Business*]
Parkinson's Law, formulated by C. Northcote Parkinson in his book of the same name in 1958, states that 'Work expands so as to fill the time available for its completion'. Parkinson also formulated the law that 'expenditure rises to meet income'. These are sometimes confused with the *Peter Principle* (formulated by Laurence Peter and Raymond Hull) that 'In a Hierarchy Every Employee Tends to Rise to His Level of Incompetence'.

PARIS see HELEN OF TROY

PARNASSUS [*Mythology*]
In Greek mythology, Mount Parnassus was sacred to the MUSES, thus to climb or scale Parnassus is to become proficient in literature, especially poetry.

PARSIFAL [*Opera*]
The title of Richard Wagner's last opera, based on one of the many medieval versions of the story of **Percival**, a holy fool, who through innocence acquires enlightenment and wisdom and finally achieves the quest of the HOLY GRAIL.

PARTING OF THE RED SEA see MOSES

PARTON, DOLLY [*Popular Culture, Music*]
This well-known country and western singer and actress is known for her petite size, mass of platinum hair, and above all the astonishingly large size of her bust. During the 1991 Gulf War American troops nicknamed the bulbous-fronted Iraqi Assad Babyle tank 'The Dolly Parton', and 'Does Dolly Parton sleep on her back?' has been used as a rhetorical question of the 'Is the Pope a Catholic?' type.

PASIPHAË see MINOTAUR

PASSEPARTOUT see PHILEAS FOGG

PATSY see ABSOLUTELY FABULOUS

PAVAROTTI, LUCIANO [*Music, Opera*]
When this famous Italian opera singer's name is used allusively, it is nearly always with reference to his large size and appetite, rather than to his singing. Newspapers have cruelly nicknamed him 'Fat Lucy'.

PAVLOV'S DOGS [*Psychology*]
The Russian scientist Ivan Pavlov (1849–1936) developed the concept of the conditioned reflex, which he demonstrated by teaching hungry dogs to expect food when they heard a bell. After a time their mouths would start watering just at the sound of the bell – this was the conditioned reflex. 'A **Pavlovian reaction**' is often used to mean an automatic or unthinking response to something.

PEABODY, PROFESSOR JOCELYN see DARE, DAN

PEACHUM, POLLY see MAC THE KNIFE

PEARCE, 'HAWKEYE' see MASH

PEARLY GATES [*Religion*]
In the Bible, Book of Revelation 21: 21, St John describes his vision

of the Heavenly City saying 'And the twelve gates were twelve pearls; every several gate was of one pearl'. From this the term 'pearly gates' has developed to mean the gates of Heaven – an image much loved by cartoonists – or simply Heaven itself.

PEASON see NIGEL MOLESWORTH

PECKSNIFF [*Literature*]
Seth Pecksniff is a character from Charles Dickens' *Martin Chuzzlewit*. Dickens describes his manner as 'soft and oily', and his chief characteristic is hypocrisy.

PEEL, EMMA [*Television*]
Leather-clad assistant to JOHN STEED in the surreal TV spy series *The Avengers* (1961–69). She was played by Diana Rigg. See also PURDEY.

PELION ON OSSA [*Mythology*]
The expression 'to pile Pelion on Ossa' – to heap up difficulties to a ridiculous extreme – comes from Greek myth, where two giants try to climb up to heaven by piling Mount Pelion on top of Mount Ossa.

PENELOPE [*Literature, Mythology*]
In HOMER's ODYSSEY, Penelope is the wife of Odysseus who remained faithfully waiting for him for the twenty years he was at the TROJAN WAR and travelling home, despite her many suitors. Sometimes she is alluded to because of the trick she used to put off these suitors, saying that she would not choose one until she had finished the piece of weaving she was doing. She would then spend the day weaving, only to unpick her work at night; but most often she is alluded to as an example of a faithful wife. See also LADY PENELOPE.

PENELOPE, LADY [*Television*]
Lady Penelope Creighton-Ward is the glamorous aristocrat who helps out the **Tracy** family in Gerry Anderson's TV puppet series THUNDERBIRDS. She is assisted by the cockney PARKER, who chauffeurs her round in her pink Rolls Royce.

PENGUIN, THE see BATMAN AND ROBIN

PENNYFEATHER, see PAUL LLANABA

PEPYS, SAMUEL [*History, Literature*]
The diary kept by Samuel Pepys from 1633 to 1703 is a vivid source of information on everyday London life of the time. Thus a Pepys is either a diarist or one who keeps a record of the minutiae of life.

PEQUOD see MOBY DICK

PERCIVAL see PARSIFAL

PERICLES see ALCIBIADES

PERRIN, REGGIE [*Television*]
The hero of a series of comic novels by David Nobbs which were made into the enormously successful TV series *The Fall and Rise of Reginald Perrin*; Reggie Perrin is a middle manager at **Sunshine Desserts**. Stressed beyond endurance, and appalled by the sycophancy surrounding the company owner **C. J.** (motto 'I didn't get where I am today by ...'), he has a nervous breakdown, fakes his suicide in a way surely inspired by JOHN STONEHOUSE, and finds a sort of peace in the simple life. The character was brought brilliantly to life by the late Leonard Rossiter.

PERSEPHONE [*Mythology*]
In Greek myth Persephone or **Proserpine** is the daughter of the goddess **Demeter** or **Ceres** who looked after the growth of crops. When HADES, god of the underworld, abducts her, Ceres abandons her duties to look for her daughter, and the crops begin to die. She tracks her to the underworld, where Hades had made her Queen of the dead. Persephone had been too miserable to eat during her stay. As she has not eaten the food of the dead she is free to leave, but at the last minute it emerges she had eaten a few pomegranate seeds, and it was declared that she had to spend half the year with Hades and only half with her mother. This explains the seasons – spring comes when Ceres looks forward to her daughter's return, autumn when the time of her absence draws near, and in winter

the crops die back as Ceres mourns the loss of her daughter.

PERSEUS [*Mythology*]
In Greek myth Perseus, son of DANAË, slays the **Gorgon** MEDUSA, whose face is so terrible it turns whoever sees it to stone. HERMES had lent Perseus his winged sandals, allowing Perseus to fly, and on his way home with Medusa's head he spots the beautiful princess ANDROMEDA chained to a rock as a sacrifice to a sea monster. Perseus rescues the princess by turning the monster to stone with the Gorgon's head.

PETER PRINCIPLE see PARKINSON'S LAW

PETERS, SUSAN AND JOHN see WORZEL GUMMIDGE

PETERSEN, CARL see BULLDOG DRUMMOND

PETRONIUS [*History, Literature*]
Petronius, a member of the court of the Roman Emperor NERO, was famous for his luxury and sense of style. Nero gave him the title of 'arbiter of elegance', hence Petronius' full name of Petronius Arbiter. Petronius probably wrote the **Satyricon**, a work of mixed verse and prose. Since only fragments of it have survived it is difficult to describe, although Fellini's film version has given it an exaggerated reputation for its sexual content. The best-known episode in the book is **Trimalchio**'s Feast, a satire on the seemingly eternal vulgar excesses of the nouveau riche. See also EPHESUS.

PEW, BLIND [*Literature*]
Blind Pew is one of the pirates in *Treasure Island* (see further under LONG JOHN SILVER). He leads the attack on the inn where JIM HAWKINS lives, and Jim and his mother are terrified by the tap-tapping of his stick along the road as he approaches the deserted inn. Although he is the first of the pirates to die – trampled to death and abandoned by his fellow pirates – his name crops up surprisingly often. See also BLACK SPOT, CAPTAIN FLINT and ISRAEL HANDS.

PEYTON PLACE [*Television*]
American TV soap opera (1964–68) depicting the dark scandals of
a small town, inspired by the 1957 novel of the same name by
Grace Metalious. Although mild by the standard of similar modern soaps such as BROOKSIDE, it was thought daringly outspoken
for its day.

PHARAOH'S DAUGHTER see MOSES

PHASER see STAR TREK

PHILISTINES [*Religion*]
The Philistines were a people who feature in the Old Testament as
the inveterate enemies of the Jewish people. They came into conflict particularly with the great hero SAMSON, who, we are told
'smote them hip and thigh with great slaughter'. The use of the
name to mean someone who has no interest in culture or the more
refined things of life only dates from the 19th century, when
Matthew Arnold wrote in *Culture and Anarchy* 'The people who
believe most that our greatness and welfare are proved by our
being very rich, are just the very people whom we call Philistines'.
This is all rather unfair to the original Philistines who were in
many ways more advanced culturally than other peoples in their
area, and whose land, Philistia, is the source of the modern place
name Palestine.

PHOENIX [*Mythology*]
The Phoenix is a mythical bird, only one of which has ever existed. Every 500 years this beautiful bird flies to Egypt where it
builds its nest in a palm tree (hence *phoenix* as the botanical name
of the palm). There it is consumed by fire, but in the ashes a worm
appears which eventually becomes the new phoenix. Phoenix is
used allusively with reference to its ability to be born again, to
'rise from its ashes', and to its uniqueness.

PHONES see STINGRAY

PHRYNE [*Sculpture*]
Phryne was a Greek courtesan of the 4th century BC, who was

used as an artist's model by, amongst others, the great sculptor Praxiteles for his statue of APHRODITE. This was often considered the most beautiful female statue ever made, so Phryne's name in turn became a byword for beauty.

PICARD, CAPTAIN see STAR TREK

PICKWICK [*Literature*]
Samuel Pickwick is the hero of Charles Dickens' *The Pickwick Papers*, which tell of Mr Pickwick's adventures as he travels round the country, meeting such characters as **The Fat Boy**, **Mr Jingle**, who cannot finish a sentence, and **Mrs Bardell** who sues him for breach of promise. Pickwick is a fat, jolly, generous man, fond of making speeches, to whom comic adventures just happen, often through ridiculous misunderstandings. His essential innocence is tempered by the worldly knowingness of his cockney servant **Sam Weller**, whose other chief characteristics are an inability to distinguish between the sound of 'w' and 'v' and an inexhaustible store of anecdote. The term **'in a Pickwickian sense'** meaning 'not meant literally' comes from a running joke in the book.

PICTURE IN YOUR ATTIC, see DORIAN GRAY

PIECE OF PAPER see MUNICH

PIED PIPER [*Folklore*]
The Pied Piper was the fantastically dressed man who freed the town of Hamlin from its plague of rats by charming them to follow the sound of his pipe, and then led them to the river to drown. When the town council refused to pay the promised fee, he took revenge by charming the town's children, who all followed him to the mountains and through a doorway into the hill that then disappeared. Only one child was not lost in this way – a little lame boy who was too slow to keep up with the others, and who spent the rest of his solitary childhood regretting the loss of his friends. This is a traditional German folktale, best known in English from Robert Browning's poem on the subject.

PIERIAN SPRING see MUSES

PIERS PLOWMAN [*Literature*]
Piers Plowman is a long, rambling 14th-century, English poem by John Langland. It opens with Piers having a dream-vision of 'a field full of fair folk'. In the early part of the poem Piers at times represents the common man and the good Christian – what he represents the rest of the time is anybody's guess, and many a scholar has made a living out of this question. In the earlier part of the 20th century there was a popular elementary history series called *Piers Ploughman's History of England* and for some older people this is the primary association of the name.

PIGLET see WINNIE THE POOH

PILATE, PONTIUS [*History, Religion*]
Pontius Pilate was the Roman governor of Judea at the time of Christ. When Jesus was accused of treason Pilate did his best to acquit Him, and finally offered to release Him as tradition decreed that someone should be freed at Passover. However, the crowd called for the release of **Barabbas**, a thief, instead. To demonstrate his disagreement, Pilate washed his hands publicly, literally 'washing his hands of the affair'. Rather than condemning Pilate, some Christian traditions look kindly on him, and he and his wife are both saints of the Coptic Church. The term 'jesting Pilate' comes from an essay by Francis Bacon (1561–1626) who wrote 'What is truth? said jesting Pilate; and would not stay for an answer'.

PILTDOWN MAN [*Pre-History, Hoaxes*]
In 1912 a skull, long thought to be the **'missing link'** that proved that man descended from the apes, was found in a Sussex quarry. In 1953 it was proved to have been a fake, made from a man's head-bones linked with an orang-utan's jaw. Thus Piltdown Man can either be used as an alternative to NEANDERTHAL, or to refer to a successful hoax.

PINK PANTHER [*Film, Television*]
The Pink Panther is used in reference to two distinct things. Firstly to the series of comic detective Pink Panther films, the first of which was made in 1978. These starred Peter Sellers as the bumbling INSPECTOR CLOUSEAU, and usually refers to the Clouseau char-

acter, rather than to anything else. (The Pink Panther is actually the name of the jewel that a thief called The Phantom was trying to steal). Secondly, it refers to a cartoon series that showed Clouseau in conflict with the cartoon pink panther which had appeared in the opening credits of the original film. This series made much play of traditional detective clichés, and the pink panther himself was remarkable for his mobile and expressive eyebrows, drawn detached from his face.

PINOCCHIO [*Children's Literature, Film*]
Pinocchio is the little wooden boy, carved by the carpenter **Gepetto**, who comes to life. His most significant characteristic is the way in which his nose grows longer each time he tells a lie. Originally written in Italian by Carlo Collodi in 1883, the story has long been translated into English, and was made into a Disney film in 1939. See also JIMINY CRICKET.

PINTERESQUE [*Drama*]
The term Pinteresque refers to the style of writing found in the earlier plays of the English writer Harold Pinter (b. 1930), particularly to their long pauses and unfinished sentences.

PITSTOP, PENELOPE see DICK DASTARDLY

PLATO'S CAVE [*Philosophy, Literature*]
In his work *The Republic*, the Greek philosopher Plato (428–c. 348 BC) explains his idea that ideal Forms of things exist, beyond human experience. He illustrates this by describing normal human experience as being like that of a man chained prisoner in a cave, facing its wall and with his back to the light. He can only interpret the world in terms of the shadows cast on the wall of this cave. These shadows are our understanding of the world, while the clarity of the ideal Forms are represented by what we would see looking directly out of the cave. The term **Platonic Love** for non-sexual love comes from a misunderstanding of Plato's writings on the subject.

PLUTO [*Mythology, Popular Culture*]
Another name for the Greek god of the underworld, HADES, par-

ticularly emphasising his role as god of the riches to be found under the earth. Also the name of MICKEY MOUSE's dog.

POBBLE [*Literature*]

'The Pobble who has no toes had once', according to Edward Lear's poem 'as many as we', until he decides to swim the Bristol Channel 'to fish for, his Aunt Jobiska's Runcible Cat with crimson whiskers'. He takes the precaution of wrapping his nose in scarlet flannel in order to protect his toes, but this is stolen by a porpoise, and his toes are mysteriously stolen away.

POIROT, HERCULE [*Literature*]

Vain, Belgian detective with a waxed moustache and 'patent-leather hair' in detective novels by AGATHA CHRISTIE. He is rather comic, but astute, relying not on physical prowess but on 'the little grey cells'. See also MISS MARPLES.

POLLYANNA [*Literature*]

Pollyanna Whittier is the heroine of the Pollyanna novels by Eleanor H. Porter (1868–1920). No matter what horrors life throws at her, Pollyanna always remains cheerful and up-beat. The term is rarely used as a compliment, and usually indicates someone who is stupidly optimistic or unrealistic.

POLYHYMNIA see MUSES

POLYNESIA see DR DOLITTLE

POMEROY'S WINE BAR see RUMPOLE OF THE BAILEY

PONTIUS PILATE see PILATE

POOH see WINNIE THE POOH

POOH-BAH [*Opera*]

Pompous and power-grabbing politician on the make in Gilbert and Sullivan's comic opera *The Mikado* (1885). He is not the Lord High Executioner, but he is **Lord-High-Everything-Else**. He is also proud 'I can trace my ancestry back to a protoplasmal primordial atomic globule. Consequently, my family pride is something in-conceivable. I can't help it. I was born sneering.'

POOTER, MR [*Literature*]
Mr Pooter is the diarist in Charles and Weedon Grossmith's *The Diary of a Nobody* (1892). Mr Pooter is a clerk clinging desperately to notions of middle-class gentility. He is easily offended and self-deluding, and almost everything he tries to do goes wrong. However, he has an essentially innocent and trusting nature, and despite the satirical content of the original, he has become a much-loved character, and 'Pooterish' has come to mean little more than 'silly old duffer', as in this description of Denis Thatcher 'For a decade the media was happy to portray him as nothing more than a Pooterish, pink-gin-and-golf bore in a silly hat' (*Independent Weekend* 13.4.96).

POPPINS, MARY [*Literature, Film*]
Mary Poppins is the nanny with magical powers in a series of children's books by P. L. Travers. However, the written character has been almost totally obscured by the character as shown in the film (1964), played by Julie Andrews, and Mary Poppins is usually used to mean excessively cheerful and wholesome, with the philosophy that 'a spoonful of sugar helps the medicine go down'.

PORLOCK, PERSON FROM [*Literature*]
The poet Coleridge was interrupted by a visit from 'a person from Porlock' when writing down the poem that had come to him in an opium vision, which is why the magnificent poem *Kubla Khan* is only a fragment. Douglas Adams makes use of this story in *Dirk Gently's Holistic Detective Agency*. A person from Porlock is thus an inconvenient visitor or someone in the wrong place at the wrong time. See also XANADU.

PORRIDGE see FLETCHER, NORMAN STANLEY

PORTER, JIMMY [*Literature*]
Jimmy Porter, in John Osborne's 1956 play *Look Back in Anger*, is the typical ANGRY YOUNG MAN. He had benefited from the social upheaval of post-war Britain. A working-class lad with a degree

and a middle-class wife, he feels guiltily cut off from his roots and yet fights to retains them, while at the same time being an intellectual snob. His frustration and alienation takes the form of destructive anger at everyone and everything, his cruelty to others being sharpened by his obvious intelligence. He sees no role for himself in society and laments that there are simply no longer any great causes left to fight for.

PORTHOS see D'ARTAGNAN

PORTIA [*History, Literature*]
There are two Portias. The first Portia or Porcia was the wife of BRUTUS, who, to prove her ability to keep a secret when her husband would not confide in her, stabbed herself in the thigh and kept the fact secret for a time, to prove to him her hardiness and trustworthiness. The second is the character in Shakespeare's *Merchant of Venice*, famous for her 'Quality of mercy' speech. This Portia is a charming and intelligent young woman, witty and wise, who disguises herself as a man in order to save, by legal argument, Antonio from death at the hands of SHYLOCK.

PORTRAIT IN YOUR ATTIC see DORIAN GRAY

POSEIDON see MINOTAUR

POSTE, FLORA see COLD COMFORT FARM

POTEMKIN [*HIstory, Film*]
Prince Grigory Alexandrovich Potemkin (1739–91) was a lover and minister of Catherine the Great of Russia, with a special interest in developing the Ukraine. When Catherine toured the area on a royal progress she was very impressed with the progress he had made, and an (untrue) story grew up that he had done this by building 'villages', which were in fact just facades, along her route to give the impression that the area was more developed than it was. Thus **'Potemkin village'** has come to mean anything that is just a facade, an impressive structure with nothing behind it. In the 19th century a battleship was named after him, and was the site of a mutiny at Odessa in the 1905 revolution. These events were

made into a film, *The Battleship Potemkin* by Sergei Eisenstein in 1925, which has frequently been voted the best film ever made.

POTIPHAR'S WIFE [*Religion*]

In the Bible (Genesis 39) we are told how Joseph, when a slave in the house of the Egyptian Potiphar, caught the eye of Potiphar's wife. She attempted to seduce Joseph, but he refused to betray his master. Infuriated at his rejection, she gets her revenge by accusing him of having tried to rape her, and Joseph is thrown into prison, where he spends two years until he is released after interpreting Pharaoh's dream of the SEVEN FAT KINE.

POUND OF FLESH see SHYLOCK

POWER RANGERS [*Television*]

The children's TV sensation of recent years, *Power Rangers* tells of the adventures of a group of ordinary teenagers at Angel Grove High School. Endowed with vaguely mystical super-human powers by **Zordon,** an extra-terrestrial wizard, and aided by a comic robot called Alpha Five, they can 'morph' into Power Rangers and save the world from invading monsters by using their **Zords,** mechanical fighting machines. The programme was reviled for its low standards and violence, but the first series did attempt to have some social worth, tackling issues such as school bullying. Now, while still maintaining its careful racial mix, it relies increasingly on unlikely action, cardboard villains and slapstick. Of the original cast – Jason, Kimberly, Trini, Zack, Billy and Tommy: Red, Pink, Yellow, Black, Blue and Green Rangers respectively – only the last two remain in the cast at the time of writing.

PRESLEY, ELVIS see GRACELANDS

PRIMROSE PATH [*Literature*]

In Shakespeare's HAMLET, OPHELIA rebukes her brother Laertes with the words: 'Do not, as some ungracious pastors do, / Show me the steep and thorny way to heaven / Whiles, like a puffed and reckless libertine, / Himself the primrose path of dalliance treads'. From this 'the primrose path' (occasionally 'way') has come to mean following pleasure, usually with dire results.

PRINCE OF DARKNESS [*Religion*]
Another term for the Devil.

PRINCES IN THE TOWER [*History*]
The princes in the Tower were Edward V (1470–83) and his brother Richard, the young sons of Edward IV. Traditional history says they were smothered by order of their wicked Uncle the hunchbacked Richard, so that he could take their throne as King **Richard III**. How much truth is there in this? All we know for sure is that the boys disappeared and Richard became king. Richard has his defenders, largely inspired by Josephine Tey's excellent detective novel *Daughter of Time* (1951), and even has a society dedicated to defending him. Certainly Richard was the victim of that expert propagandist Henry VII, and Shakespeare's play, based on such propaganda, has done him no favours; nor have various Victorian pictures of the princes as innocent little angels (Shakespeare at least has the grace to show them as brats). Richard was not hunchback, and seems to have been an effective king. No one will ever know what really happened, which has benefited a number of romantic novelists, but one recent, dispassionate study of Richard has concluded that on balance he probably did do away with his nephews, but that this was no worse than the behaviour of his predecessor Edward IV who probably ordered the killing of his own brother (although Shakespeare blames Richard for this, too – see MALMSEY), or of his successor Henry, who took the throne by force and arranged the judicial murder of those of Richard's relatives that survived.

PRISONER OF ZENDA see RURITANIA

PROCRUSTES [*Mythology*]
In Greek myth Procrustes was a robber who boasted that he had a bed that would fit any guest. To do this his 'guests' would either be stretched on a rack or have their limbs cut off so they fitted. He was finally killed by **Theseus** (see further under MINOTAUR). Thus **Procrustean** has come to mean forcing people to fit in or confirm.

PRODIGAL SON [*Religion*]
In the Bible (Luke 15: 30) the Prodigal Son asks his father for his

share of his inheritance, leaves home and proceeds to squander the money. He is reduced to destitution and forced to take a job looking after pigs (the lowest of the low in a society which regards the pig as an unclean animal). He returns home, not expecting to be welcome, but asking for a job as a servant. His father, to his brother's disgust, welcomes him home with open arms and kills a calf to hold a feast (This is the origin of the term 'to kill the fatted calf' for a lavish welcome).

PROMETHEUS [*Mythology*]
In Greek myth Prometheus was an immortal who made mankind out of clay, and after the gods breathed life into him taught him how to survive. ZEUS had forbidden him to give them the gift of fire, but Prometheus took pity on mankind's cold and misery and stole fire from the gods. As a punishment he was chained to a mountain and an eagle sent to eat his liver every day, the liver growing again each night. He suffered this torment until HERCULES shot the eagle. Prometheus was worshipped by craftsmen as the supreme artificer, and **Promethean** means skilled, cunning, creative. See also PANDORA.

PROMISED LAND [*Mythology*]
In the Bible the Promised Land is the land of CANAAN, a land 'flowing with milk and honey', promised by God to the Jewish people. Thus the term is used of any long-sought, longed for place or thing, and as a term for heaven.

PROSERPINE see PERSEPHONE

PROSPERO [*Literature*]
Prospero is the exiled Duke of Milan who now rules the magic isle in Shakespeare's *The Tempest*. He controls the events of the play, and creates numerous magical illusions, and in the end chooses reconciliation rather than revenge. Much of his magic is carried out by **Ariel**, a spirit of the air he has saved from torment. His daughter **Miranda**, innocent of all to do with the world, falls in love with her cousin Ferdinand, son of Prospero's usurping brother, and harmony is restored. See also BRAVE NEW WORLD, CALIBAN.

PROUDIE, BISHOP AND MRS see BARSETSHIRE

PROUST, MARCEL [*Literature*]
Proust (1871–1922) was the author of the series of novels *A la recherche du temps perdu* (Remembrance of Things Past), which show life in late 19th-century France in great psychological detail. The series has a famous opening scene where the eating of a madeleine cake brings with it a flood of detailed memories and nostalgia for the past, and the term **Proustian** usually refers to this sort of intense recall, triggered by a sight, sound, smell or other apparently unconnected sensation.

PROZAC [*Medicine*]
An anti-depressant drug which has been taken up as the solution to ordinary, everyday dissatisfaction with life. It is thus used to mean seeing life in an artificially optimistic sense, or simply drugged.

PSYCHO see BATES, NORMAN

PUDDLEGLUM see NARNIA

PUGSLEY see ADDAMS FAMILY

PUMPHREY, MRS [*Literature*]
A character in James Herriot's *All Creatures Great and Small* who dotes obsessively on her absurdly spoilt lapdog, **Tricky Woo**.

PUNCH AND JUDY [*History, Entertainment*]
The traditional plots of the Punch and Judy shows vary, but Mr Punch is always a violent and disreputable character. The basic plot usually involves Mr Punch betting bitten by his dog **Toby** and some comic business with some sausages, before **Judy** gives Mr Punch their baby to look after. When the baby cries he loses his temper and throws it in the audience or out of a window. When Judy gets home and finds what he has done she hits him and he kills her. The Constable comes and arrests him and he is taken to be hanged by **Jack Ketch** (a traditional name for a hangman named after a famous real-life 17th-century hangman). Punch

tricks Ketch into hanging himself with his own rope. In the end Punch gets his just deserts when the **Crocodile** (originally the Devil) comes and carries him off. This used to be considered healthily anarchic entertainment for children, but there in now a tendency to regard Mr Punch as dangerously antisocial.

PURDEY [*Television*]
A character in the cult spy series *The New Avengers* (1976), played by Joanna Lumley. Her name was probably inspired by the make of gun. See also EMMA PEEL and JOHN STEED.

PUSH-ME-PULL-YOU see DR DOLITTLE

PYGMALION [*Mythology, Drama*]
According to legend, Pygmalion was a Greek sculptor who rejected real women, and instead made a statue of his ideal woman. To punish him the goddess of love APHRODITE made him fall in love with his creation, but then moved by his prayers, caused her to come to life. Pygmalion is sometimes incorrectly used for the statue, but her name was **Galatea**. The story lies behind George Bernard SHAW's play *Pygmalion*, which later became the musical *My Fair Lady* (see under ELIZA DOOLITTLE).

PYRRHIC VICTORY [*History*]
In 279 BC Pyrrhus, King of Epirus, fought the Romans at the Battle of Asculum. He just barely won, but lost two-thirds of his men in the process, and was never again able to mount an effective attack against the Romans. Thus a Pyrrhic victory is one that is won at too great a cost to the victor.

QUANTUM LEAP [*Physics, Television*]
Although quantum leap has become a popular term to describe a big jump or great advance, quantum is in fact a specific amount of a physical quantity – for example, energy – and its size is incredibly small. The TV programme of the same name is based on the main character's ability to travel through time. In terms of human life-spans this would usually be a huge jump in time, but in terms of the age of the universe it is tiny.

QUARK see STAR TREK

QUASIMODO [*Literature, Film*]
Quasimodo is the hunchback of Notre Dame in **Victor Hugo**'s novel *Notre-Dame de Paris* (1831). The image of Quasimodo has been strongly influenced by Charles Laughton's performance in the 1939 film *The Hunchback of Notre Dame*, and by LON CHANEY's 1923 film of the same name. At least five other films have been made of the book. Quasimodo was portrayed in the Disney film of 1996 as a kind, gentle and clever man beneath his ugly exterior. This was attacked by some critics as being overly politically correct, but children seemed to enjoy the character. Cartoonists love to show him swinging from the bells (he is the cathedral bell-ringer), and the Laughton film made catchphrases of 'The bells, the bells! and 'Sanctuary! Sanctuary!'.

QUATERMAIN, ALLAN [*Literature*]
Allan Quatermain is the wise old Africa hand who led the expedition to **King Solomon's mines** in the book of that name, and who has numerous other adventures in the series of novels that H. Rider Haggard (1856–1925) wrote about him. He visits many remote races and lands, and inspires loyalty in his companions such

216

as **Sir Henry Curtis**, and the majestic **Umbopa**, who turns out to be the lost heir to the throne of those who guard King Solomon's mines. There have been various depictions of him on film, which have made the character more of a prototype for INDIANA JONES.

QUATERMASS [*Television*]
Professor Bernard Quatermass was the hero of a series of three outstanding science-fiction thrillers shown on BBC TV between 1953 and 1959, with a revival in 1979. Brilliant and pig-headed, Quatermass saves mankind from threats from outer space, usually brought about by those, particularly the military, who have pushed science ahead without thinking through the consequences. For their day the programmes were technically and creatively very advanced, genuinely frightening and were a landmark in this kind of TV.

QUEEG, CAPTAIN [*Film, Literature*]
Unstable, domineering, petty and cowardly captain of the mine sweeper *Caine* in *The Caine Mutiny*. Although Herman Wouk's 1951 novel was a best-seller, Humphrey Bogart's much imitated performance as Queeg in the 1954 film is better known. Queeg's pettiness is summed up by his obsession with who ate the strawberries from the wardroom icebox, while his attitude to his crew is shown in the lines 'There are four ways of doing things on board my ship. The right way, the wrong way, the navy way and my way. If they do things my way, we'll get along'.

QUEENSBERRY, MARQUIS OF [*Sport, History*]
The eighth Marquis of Queensberry (1844–1900) was a keen sportsman who in 1867 supervised a new set of rules governing boxing, making the sport much safer, and which have been known ever since as the Queensberry Rules. This same man also objected to the relationship between his son, Lord Alfred Douglas, and OSCAR WILDE, and made his views widely known. At Douglas' urging, Wilde foolishly sued him for libel, and it was the failure of this case which led directly to Wilde's trial for homosexuality.

QUEEQUEG see MOBY DICK

217

QUELCH, MR [*Children's Literature*]
Mr Quelch is the short-tempered schoolmaster in the BILLY BUNTER stories, and Bunter's nemesis. He is devoted to Latin and adept at delivering 'whops' to errant schoolboys.

QUIXOTE, DON [*Literature*]
Don Quixote, the man from La Mancha, is the hero of Miguel de Cervantes' novel of that name, first published in Spanish in 1605, with part two appearing in 1615. By 1616 it had been translated into English. Don Quixote, a poor, mild gentleman, has his brains addled by reading too many chivalric romances, and sets off to emulate the heroes he has read about. His old, lean horse **Rosinante** he imagines is a great war horse, SANCHO PANZA is his squire, and a pretty village girl is given the name **Dulcinea** and made the lady of his heart. The most famous incident in the book is when Quixote believes that a group of windmills are giants and attacks them. This has given us the expression 'tilting at windmills', while his unworldliness and determination to pursue his romantic ideals regardless of the dictates of reality has given us the term **Quixotic**.

R2–D2 see LUKE SKYWALKER

RABBIT see WINNIE THE POOH

RABELAIS, FRANÇOIS [*Literature*]
The earthy humour of François Rabelais (c. 1494–c. 1553) has given us the term **Rabelaisian**. He was a scholar and doctor, but his achievements in many fields have become swamped by the fame of his rollicking satires featuring the giants **Pantagruel** and GARGANTUA. In these fantasies pigs and even sausages really can fly, vast meals are eaten, giants wipe their bottoms on goose's necks and found the Abbey of **Theleme** where monks and nuns live together under the motto 'Do what you like' (*Fay ce que vouldras*).

RAFFLES [*Literature*]
A. J. Raffles is the gentleman-thief in the fiction of E. W. Hornung (1866–1921). One of the best cricketers in the country, he is invited to all the best houses, and uses his athleticism for daring heists, usually from thoroughly unattractive victims. Needless-to-say, in these rather snobbish books, Raffles does it for the kicks, rather than the money. His adventures are told by his sidekick **Bunny**, his former public-school fag. There was also a real Raffles, **Sir Thomas Stamford Raffles** (1781–1826) founder of both Singapore and London Zoo, after whom the famous Raffles Hotel is named.

RAFT OF THE MEDUSA see MEDUSA

RAGNARÖK see GOTTERDÄMMERUNG, LOKI

RAMBO [*Literature, Film*]
John Rambo is the hero of David Morrell's 1972 novel *First Blood*, but is better known from the series of films starring the muscular

Sylvester Stallone. Best known is the 1985 film *Rambo: First Blood Part Two* where the tough Vietnam War veteran is sent back to 'Nam to rescue some American prisoners. This film was praised by the US President Ronald Reagan, who acquired the nickname 'Rambo' for a while. Rambo is a by-word for single-handed heroics, shoot-first action and excessive violence.

RANGER, THE see YOGI BEAR

RAPUNZEL [*Folklore*]
Rapunzel is the long-haired beauty in the fairy story who is locked in a tower by a witch. The only access to her is to call out 'Rapunzel, Rapunzel, let down your long hair' and to use her tresses as a rope, a method used by both the witch and the prince who falls in love with her. 'Steven Waddington plays the disgraced Crusader hero, back in disguise to clear his name, regain his inheritance and dally with Rapunzel-tressed damsels' (*Guardian* 11.1.97).

RASPUTIN [*History*]
Grigori Rasputin (c. 1871–1916) was a Russian monk who claimed mystical powers. He seemed to be able to help the haemophilia of the young Tsarevich, and so gained a place in the court of Tsar Nicholas II. Despite his poor personal hygiene, he was a charismatic figure, with piercing eyes and a remarkable ability to make sexual conquests (his name is actually a nickname from the Russian word meaning 'debauchee') and he won considerable influence at court, so much so that a group of politicians finally decided to murder him. He proved remarkably difficult to kill, and after being poisoned and twice shot, he was finally drowned. Rasputin is used as a term for a person who exercises malign power through those in control, or less often, for someone or thing difficult to kill.

RATTY see TOAD OF TOAD HALL

RAVEN, THE [*Literature*]
The Raven (1845) is a poem by Edgar Allan Poe in which a man sitting alone brooding over his dead love is visited by a Raven, a

'grim, ungainly, ghastly, gaunt and ominous bird of yore'. The best-known lines from the poem are 'Take thy beak from out my heart, and take thy form from off my door! / Quoth the Raven "Nevermore" '.

REBECCA [*Literature, Film*]
Rebecca is the name of the first wife of **Maxim de Winter**, romantically mysterious owner of the great house, **Manderley**. Daphne Du Maurier's 1938 novel of the same name is narrated by the second Mrs de Winter – we never learn her first name – a naive girl overawed by the magnificence of Manderley, and tells how their marriage nearly breaks down thanks to the machinations of MRS DANVERS, the housekeeper, who is devoted to Rebecca's memory.

REBEL WITHOUT A CAUSE [*Film*]
This key teenage film, made in 1955, was important (and caused a stir at the time) as it suggested that teenage angst and violence did not come only from the slums; for JAMES DEAN, who was made a star by the film, plays what the publicity called 'the bad boy from a good family'.

RED-BEARDED DWARVES see BEACHCOMBER

RED DWARF [*Television*]
Wacky science fiction TV series chronicling the comic misadventures of the slobbish **Lister**, the sole surviving human on his spaceship and his incompatible companions **Rimmer**, an obnoxiously conceited hologram, **Cat**, an image-obsessed humanoid who has evolved from the ship's cat, and the android **Kryten**, on whom see further under CRICHTON.

RED PLANET [*Astronomy*]
Another name for the planet MARS. It gets its name both from its red colour, and from the fact that Mars is the god of war.

REGAN see GONERIL

REITH, LORD [*Television*]
Lord Reith (1889–1971) was the first manager of the BBC. He was

an authoritarian man of high-minded principles who believed that the BBC's role as a public broadcasting service was to educate and inform as much as to entertain. The term **Reithian** is used of this rather dour, paternalistic approach. See also AUNTIE.

RELIANT ROBIN [*Transport, Technology*]
This British-made three-wheeled car has always been something of an object of fun, despite the fact that it is in many ways the ideal town car. RODNEY TROTTER drives one, and its low-powered engine inspires such comparisons as 'CD-Rom drives are as fast as Porches, but is there any advantage when your processor is more of a Reliant Robin?' (*Independent Network* 13.5.96).

REMUS, UNCLE [*Children's Literature*]
Uncle Remus is the creation of the American Joel Chandler Harris who published a series of books between 1881 and 1910 in which the old slave Uncle Remus told stories to the small son of the plantation owner. These stories, derived from Harris' extensive knowledge of Black folk-tale, are mainly the adventures of various animals, particularly **Brer Rabbit** and **Brer Fox**, and are mostly ultimately African in origin. At one time they were the staple fare of childhood, and everyone grew up knowing about Brer Rabbit and the **Tar Baby**, but they have now fallen out of fashion, perhaps because people are no longer comfortable with the dialect in which they are written.

RETREAT FROM MOSCOW see NAPOLEON

REVERE, PAUL [*History*]
Paul Revere (1735–1818) is one of the great folk-heroes of the American Revolution. He was actively involved in the events that let up to the outbreak of war, but is best known for the ride he made through the night of 18 April 1775, warning the people in the Boston area that 'The British are coming'. It was this warning that allowed the American troops to be ready to face the British at the Battle of Lexington.

RICE, ARCHIE [*Drama*]
Archie Rice is a seedy music hall comedian, a disillusioned

ROC

'cheeky-chappie' past his sell-by date, in John Osborne's 1957 play *The Entertainer*.

RICHARD III see PRINCES IN THE TOWER

RIGBY, ELEANOR   [*Song*]
In The Beatles' 1966 song *Eleanor Rigby* is one of 'all the lonely people', with no significance, only dreams, in their lives. In the end she 'died and was buried along with her name'.

RIGHTS OF MAN see TOM PAINE

RIMMER see RED DWARF

RIN TIN-TIN   [*Film*]
Rin Tin-Tin (1916–32) was the great dog star of the silent film era. Compare LASSIE.

RIZZO, RATSO   [*Film*]
In the 1969 film *Midnight Cowboy*, Ratso Rizzo is the consumptive conman who promotes, and is supported by, the naive Texan **Joe Buck** who comes to New York to make it as a stud to rich women. He sums up seedy, low-life New York.

ROBBEN ISLAND   [*History*]
Robben Island is the notorious South African prison-island where many political prisoners, including Nelson Mandela, were kept under apartheid.

ROBIN, THE BOY WONDER see BATMAN

ROBSART, AMY   [*History*]
Amy Robsart was the wife of Queen Elizabeth I's favourite, Robert Dudley, Earl of Leicester. She was found dead at the bottom of a flight of stairs, and controversy has raged since as to whether she jumped, fell or was pushed. A fictionalised version of her story is told Sir Walter Scott's *Kenilworth*.

ROC see SINBAD

223

ROCHESTER, MR see EYRE, JANE

ROCKEFELLER [*Business, Finance*]
John D Rockefeller (1839–1937) was an American business man
who founded the Standard Oil Company which at one time had a
near monopoly of the US oil business, and made him immensely
rich. Hence the near proverbial expression 'as rich as Rockefeller'.

ROCKWELL, NORMAN [*Popular Culture*]
The painter and illustrator Norman Rockwell (1894–1978) specialised in magazine covers showing an idealised, sanitised
America of Mom and apple pie, typically showing healthy, nauseatingly cute kids welcoming home a kindly pipe-smoking Dad,
while Mom stood by in a frilly gingham apron. He has come to
represent this idealised world of the USA in the 'perfect' '50s and
'60s.

ROCKY HORROR SHOW [*Drama, Music, Film*]
Richard O'Brien's stage musical, filmed in 1975, is a spoof of the
FRANKENSTEIN and DRACULA genre, which has developed a cult following. It tell of the experiences of an innocent honeymoon couple who become involved with Dr Frank N. Furter 'a sweet trans-
vestite from transexual Transylvania'.

ROGAN, ROCKFIST [*Popular Culture*]
Rockfist Rogan was the fighter-pilot hero of a strip cartoon that
ran for many years in the boy's comic *Champion*. He was created
by Frank Pepper.

ROGERS, BUCK [*Popular Culture, Film, Television*]
Buck Rogers in the 25th Century started life as a strip cartoon, and
has been through just about every possible medium since. Buck is
a twentieth-century spaceman who, through a freak accident, is
kept in suspended animation until the 25th century where he is
rescued. Once in the 25th century he performs innumerable deeds
of daring, saving the world over and over with the help of his
beautiful side-kick **Wilma Deering** and the inventions of **Dr
Huer**. Buck Rogers has become identified with the thrilling adventures, space-man-as-modern-cowboy school of science fiction.

ROGERS, ROY [*Music, Film, Television*]
From the 1930s to the 1950s Roy Rogers (1912–) was the great cow-boy filmstar. He had started out as a country-and-western singer, and continued singing in his films. He typically appeared dressed in fancy buckskins with his wife Dale Evans, 'The Queen of the West', and his 'four-legged friend', his horse **Trigger**, who usual-ly rescued him from some dangerous situation. Later on he appeared in a TV series.

ROLAND AND OLIVER [*Folklore*]
In the French medieval epic of *The Song of Roland*, and in many later romances, Roland and Oliver are the outstanding warriors of the court of the Emperor Charlemagne – the DAVID and Jonathan of their day and similarly used as examples of male friendship. Roland quarrels with his stepfather **Ganelon**, who decides to get his revenge by betraying the French to the Saracens. As a result Ganelon's name is used to mean 'traitor', an alternative to JUDAS. Roland and Oliver are set to command the rear guard as the French army goes through the Pyrenean pass of **Roncevalles**, but thanks to Ganelon are ambushed. After a great battle, in which the warrior-priest **Archbishop Turpin** also performs great deeds, the two heroes are killed, but not before Roland has been able to sound his great horn **Oliphant**, and summon Charlemagne to avenge him.

ROMEO AND JULIET [*Literature*]
Romeo Montague and Juliet Capulet are the teenage lovers who are unable to declare their love and marriage because of their war-ring families. Despite the fact that he is faithful even unto death, Romeo's name tends to be used for a smooth-operating womanis-er, a LOTHARIO, while poor Juliet's name is used of a type of wed-ding head-dress, rather inappropriately considering their secret marriage. **Capulets and Montagues** is used of any warring fami-lies.

ROMULANS see KLINGONS, VULCANS

ROMULUS AND REMUS [*Mythology*]
In Roman mythical history Romulus and Remus are twins, sons of

the god MARS and the rightful heirs to the throne of Alba Longa. They are set adrift on the Tiber by their wicked uncle who had deposed their grandfather, but their divine father sees that they come safely ashore, where they are found and suckled by a she-wolf. They later restore their grandfather, and go off to found a new city. They quarrel over who is to be king, and when Remus jumps derisively over the city walls that Romulus is building, Romulus kills him in anger. Thus the new city, Rome, is named after the surviving twin.

RONCEVALLES see ROLAND AND OLIVER

ROO see WINNIE THE POOH

ROSINANTE see QUIXOTE

ROUND TABLE [*Mythology*]
KING ARTHUR and his knights used a round table to promote harmony. There is no head or foot to a round table, so no one could be said to be seated in a more honourable position than another, thus avoiding inter-knight rivalry. Among the seats at the Round Table was the **Siege Perilous**, the seat that could only be sat in without immediate death by the knight who was to win the HOLY GRAIL. The Round Table became symbolic of Arthur's court, until the harmony of the knights was broken firstly by the quest for the Holy Grail, and then by the scandal of the love affair between Arthur's premier knight, **Lancelot,** and his queen **Guinevere**.

ROVERS RETURN [*Television*]
The Rovers Return is the local pub in the long-running soap of working-class northern life, CORONATION STREET. Run originally by **Annie and Jack Walker**, it later acquired the tarty, brassy **Bet Lynch** as a barmaid. See also ENA SHARPLES.

ROXANNE see CYRANO DE BERGERAC

ROY, ROB [*History, Literature*]
Rob Roy Macgregor (1671–1734) plays in Scottish tradition something of the role of a ROBIN HOOD, thanks in part to the image of

him in Sir Walter Scott's 1818 novel *Rob Roy*. The name Rob Roy ('Red Rob') came from his dark red hair. A prominent member of the banned MacGregor clan, Rob became an outlaw and freebooter, raiding the cattle of his enemies and protecting his supporters, robbing the rich and helping the poor. His hairbreadth escapes and cunning stratagems became the stuff of folktales.

RUBBLE, BARNEY AND BETTY see FRED FLINTSTONE

RUBENS, RUBENESQUE [*Art*]

Usually used of naked women and a polite way of saying 'fat, but shapely', this term comes from the liking of the Flemish painter Peter Paul Rubens (1577–1640) for painting well-fleshed female nudes.

RUBICON [*History*]

In 49 BC JULIUS CAESAR took his army across the Rubicon, a small Italian river just north of Rimini. Since this river marked the boundary between the province of Gaul, of which Caesar was governor, and Republican Rome, the crossing of the river was in fact a declaration of his intention to seize power in Rome. This event gives us both the expression 'to cross the Rubicon' and 'the die is cast', supposedly Caesar's words at the time, both indicating there is no going back.

RUMPELSTILTSKIN [*Folklore*]

Rumplestiltskin was the name of the deformed dwarf in the fairy-tale, who helped the miller's daughter spin straw into gold. This miracle having been performed, the girl is married by the king, but the price she had to pay was to give up to Rumpelstiltskin her first child unless she could guess his name in three goes. Luckily, Rumpelstiltskin had been overheard singing to himself of his cleverness, and she was able to do so, at which the dwarf died from rage. His name means 'rumpled foreskin'.

RUMPOLE OF THE BAILEY [*Literature, Television*]

Horace Rumpole is the hero of a series of short stories, and their televised versions, by John Mortimer. Rumpole cares passionately about justice, but otherwise is not ambitious, and is disillusioned by the behaviour of most other barristers, such as the calculating **Erskine-Brown** and the social climbing **Guthrie Featherstone**. His clients are usually as downbeat as he is, but his unconventional approach to their defence often sees justice triumph. He is married to the domineering Hilda, 'SHE who must be obeyed', from whom he takes refuge in **Pomeroy's Wine Bar**.

RUNYON, DAMON [*Literature*]

Damon Runyon (1884–1946) was the author of a vast number of short stories about low-life New York, particularly about bootleggers and other criminals in the 1920s and '30s. They are both poignant and comic, usually ending with a twist, told in the first person in an extraordinary, laconic language that only uses the present tense as in ' "You are snatching a hard guy when you snatch Bookie Bob. A very hard guy, indeed. In fact," I say, "I hear the softest thing about him is his front teeth." ' These stories are the basis of the musical *Guys and Dolls*.

RURITANIA [*Literature*]

Ruritania is an imaginary country in south-east Europe, the setting for Anthony Hope's romantic adventure novels *The Prisoner of Zenda* (1894) and *Rupert of Hentzau* (1898). **Ruritanian** is used of any setting for such adventures, often nowadays rather scornfully to suggest not so much intrigue, but the sort of place that may run to fancy, romantic uniforms and ceremonial, but has little solid behind it.

RYDER, CHARLES see BRIDESHEAD

SAFFRON see ABSOLUTELY FABULOUS

ST HELENA see NAPOLEON

ST TRINIAN'S [*Popular Culture, Film*]
St Trinian's was a run-down girls' boarding-school inhabited by hell-cats, created in 1941 by the cartoonist Ronald Searle (1920–). In many ways it is the counterpart of MOLESWORTH'S St Custard's, also illustrated by Searle. The gym-slip wearing, hockey-stick wielding girls gained wider fame through a series of St Trinian's films, where the older girls were helped in their precocious forays into such things as betting by George Cole's FLASH HARRY.

ST VALENTINE'S DAY MASSACRE see AL CAPONE

SALAMIS see THERMOPYLAE

SALEM [*History*]
The Salem witch trials, made famous by Arthur Miller's 1953 play *The Crucible* which showed up the parallels between the witch trials and contemporary MCCARTHYISM, occurred in 1692. Amid the Puritan atmosphere of Massachusetts at the time, it was easy for mass religious hysteria to spread, and this is what happened when some girls, influenced by the voodoo stories of a black slave, claimed they were possessed by the Devil. They accused three women of witchcraft, and as fears spread, so did the accusations. In the end 19 were executed for witchcraft and more imprisoned before people came to their senses, released the remaining prisoners and tried to forget it had ever happened.

SALOME [*Religion*]
According to the Bible (Matthew 14 or Mark 6) JOHN THE BAPTIST

had been criticising King Herod for having married Herodias, his brother's widow, which under Jewish law was incest. John was already in prison when Herod held a birthday party at which his step-daughter, Salome, dance for him (this became in later tradition the notorious **Dance of the Seven Veils**). Herod was delighted with her performance, and promised to give her anything she wanted as a reward. Salome consulted with her mother Herodias, and came back and asked for the head of John the Baptist 'on a charger [dish]'. Because of his promise Herod reluctantly agreed. Ever since, Salome's name has been symbolic of the use of eroticism to entice and betray (Compare Delilah under SAMSON AND DELILAH).

SALT, VERUCCA see MIKE TV AND VERUCCA SALT

SAM, UNCLE   [*Popular Culture*]
Uncle Sam is the embodiment of the USA in the same way as JOHN BULL is of England. He is usually shown as a man with long white hair and beard, dressed in 19th-century clothes: a swallow-tail coat, striped trousers and a stove-pipe hat. He did not appear until the nineteenth century, apparently as a development of the letters US (United States) stamped on army supply boxes in the war of 1812. Previously the embodiment of America had been the Puritan **Brother Jonathan**.

SAMSON AND DELILAH   [*Religion*]
Samson is one of the great heroes of the Old Testament. A man of incredible strength, capable of killing a lion with his bare hands, and with a hatred for PHILISTINE men, which he killed at every opportunity, but a weakness for Philistine women. He falls in love with Delilah and she agrees to betray him by finding out the secret of his strength. After long nagging Samson finally tell her that he is so strong because his hair has never been cut, and if it is once cut, he will be no stronger that other men. She cuts his hair while he is asleep and the Philistines capture him. Hence, like SALOME, Delilah's name is used of women who use their sexual attractiveness to betray.

SANDHURST see ALDERSHOT

SARAJEVO [*History*]
The name of the city of Sarajevo has gained a new set of associations from the civil war in former Yugoslavia, but allusions to it usually refer to the events of 28 June 1914. On that day a Serbian nationalist shot the Archduke Franz Ferdinand, the heir to the ailing Austro-Hungarian Empire. The political events that followed on from the assassination led directly to the outbreak of the First World War.

SARTRE [*Philosophy*]
The French philosopher and writer Jean-Paul Satre (1905–80) was a leading exponent of that depressing philosophy, existentialism. Consequently, his name is often used to imply depression, despair or a general disillusionment with the world.

SATYR see DIONYSYS

SATYRICON see PETRONIUS

SAURON see MORDOR

SAWYER, TOM [*Literature*]
The hero of Mark Twain's *The Adventures of Tom Sawyer* (1876) feels he has many crosses to bear in what is really an ideal childhood, but the worst of these is his Aunt Polly's attempt to civilise him. This leads to frequent punishments, including being made to whitewash the fence. He cunningly pretends to enjoy this, and so gets other children to part with their treasures for the privilege of doing his work for him. See also HUCKLEBERRY FINN.

SCARECROW see WIZARD OF OZ

SCARLET PIMPERNEL [*Literature*]
The foppish, dull-witted man-about-town **Sir Percy Blakeney**, who seems to be interested in nothing but clothes and London society, only uses this front to hide the fact that he spends the rest of his time spiriting French aristocrats caught up in the Terror of the French Revolution away from the very jaws of the guillotine. He remains anonymous even to those he rescues, but leaves the

symbol of the little red flower, the scarlet pimpernel, behind as his calling card. As Sir Percy he makes up a rhyme about the Scarlet Pimpernel 'They seek him here, they seek him there / Those Frenchies seek him everywhere. / Is he in heaven or is he in hell / That demned elusive Pimpernel'. The chief among the French seekers is the fanatical **Citizen Chauvelin** who has made it his life's work to capture The Scarlet Pimpernel.

SCARLET WOMAN [*Religion*]

The figure of the Scarlet Woman in the APOCALYPSE of St John (Revelations chapter 17) is interpreted by theologians as representing pagan Rome, and later by some Protestants as standing for the Roman Catholic Church with its gaudy robes and pageantry. However, since St John describes a woman 'arrayed in purple and scarlet colour, and decked with gold and precious stones and pearls, having a golden cup in her hand full of abominations and filthiness of her fornication' and elsewhere as 'the great whore' and 'the mother of harlots' it is not surprising that in popular usage the term is used for a sexually promiscuous woman or prostitute.

SCARLETT, WILL see ROBIN HOOD

SCARPIA [*Opera*]

Baron Scarpia is the sinister and vindictive chief of police in Puccini's opera *Tosca* (1900). Tosca is a famous singer that Scarpia – described by one of the characters in the opera as 'a bigoted satyr and hypocrite, secretly steeped in vice, yet most demonstratively pious' – lusts after. He takes the opportunity of Tosca's lover's involvement in hiding a republican revolutionary to have him arrested and tortured in her hearing. He offers to spare the lover if Tosca will sleep with him. Tosca reluctantly agrees and Scarpia says that a mock execution must be gone through, but that he will write a safe conduct for them both. Tosca impulsively stabs Scarpia rather than go through with her side of the bargain, and then finds that Scarpia has not kept his word either, and that the execution is for real. She kills herself, so like all the best operas everyone ends unhappily.

SCATTERBROOK FARM see WORZEL GUMMIDGE

SCHEHEREZADE see ARABIAN NIGHTS

SCHNORBITZ THE DOG [*Entertainment*]
Schnorbitz the dog was a huge, immensely popular St Bernard dog that used to appear on stage with the English comedian Bernie Winters.

SCHWARZENEGGER, ARNOLD see CONAN THE BARBARIAN, TERMINATOR

SCOOBY DOO AND SCRAPPY DOO [*Television*]
Scooby Doo is a large, strangely knobbly dog in a series of Hanna–Barbera cartoons named after him. Scooby and his owner the shambolic, cowardly **Shaggy** are interested only in eating and saving their skins, but Scooby's combative nephew Scrappy Doo is always ready for a fight whatever the odds. They, along with the all-American Daphne and Freddy, and plain-but-bright Velma, travel round the States in a battered camper called **The Mystery Machine**, solving spooky mysteries, which typically turn out to be some pillar of society posing as a ghost in order to make a fast buck.

SCROOGE [*Literature*]
Ebenezer Scrooge is the heartless miser in Charles Dickens' *A Christmas Carol* (1843). Having sacrificed everything in his life to making money and dismissed Christmas with a 'Bah! Humbug!', he is given one last chance by a midnight visit first from the ghost of **Jacob Marley**, his old partner who is now paying for his sins in life, and then from the ghosts of Christmas Past, who reminds him what things were like, Christmas Present, and Christmas Yet To Come who predicts a miserable, unmourned death if he does not change his ways. He reforms, buying gifts for his ill-treated employee BOB CRATCHIT, and being a changed man for the rest of his days. The work was immensely popular, and Scrooge has come to be a common term for anyone mean, as in the business-section headline 'Banks cast as Scrooge while mutuals up rates' (*Guardian* 21.12.96).

SCULLY, AGENT see X-FILES

SEAGOON, NEDDIE see GOONS

SEMIRAMIS see BABYLON

SERPENT see EDEN

SESAME STREET see MUPPETS

SEVEN DEADLY SINS *[Religion]*
The Seven Deadly Sins are: Pride, Lust, Avarice, Gluttony, Envy, Wrath and Sloth. The list is not found in the Bible, but was developed by early Christian writers.

SEVEN DWARFS see SNOW WHITE AND THE SEVEN DWARFS

SEVEN FAT/LEAN KINE/COWS/YEARS *[Religion]*
In the Bible we are told that the pharaoh of Egypt had a dream in which he saw seven fat kine (cows) come up out of a river and feed in a meadow. Then seven lean kine came out of the river 'And the ill favoured and lean-fleshed kine did eat up the seven well favoured and fat kine'. Puzzled by this dream, pharaoh calls Joseph out of prison where he was thrown after being accused by POTIPHAR'S WIFE, and had him interpret it. Joseph explains that the seven fat cows are seven fat or prosperous years, when harvest will be good, but that seven lean years of famine will eat up the produce of the previous years. The answer is to build granaries (the pyramids were traditionally interpreted as these granaries) to store the produce of the fat years against the lean ones.

SEVEN-PER-CENT SOLUTION see SHERLOCK HOLMES

SEVEN SEAS *[Oceanography]*
The Seven Seas, used to indicate the whole world, are arrived at by splitting the Pacific and Atlantic Oceans into North and South sections and adding on the Arctic, Antarctic and Indian Oceans.

SEVEN SLEEPERS OF EPHESUS see EPHESUS

SEXTUS see TARQUIN

SHADRACH, MESHAK AND ABEDNIGO [*Religion*]
The Bible (Daniel 3) tells the story of how NEBUCHADNEZZAR made a great golden idol and ordered everyone 'that what time ye hear the sound of the cornet, flute, harp, sackbut, psaltry, dulcimer, and all kinds of musick, ye fall down and worship the golden image that Nebuchadnezzar the king hath set up' on the penalty of being cast into a burning **fiery furnace**. Three captive Jews, Shadrach, Meshak and Abednigo, refuse to worship the idol, and are thrown into the furnace. However, they are totally unaffected by the flames, even though the furnace was so hot that the men who threw them in were killed. Instead, a fourth figure, an angel sent by God to protect them, is seen in the flames with them, and when they emerge from the furnace, they do not even smell of the fire.

SHAGGY see SCOOBY DOO

SHANDY, TRISTRAM [*Literature*]
Lawrence Sterne's delightful, long, rambling novel *The Life and Opinions of Tristram Shandy* (1759–67), filled with digressions and narrative devices which, if used today, would be called experimental. It has won a fond place in the hearts of many who have not been put off by its slow pace, for its joy in exploring ideas to their limits, gentle humour and warm depiction of English eccentricity. Fairly typical of the book is that it opens with his father going to wind up the clock on the evening on which the narrator, Tristram, is conceived, and does not get round to his birth until volume three. One of the most popular characters in the book is **Uncle Toby**, whose life, since he had to retire from the army after being severely wounded in the groin, is devoted to building scale replicas of siege-works in the garden with the help of the faithful **Corporal Trim**, and who would far rather be doing this than coping with the advances of the amorous widow **Mrs Wadman**. 'His book is a **Shandean** assembly of (more or less) sea-related digressions' (*Independent on Sunday* 28.6.92).

SHANGRI-LA [*Literature*]
James Hilton's 1933 novel *Lost Horizon*, which spawned innumerable imitators, tells of a hidden valley, Shangri-la, in the mountains of Tibet where the climate is ideal, despite the height, and where the Lamas have found the secret of eternal youth. However, the cost of this is that the status quo must be accepted and all change and enterprise abandoned, for if you leave the valley the years catch up, and the ancient ones will wither into a handful of dust. This downside has usually been forgotten, and the term Shangri-la is usually used to mean an earthly paradise or UTOPIA.

SHANKILL ROAD see FALLS ROAD

SHAPESHIFTER see STAR TREK

SHARPEVILLE [*History*]
In 1960 the Pan-African Congress organised what was meant to be a non-violent protest at the black township of Sharpeville against the South African pass laws, the major vehicle of apartheid. A crowd of 20,000 turned up near the Sharpeville police station and began throwing stones at the police. The police replied with sub-machine guns and at least 67 were killed, and 186 wounded. In the following crackdown 1700 were arrested. These events shocked the rest of the world and greatly strengthened opposition to apartheid. Sharpeville has now become a standard for excessive repression and police over-reaction.

SHARPLES, ENA [*Television*]
In the early days of the TV soap opera CORONATION STREET, Ena Sharples was the terrifying battle-axe who was caretaker of the Glad Tiding Mission. Grim-faced and wearing a hair net, she would sit in the snug of the ROVERS RETURN with meek little **Minnie Cauldwell** and nondescript **Martha Longhurst** and over a glass of milk stout tear the whole street to shreds. In these pre-Women's Liberation days Ena would have had no nonsense about women being equal to men – she knew very well there was no man in the street that was anything like a match for her sharp tongue.

SHE WHO MUST BE OBEYED [*Literature*]

In H. Rider Haggard's 1887 novel *She* Ayesha is the 2000-year-old, indescribably beautiful, blonde, white-skinned absolute ruler of the lost city of Kôr who bears the title 'She Who Must Be Obeyed' (a title RUMPOLE applies to his wife). At one time there were three of her kind, a priest and two women, but the priest preferred the other woman, so She killed him, and the other woman, now pregnant, fled. Later, She gains eternal youth by passing through the flame of life. Meanwhile the descendants of the other woman have retained over the centuries a memory of their descent, and the last of their line, Leo Vincey, determines to find his lost ancestry. When he and a group of English explorers arrive at Kôr She falls in love with him and offers him the chance of immortal life with her. To prove he need fear nothing from the flame of life she steps into it again, but it is not possible to pass through it twice, and She dies. *She* was so successful that Haggard later had the character reincarnated in other times, and thus managed to get her to meet his other great creations QUATERMAIN and UMSLOPAGAAS.

SHELOB see MORDOR

SHERE KHAN see MOWGLI

SHERGAR [*Sport, Crime*]

In 1981 the race-horse Shergar had won the Derby by a record margin. In 1983 this champion horse was kidnapped from its Irish stables and a ransom of two million pound demanded for its safe return. Although every effort was made to get the horse back, no one knows what happened. Something must have gone wrong with the kidnappers' plans, for the horse was never seen again, and Ireland is full of stories about where the body in buried.

SHERWOOD FOREST see ROBIN HOOD

SHYLOCK [*Literature*]

In Shakespeare's *The Merchant of Venice* Shylock is a money lender, whose bitterness against the Christians acts as a reflection of their own anti-Semitism. He gets the virtuous Antonio to sign an agreement whereby if he does not repay a loan on time Shylock will be entitled to take from him a **pound of flesh** (the expression's origin), which will lead to Antonio bleeding to death. When Antonio cannot repay him Shylock goes to court. The law is on his side, but in the ensuing case clever PORTIA, disguised as a barrister, argues that while Shylock is entitled to his pound of flesh, the agreement does not cover blood, and he must take it without spilling a drop of blood. This obviously cannot be done, and Shylock finds himself punished, rather than winning his case. 'A Shylock' is used as an expression to mean a heartless or demanding creditor.

SIBERIA [*History*]

Internal exile to the chilly and remote area of Siberia where the extreme climate meant great hardship and a good chance of an early death was a punishment well-established in Tsarist Russia, but more notorious under STALIN, who had many GULAGS there. Thus to be sent to Siberia is used to mean to be sent to a remote or undesirable place or to be ostracised.

SIBYLLINE BOOKS [*Mythology*]

In the classical world a sibyl was a term for a prophetess, and the most famous of these was the Sibyl of Cumae, south of Rome. The Romans had a story that at one time the prophesies about Rome's future were gathered together by the Cumaean Sibyl and offered to the king TARQUIN the Proud for a high sum. He objected to the price, so she burnt a third of them and demanded the same price for what remained. When he demurred again she burnt another third and finally sold him what remained for the original price. Thus the Sibylline Books stand for both knowledge of the future and the loss of something precious and irreplaceable. 'If the material is not acquired for the British Museum ... it will be as though another Sibylline Book has been taken up and burnt. Posterity will blame us for our philistinism' (*Current Archaeology* 139).

SIEGE PERILOUS see ROUND TABLE

SIKES, BILL [*Literature*]

In Charles Dickens' 1838 OLIVER TWIST Bill Sikes is a violent, bullying burglar. After killing his faithful **Nancy**, he meets his end by falling and choking to death when fleeing justice across the rooftops.

SILENCE OF THE LAMBS, THE see LECTEUR, HANIBAL

SILENUS see DIONYSUS

SILVER see LONE RANGER

SILVER, LONG JOHN   [*Literature*]

Long John Silver is the dominant character of R. L. Stevenson's adventure novel *Treasure Island* (1883). He is a one-legged sailor with a parrot on his shoulder (the original of this image), who once sailed with the evil pirate CAPTAIN FLINT. After BLIND PEW fails to get the map showing where Flint's treasure is buried from JIM HAWKINS, Silver joins the *Hispaniola*, which has been hired to search for the treasure, as ship's cook and sees to it that most of the crew are his men. He soon emerges as the most intelligent of the pirates and as their leader. He is a curious mixture of the attractive and totally repellent, and there is an ambiguous attitude to him throughout the book. He is the only pirate to escape at the end of the book. See also ISRAEL HANDS, BEN GUNN.

SINBAD   [*Folklore*]

The ARABIAN NIGHTS stories of Sinbad the Sailor were originally Arabic, but have now become international. Sinbad gains great riches through his seven voyages, but his adventures also involve much suffering. The most famous of his adventures is his encounter with the giant bird called the **Roc**.

SINK THE BISMARCK see BISMARCK

SIRENS   [*Mythology*]

In Greek myth the Sirens are sea nymphs whose enchanting singing from rocky islands lures sailors to their deaths. They are usually described as beautiful women, and are obviously one source of the later mermaid legends, but are sometimes shown as much less alluring birds with female heads. They were encountered both by the heroes on the *ARGO* (who drowned out their song by harp playing) and by ODYSSEUS, who became the only man actually to survive hearing their song when he blocked his crew's ears with wax, but had himself tied to the mast of the ship. A Siren is thus anyone or anything, particularly an attractive woman, that lures you out of your path in life, but the word has also been productive in other ways. Because of the noise they made, our word 'siren' for a warning signal comes from the Sirens, and their name has also been given to a type of American amphibian.

SISTINE CHAPEL [Art]
The Sistine Chapel is chiefly alluded to for its famous paintings by Michelangelo, including the much-exploited one of God stretching out his hand to instil life in Adam. It is also referred to for the amazing physical feat involved, which for Michelangelo meant years working on his back painting the ceiling. This became the subject of the 1965 film *The Agony and the Ecstasy*.

SISYPHUS [Mythology]
In Greek myth Sisyphus was punished after death in **Tartarus**, that part of HADES reserved for the wicked, for his earthly sins by being forced to roll a large stone up a hill. Just as he was reaching the top every time, the stone would slip and roll down to the bottom, so that Sisyphus' task never ended. Thus a job that seems endless or futile can be called **Sisyphean**. 'Most scarabs are less than an inch long: their labours can reasonably be described as HERCULEAN, or Sisyphean – the work is recurrent, endless and largely solitary' (*Guardian* 10.5.96).

SITTING BULL see BUFFALO BILL, CUSTER'S LAST STAND

SIX MILLION DOLLAR MAN see BIONIC WOMAN

666 see NUMBER OF THE BEAST

SKIPPY [Television]
The TV series *Skippy, the Bush Kangaroo* (1967–69) with its catchy theme song, was an Australian answer to LASSIE. Skippy was the devoted pet of the son of a national park Ranger who had nursed the injured kangaroo back to health. Skippy repaid him by frequently saving him and various others from certain death by its amazing ability to understand what humans wanted from it. 'Skippy' is often simply used as a substitute for 'kangaroo', as in

the newspaper report during the BSE scare 'Skippy could soon be served up on a sesame bun in school canteens as a substitute for beef' (*Evening Standard* 29.3.96).

SKYWALKER, LUKE [*Film*]
Luke Skywalker is the young, impetuous and naive hero of the STAR WARS films. A boy from a backwoods planet, he is destined by inheritance and innate abilities to become the last of the JEDI KNIGHTS. Over the three films we watch him grow and develop as he is trained first by OBI-WAN KENOBI and then YODA in the ways of the Jedi and fighting with a **light sabre** and, with the beautiful **Princess Leia,** HAN SOLO and **Chewbacca** and the robots **C-3PO** and **R2–D2,** fights against the evil Empire and its general DARTH VADER.

SLAUGHTER OF THE INNOCENTS see HEROD

SLEEPING BEAUTY [*Folklore*]
The fairy tale of The Sleeping Beauty tells of the princess condemned to die by the wicked fairy who is angry at not having been invited to her christening, and how the curse is modified into sleeping for a hundred years by a (good) fairy godmother. It is the source of the image of the sleeping princess being woken by a kiss from a prince (but see also SNOW WHITE) which has been much used elsewhere. 'Imagine you've just kissed the sleeping princess in the enchanted castle, as she stirs, and opens her eyes, and turns her head, and then you notice the book beside her bed is called 10001 Cures for Chronic Insomnia' (Tom Holt *Here Comes the Sun* 1993).

SLOPE, REVEREND OBEDIAH see BARSETSHIRE

SMERSH see JAMES BOND, ROSA KREB

SMIKE see DOTHEBOYS HALL

SMITH, WINSTON see 1984

SMURFS [*Popular Culture*]
The Smurfs are small, blue pixie-like creatures in white pointy

hats, who live in forest glades and have adventures the attractions of which are a mystery to adults, but which go down well with small children. Their natural history is also something of a mystery, as there only appears to be one female member of the race. Allusions to them are usually mocking, as in 'The poor are still with us, as are the terrorists, the Tories and the Smurfs' (*Guardian* 2.9.96).

SNOOPY [*Popular Culture*]
Snoopy is the simply-drawn, philosophising white beagle who is probably the most popular of the characters in the strip-cartoon *Peanuts* by Charles Schulz.

SNOOTY, LORD [*Popular Culture*]
A strip which ran for many years in the children's comic paper *The Beano*, Lord Snooty and his Pals showed the top-hatted, Eton-uniformed Lord Snooty at play with the poor children of Ash-Can Alley.

SNOW WHITE AND THE SEVEN DWARFS
[*Film, Folklore*]
Snow White is one a the main sources of the image of the wicked step-mother, this time the wicked queen-witch with her magic 'mirror, mirror on the wall'. The poisoned apple with which the queen apparently kills Snow White (until the prince kissing Snow White dislodges the apple from her mouth) is also alluded to. The names given the dwarves in the Disney cartoon film – Dopey, Grumpy, Sneezy, Bashful, Sleepy, Happy and Doc – have become well established even thought they were invented for the film. Snow White is one of the fairytales least liked by feminists as her role is essentially passive or domestic.

SNOWY see TIN-TIN

SNOZZCUMBERS [*Literature*]
The **BFG** (Big Friendly Giant) in Roald Dahl's *The BFG* (1982) is a convinced vegetarian, unlike the other giants who feed off sleeping children. Unfortunately for him, the only food that grows in Giant Land are snozzcumbers, the most 'disgustulous' (the BFG

has his own ideas about words) food in the world. Luckily for him with the help of orphan Sophie and the Queen of England he saves the world from the giants and gets to live in England with all the nice food he can eat.

SOCRATES [*Philosophy*]

No writings of the Greek philosopher Socrates (c. 470–399 BC) have survived, but he is the major character in the dialogues of his pupil **Plato** (see PLATO'S CAVE) which are supposed to be a record of his teaching. The **Socratic method** derives from these dialogues. This consists of instuction by questions (by Socrates) and answers (by his pupil/victim) in order to draw out truths that Socrates felt were known by all rational beings. The term **Socratic irony** is used to describe the way in which pretended ignorance by a skilful questioner can be used to show up the answerer's own fundamental ignorance. See also ALCIBIADES.

SODOM AND GOMORRAH [*Religion*]

The Cities of the Plain were hotbeds of sin and iniquity, and were destroyed by God as a result, according to the Bible (Genesis 19). Two angels are sent to test the cities and Lot invites them to be his guests. While they are eating the men of Sodom come to rape the men (hence the use of Sodomite for homosexual), but Lot will not let them get at the men for they are his guests, and even offers to hand over his daughters instead. The wicked Sodomites are then struck blind. God decides to destroy the cities. Lot, his wife and daughters are told to flee, but on no account must they look behind them. But **Lot's wife** looked behind her, and was turned into a pillar of salt. In the words of the Bible 'the Lord rained upon Sodom and upon Gomorrah brimstone and fire from the Lord out of heaven; And he overthrew those cities, and all the plain, and all the inhabitants of the cities, and that which grew upon the ground.' The Dead Sea with its low-lying position and high chemical content is traditionally said to lie over these cities.

SOLO, HAN [*Film*]

The swashbuckling co-hero, with LUKE SKYWALKER, of the STAR WARS trilogy, Han Solo is a professional smuggler who likes to shoot first and ask questions later. He claims that he is only motivated by self-interest, but events ultimately show that he is not as cynical and hard-bitten as he likes pretend. His great love is his ship the *Millenium Falcon* which he pilots expertly with the help of his friend and side-kick **Chewbacca**. This is an enormously tall and strong creature covered in unkempt long fur and known as a **Wookie**.

SOLO, NAPOLEON see MAN FROM UNCLE

SOLOMON [*Religion*]
In the Bible Solomon is a 10th-century BC king of Israel famous for his wisdom, which has become proverbial. The **Judgement of Solomon** refers to an occasion when two women both claimed the same baby as their own. Solomon suggested that as there way no way to tell which was the true mother, the child should be cut in half and they have half each. One woman agreed, but the other immediately withdrew her claim. Solomon then awarded the baby to the second woman on the grounds that the true mother was the one who would do anything to stop her baby being harmed.

SOUP DRAGON [*Television*]
Between 1969 and 1974 there appeared a five–minute children's TV series called *The Clangers*. **Clangers** were pink, stockinet, rather mouse-like creatures which communicated with each other in surprisingly eloquent, melodious whistles, and lived a simple life on a small planet, recycling things that fell from space. Many meteors also fell on the planet so their homes were underground, sealed off by dustbin lids. Their main source of food was soup, which they got from the Soup Dragon which lived in the soup wells and dispensed wisdom and advice along with the soup.

SOUTH SEA BUBBLE [*History, Finance*]
In the early 18th century the South Sea Company took over the British national debt in return for a monopoly of trade with the South Seas. This led to feverish speculation in their stock, which in 1720 collapsed like a pricked bubble (hence the term), ruining many. Since then any financial event that has blown up like a bub-

ble and then collapsed rapidly has been compared to the South Sea Bubble.

SPADE, SAM see MALTESE FALCON

SPAGHETTI JUNCTION [*Transport*]
After the opening in 1972 of Gravelly Hill Interchange at Birmingham, the meeting place of four major roads and many interchanges and underpasses, it quickly gained the nickname 'spaghetti junction', for the roads were felt to be as tangled together as a heap of spaghetti. Since then the term has come to be applied to any similar interchange.

SPANISH INQUISITION [*History, Religion*]
Many legends and rumours surround the workings of the Spanish Inquisition, the Spanish branch of the **Inquisition**, a department of the Church dedicated to find and suppressing heresy. The Spanish Inquisition flourished particularly from the 15th to 17th century and swiftly gained a reputation for fierce cross-questioning, cruelty and torture. Since then any form of persecution has been compared to them. The catch phrase 'Nobody expects the Spanish Inquisition' comes from a MONTY PYTHON sketch. See also TORQUEMADA.

SPART, DAVE [*Popular Culture*]
Invented by *Private Eye*, but now used more generally, Dave Spart represents a typical, jargon-spouting, left-wing activist. So we get allusions to such things as 'the crazed Spartist headmistress of one of the borough's primary schools' (*Evening Standard* 19.1.94).

SPARTA [*History*]
The citizens of the ancient Greek city of Sparta were a ruling elite holding down a much larger population of mistreated virtual slaves called **Helots**. They were in constant fear of rebellion, and to avoid this, they evolved a highly militaristic and disciplined way of life, which involved doing away with most of family life and the comforts of life in order to develop a race of hardy warriors. Such was the austerity of life that when a visitor tasted the famous black broth which formed the staple diet, he remarked

'Now I know why Spartans are not afraid to die'. Thus **Spartan** means very strict or austere or, since they were famous for being men of few words, taciturn or laconic, a word that comes from Laconia, the region of which Sparta was the capital.

SPARTACUS [History]

Spartacus was a Thracian gladiator of the first century BC. He escaped from a gladiatorial school outside Rome and for two years led a slave revolt in southern Italy, before he was captured and crucified (the traditional punishment for rebelling Roman slaves) along with his followers. Spartacus has been used to represent the urge of the oppressed for freedom. In 1960 a film was made of his life starring action man Kirk Douglas. 'Dreadlocked singer MacAlmont, of a campness to make QUENTIN CRISP seem like Spartacus' (Evening Standard 15.4.96).

SPEEDY GONZALES [Popular Culture]

Speedy Gonzales is an incredibly fast-moving Mexican mouse in a series of Warner Brothers animated cartoons.

SPIDER MAN [Popular Culture]

Spider Man is one of the many super-heroes, in the mould of SUPERMAN and BATMAN, who appeared in American comics in the 1950s and '60s. In this case he is one **Peter Parker** who, after being bitten by a mutant spider, finds he has spider-like powers such as the ability to climb up the sides of buildings. Armed with his 'web-shooter' which he can use to trap and entangle people, he fights crime.

SPINAL TAP [Film]

The 1984 film *This is Spinal Tap* is a spoof documentary of a British heavy metal rock band making a comeback tour in the USA. It satirises all the clichés of the rock world and its hangers on.

SPOCK, MR [Television]

In the original STAR TREK series Mr Spock is the USS *Enterprise*'s science officer. He is half-human, half-VULCAN, but favours his Vulcan nature, typically suppressing his emotions (although they sometimes show through nonetheless) and emphasising his dependence on logic. It is this, rather than his pointed Vulcan ears, that sets him apart from the rest of the crew, and his sharply slanting eyebrows often shoot up at the emotional illogicality of mere humans.

SPODE, RODERICK see BERTIE WOOSTER

SPOTTY DOG see THE WOODENTOPS

SQUEERS, WACKFORD see DOTHEBOYS HALL

STALIN, JOSEPH [*History*]
Joseph Stalin (1879–1953) became leader of Russia in 1922 and remained in power until his death. He created a totalitarian state, ruthlessly crushed all opposition and ruled by decree and through a rigid bureaucracy. Millions died, either as a direct result of purges such as those of 1934 to 1937 when thousands were imprisoned in the GULAGS, shot or sent to SIBERIA, or through starvation as a result of his enforced collectivisation of agriculture. Carrying out the central plan was much more important to Stalin and his followers than what happened to the people affected. Thus the accusation of **Stalinism** can be hurled at any regime which is felt to be totalitarian and to put theory before people. Labour leader and Prime Minister Tony Blair complained of the images of him created in the press with 'last year I was BAMBI; this year I am Stalin!' (*Guardian* 31.7.96).

STALKY AND CO [*Literature*]
Rudyard Kipling's schoolboy stories *Stalky and Co* tell the adventures of three boys, **Beetle** (based on Kipling himself). **M'Turk** and Arthur Corkran, known as **Stalky**. (The school slang for cunning was 'stalky' and Stalky was the prime exponent of the clever schoolboy prank). These three boys go to school at a boarding school in Devon (the setting is largely autobiographical, and reflects Kipling's own school Westward Ho!), have a wonderful time running round the countryside, and getting into trouble and battling with the Latin-loving schoolmaster **King** – 'a beast but a just beast', as the boys admit – who actually understands them much better than they realise.

STAR TREK [*Television, Film*]

The TV series (started 1966) and films based on Gene Rodden-berry's *Star Trek* have introduced many a concept and catch-phrase into the language. **Warp factor** (a faster-than-light velocity) has become a familiar expression of speed: 'Should the conditions be right you can keep going to Warp-factor 9' (car review, *Top Gear* 25.4.96). The giant spaceship USS *Enterprise*'s version of the death-ray, the **phaser**, and the **transporter** technology that allows people to be 'beamed' from one place to another once the system has been 'energised' are also familiar. One prominent British politician is regularly described as a VULCAN (although this should really be a **Romulan**), and there have even been two rival transla-tions of parts of the Bible into KLINGON. Catch-phrases from the first series include 'Beam me up, Scotty' (supposedly said by Captain **Kirk** to his engineer, but in fact never used in the TV series, although it was worked into one of the films after having become a catch-phrase); engineer Scott's horrible cod-Scotch accent, saying, 'The dilithium crystals willna' take it'; Dr 'Bones' McCoy telling his captain, 'It's life, Jim, but not as we know it', and the captain's famous opening voice-over, which includes the words 'Space – the final frontier … ' and that notorious split infinitive: 'its five-year mission – to boldly go where no man has gone before'. The next series was *Star Trek: The Next Generation* where a new *Enterprise* is captained by Jean-Luc **Picard** (whose catch-phrase instruction is '**Make it so**'), and its crew include his dash-ing 'Number One' Will **Riker**, and the earnest SPOCK-like android **Data**. *Deep Space Nine*, another spin-off, is set on a vast space sta-tion by the wormhole in space above the planet **Bajor** (see KLIN-GON), and introduced the **Shapeshifter**, **Odo**, and the delightfully amoral **Ferengi**, **Quark**. The latest series, *Voyager*, with its female captain Kathryn Janeway, has not been going long enough to have had much impact.

STAR WARS [*Film*]

George Lucas' trilogy of *Star Wars* films – *Star Wars* (1977), *The Empire Strikes Back* (1980) and *Return of the Jedi* (1983) – was designed to create a substitute mythology for the young at a time when the adventure film was in the doldrums, and it eminently succeeded. So much so that the USA's Strategic Defence Initiative which proposed using satellites armed with lasers to shoot down enemy missiles from space was almost universally referred to as Star Wars, and the term 'Evil Empire' taken from the films to refer to Russia. The Star Wars films' themes were based on both earlier cowboy films and classic American science fiction with its stress on democracy and individualism, and told of young LUKE SKY-WALKER, good baddie HAN SOLO and feisty **Princess Leia** as they fought against the Empire and is warriors led by DARTH VADER, aided by what was left of the JEDI knowledge, and dealt with such master criminals such as **Jabba the Hutt**, a revolting sort of over-developed slug, on the side. See OBI-WAN KENOBI, YODA and cross-references for other characters.

STARDUST, ZIGGY [*Music, Popular Culture, Film*]
Ziggy Stardust was the persona adopted by the singer David Bowie (1947–) on stage and for the album *The Rise and Fall of Ziggy Stardust and the Spiders from Mars* (1972). This coincided with the rise of glam-rock and with other space-theme interests of Bowie's such as a the *Space Oddity* album (1969 in Britain, but not a hit single in the USA until 1973) with its well-known line 'Ground control to Major Tom' and the film *The Man Who Fell to Earth* (1976) and these have all rather got blurred together. It is rather difficult, in retrospect, to see what all the fuss was about, but it seemed very significant at the time, and Ziggy Stardust is still used regularly of David Bowie or of the style of the time.

STARKADDERS see COLD COMFORT FARM

STARSKY AND HUTCH [*Television*]
The high-action TV series *Starsky and Hutch* told of the adventures and car chases of two undercover Los Angeles cops, Dave Starsky and Ken 'Hutch' Hutchinson. It was one of the great buddy-buddy series, with great emphasis being put on the personal relationship and trust between the two. Their hip, street-wise under-world contact **Huggy Bear** became a minor cult figure, but the series is mostly remembered now for the amazingly chunky cardigans worn by Starsky.

STEED, JOHN [*Television*]
In the TV series *The Avengers* (1961–68) and *The New Avengers* (1976–77) the attractive females might come and go (see under EMMA PEEL and PURDEY) but suave, sophisticated, John Steed was a constant. Rarely seen without his bowler hat and furled umbrella, and with a ready quip on his lips, Steed was always the perfect gentleman to his assistants, although ruthless with the series of weird and wonderful villains attempting to take over the world that it was his lot to combat.

STEERPIKE see GORMENGHAST

STENTOR [*Literature, Mythology*]
In HOMER's *The Iliad* Stentor is the herald of the besieging Greeks whose voice could be heard throughout the camp. Thus **stentorian** means 'uncommonly loud'.

STEPFORD WIVES [*Film*]
The 1974 film *Stepford Wives* told the story of a newly married couple who move to the New York commuter village of Stepford. The wife cannot understand how the other women there are content to devote themselves to looking good and pandering to their husbands' needs without appearing to have any other interest in life, until she realises that the chauvinistic husbands have had their wives replaced by androids. The term 'Stepford Wife' has been used to indicate a zombie-like person, or someone mindlessly devoted to domesticity. 'The parents, Susan and Richard, had a slight Stepford Wives look about them as they stood proudly outside their home. (*Evening Standard* 13.3.96).

STEPTOE AND SON [*Television*]
The comedy series *Steptoe and Son* ran on BBC TV from 1962 to 1965 and from 1970 to 1974. It told the story of Harold Steptoe, a middle-aged bachelor always trying to better himself and of his love-hate relationship with his elderly father Albert, dirty in mind and body, and of their rag-and-bone business. The series spawned the catch-phrase 'You dirty old man', regularly used by Harold to Albert.

STIG OF THE DUMP [*Children's Literature*]

In Clive King's classic children's novel *Stig of the Dump* (1963) a lonely child, **Barney**, meets a cave-boy who lives in a cave at the bottom of an old chalk pit which is now being used as a rubbish dump. There they take and ingeniously adapt other people's rubbish to provide the necessities of life, and each boy learns useful skills from the other. The story's recycling element is perhaps its most memorable, and plans to turn a Cornish clay pit into the largest greenhouse in the world were described as 'Stig of the Dump meets the Palm House at Kew' (*Farming Today*, Radio 4, 29.4.96).

STINGRAY [*Television*]

Stingray was a children's TV puppet series (1964–65) which had the distinction of being the first British TV series to be filmed in colour. It opened with a voice-over saying 'Stand by for action. Anything could happen in the next half hour!' which is still to be found used as a catch-phrase, and told of the adventures of **Troy Tempest**, **Phones** and the mute, underwater girl **Marina** in the atomic sub Stingray. Marina came from the undersea world of Pacifica, but not all underseas people were friendly, and Stingray was always coming into conflict with Titan, ruler of Titanica, whose fleet of **Terror Fish** fired missiles from their mouths. On shore Marina and the commander's daughter **Atlanta** fought for Troy's affections.

STONEHOUSE, JOHN [*History*]

John Stonehouse (1925–1988) was a Labour cabinet minister in 1974 when his clothes were found on a Florida beach with no evidence of what had happened to their owner. A swimming tragedy swiftly became presumed suicide as evidence of criminal financial dealing emerged, but no body was ever found. Then Stonehouse was found to be living in Australia, for he had done a REGGIE PERRIN, and faked suicide to start a new life. He was eventually extradited, brought back to Britain and tried and imprisoned for embezzlement.

STRABISMUS, DR see BEACHCOMBER

STRANGELOVE, DR [*Film*]

The 1963 satirical film *Dr Strangelove, or How I Learned to Stop Worrying and Love the Bomb* is an attack on nuclear war and its inevitable results, with such lines as a general saying reassuringly that 'I don't say we wouldn't get our hair mussed, but I do say no more than ten to twenty million people killed'. Dr Strangelove himself is a mad Nazi scientist now working for the USA military who has invented a world-destroying weapon and whose arm automatically rises in a Nazi salute at every opportunity. Strangelove is used to indicate right-wing, militaristic fanaticism.

STRUWWELPETER [*Children's Literature*]

Struwwelpeter, usually translated as *Shockheaded Peter* but also as *Slovenly Peter* and sometimes anglicised as Struwlpeter or Straw Peter is a collection of comic and cautionary tales by the German Heinrich Hoffmann (1809–74) which was first published in 1845. Until recently it was a staple of every childhood, but some parents today feel that the themes – it contains such things as children who suck their fingers having them cut off by the Scissorman – are rather too violent. Peter himself is a tall thin boy with blond hair standing on end.

STUFFED OWL [*Literature*]

A stuffed owl is a really bad or boring bit of work by someone who can do better, particularly writing by the famous. The term comes from *The Stuffed Owl: An Anthology of Bad Verse* by D. B. Wyndham Lewis (not to be confused with Percy Wyndham Lewis the painter and novelist) and Charles Lee, which was enormously successful in the 1940s. The stuffed owl of the title came from a particularly poor poem written by Wordsworth in his later years about a sick child with a stuffed owl over its bed. Lewis was a remarkable man: a considerable scholar, literary editor of the *Daily Express* and the man who was the predecessor of J. B. Morton on, and largely the moulder of the form of, the BEACH-COMBER column.

STYX [*Mythology*]

One of the five rivers of HADES, the others being LETHE, Acheron, Cocytus and Phlegethon.

SUDETENLAND see MUNICH

SUE, GRABBIT AND RUNNE   [*Popular Culture*]
A firm of solicitors invented by *Private Eye*. The name has been widely adopted to stand for lawyers in general, particularly those involved in libel cases.

SUKEBIND see COLD COMFORT FARM

SUN KING   [*History*]
The Sun King was a title given to King Louis XIV of France (reigned 1643–1715) to emphasise his glory, and can be found used ironically of anyone vainglorious or with aspirations to absolute power in their sphere.

SUNNYBROOK FARM   [*Literature*]
Sunnybrook Farm is the home of Rebecca Randall in *Rebecca of Sunnybrook Farm* (1903) by Kate Douglas Wiggins. She is plucky, enterprising, hardworking and dutiful, and her name and that of Sunnybrook Farm have come to stand for things which are too good to be true.

SUNSHINE DESSERTS see REGGIE PERRIN

SUPERMAN   [*Popular Culture*]
Mild-mannered **Clark Kent** is a shy reporter on the *Daily Planet*, overshadowed by the feisty fellow-reporter **Lois Lane**. However, when danger threatens off come the glasses and grey clothes and he becomes Superman, the last survivor of the lost planet **Krypton**, a flying hero with x-ray vision and incredible strength. Superman started off as a comic-book hero in 1938, and his distinctive outfit of cape, tights and a sort of leotard which has led to endless jokes about Superman wearing his underwear outside his trousers, have now appeared in most media. The radio version was very popular in the States from the 1940s, and introduced such catchphrases is 'Up, up and away', 'Faster than a speeding bullet', and 'It's a bird! It's a plane! It's Superman!' (Often found in the form 'Is it a bird? Is it … '). For the philosophical concept of the superman see NIETZSCHE.

SVENGALI [*Literature*]
Svengali is the sinister villain in George du Maurier's 1894 novel *Trilby*. Trilby O'Ferral (the hat is named after one she wears in illustrations in the book) is an artist's model who, when hypnotised by Svengali, becomes a brilliant and successful singer; but such is Svengali's power over her that when he dies she loses her voice and finally dies herself. A Svengali is thus used of someone who has sinister control over another, especially in the entertainment business. 'Alan Bates, as her Svengali-like manager, is one of Hollywood's long line of English-accented villains (*Evening Standard* 10.10.96). 'Experienced music business managers have long-running relationships with the A&R departments of all the major players. These Svengalis can turn out to be ARTHUR DALEYs, so choose carefully'. (*Independent* 15.2.96).

SWAMP, THE see MASH

SYBIL see FAWLTY TOWERS

TALLEYRAND [*History*]
Prince Charles-Maurice de Talleyrand-Périgord (1754–1838), one-time bishop of Autun until excommunicated by the Pope for his support of the French Revolution, is famous for his cunning, manipulative skills and ability to survive. As well as having risen high in the Church (largely due to family connections and despite the fact that he was expelled from his seminary for taking a mistress) he held high office during the French Revolution, under Napoleon, under the restored Bourbon kings of France and even under King Louis Philippe who replaced them.

TALOS, TALUS [*Mythology*]
The Greeks' idea of a robot. In Greek myth he is a gigantic man of brass who guarded the coast of Crete destroying everyone who tried to land. His only vulnerable place was in his heel, where there was a stopper that held in his vital fluid, and he was finally destroyed by removing this.

TANNOCHBRAE see DR FINLAY

TANTALUS [*Mythology*]
Along with SISYPHUS, Tantalus is the best-known inhabitant of **Tartarus**, Greek myth's equivalent of Hell. His crime is variously described – stealing nectar, the food of the gods from OLYMPUS, revealing the gods' secrets, or most commonly cooking up his own son and serving him as food to the gods. For his crime he was afflicted with a raging hunger and thirst and now stands in Tartarus in water that recedes when he tries to drink it and under fruit that moves away as he reaches for it. His fate gives us the word 'tantalising'.

TAR BABY see UNCLE REMUS

TARA [*Mythology*]

The hill of Tara in County Meath, Ireland, is the ancient, sacred seat of the Irish Kings. In *Gone With the Wind* this is the name that has been transferred to the estate that SCARLETT O'HARA fights so hard to preserve, and so the name has come to be used as a home that is valued above all else.

TARANTINO, QUENTIN [*Film*]

The films of Quentin Tarantino have a reputation for bloody violence and strong language, and allusions to him are usually for this: 'Prepare yourselves for Gary's nightmares – bloodbaths that would make Quentin Tarantino envious.' (*Radio Times* 6–12.7.96).

TARDIS [*Television*]

The Tardis is the Time And Relative Dimensions In Space ship used by DR WHO in the long-running children's TV series. Disguised as an old-fashioned, blue, wooden police phone-box, it has the remarkable ability not only to distort the dimensions (it is many times bigger inside than out) but can also travel in time and space as its name suggests. However, it is a temperamental machine, only nominally under the Doctor's control, and is capable of landing him in adventures in almost any time or anywhere apparently at whim.

TARQUIN [*History*]

The Tarquins were the kings of early Rome. The last of their line **Tarquin the Proud** (*Tarquinius Superbus*), was deposed by BRUTUS after the rape of **Lucretia** (Shakespeare's Lucrece). In this famous incident **Sextus**, Tarquin's son, was staying with a Roman nobleman and his virtuous wife, Lucretia. One night he came to Lucretia's room and told her that if she did not sleep with him he would take a slave, cut his throat and place him in her bed and declare he had caught her with the slave. Terrified, Lucretia let him have his way, but the next day she called all her male relatives (including BRUTUS, who was Tarquin's nephew) to the house, told them what had happened and killed herself as she could not bear the shame. Horrified by this final act of tyranny from Tarquin's family the people united behind Brutus and drove out their kings forever and became a republic. See also HORATIUS, SIBYLLINE BOOKS.

TARTARUS see SISYPHUS, TANTALUS

TARZAN [*Literature, Film*]
By birth John Clayton, **Lord Greystoke**, Tarzan got his name from
the fierce apes who brought him up. Tarzan is the creation of
Edgar Rice Burroughs (see also BARSOOM), and in the original
book, *Tarzan of the Apes* (1914), his parents had been marooned in
the African jungle, and both die soon after his birth. The new-born
infant is found by Kala, (**Cheeta** the chimpanzee is a much later
addition to the legend), an ape whose own baby had just been
killed, and she takes him to replace her lost baby. Tarzan grows up
without contact with humans, but first meets with the local primitive people (depicted in a racist way that would now be totally
unacceptable), then one day sees some white people in the jungle,
including Jane Porter, the **Jane** of 'Me Tarzan, you Jane' fame. He
rescues her from various dire fates, and eventually comes to rejoin
civilisation. Rice Burroughs went on to write 23 other Tarzan
books, and other writers have taken up the theme. The myth has
also become more complex through the many films based on the
character.

TELL, WILLIAM [*History, Folklore*]
William Tell is a legendary Swiss hero (though some would claim
he actually existed) who, it is said, about the turn of the 13th and
14th centuries defied the power of the Austrian governor. In the
best-known version of the story the hat of the Governor **Gessler**
was placed on a pole and the Swiss humiliated by being forced to
honour it, which Tell refused to do. Since he was a famous marks-
man he was punished by being forced to shoot an apple off the
head of his small son. He took two arrows with him, and with one
split the apple, and with the second shot Gessler, thereby rousing
the locals to rebellion. 'Arguing that BRUCE never encountered the
energetic arachnid is akin to claiming that William Tell was a bad
shot, that GEORGE WASHINGTON framed the footman for the cherry
tree incident or that EL CID couldn't handle a horse' (*Times* 22.6.96).

TEMPEST, TROY see STINGRAY

TEN COMMANDMENTS see MOSES

1066 AND ALL THAT [*Popular Culture*]

W. C. Sellar and R. J. Yeatman's 1930 parody of history books, *1066 And All That* (1066 being the only date in English history that everyone knows) has become a symbol of jingoistic, over-simplistic interpretations of historical events.

TERMINATOR, THE [*Film*]

In this film and its sequel **Arnold Schwarzenegger** (see further at CONAN) plays a killing machine sent from the future. Well-known lines from the films include 'I'll be back' and 'Hasta la vista, baby'.

TERPSICHORE see MUSES

TERROR FISH see STINGRAY

THAÏS [*History*]

Thaïs was a fourth-century BC Greek courtesan, famous for her beauty. She was in turn mistress of Alexander the Great and wife of Ptolomy I, King of Egypt.

THALIA see MUSES

THELEME see RABELAIS

THEOSOPHICAL SOCIETY see MADAM BLAVATSKY

THERMOPYLAE [*History*]

The Battle of Thermopylae (sometimes referred to as 'the hot springs', the meaning of the name) in 480 BC is famous on a number of counts. Greece was being invaded by a vast army of Persians under their Emperor XERXES and they had already taken over the northern part of Greece. Thermopylae was the perfect spot for a small army to hold off a large army, for it was then a narrow pass between the mountains and the sea, although silting has since made it a wide passage. Thus, like HORATIUS on the bridge, Thermopylae has become a classic case of the few holding back the many. It is further known as a famous last stand, for after the Greeks under the Spartan general **Leonidas** had held the pass for three days, a Greek traitor, **Ephialtes**, showed the Persians a path through the mountains that outflanked Leonidas' army. Leonidas sent most of his troops back south to safety, but remained behind (possibly because of an oracle which said that for the Persians to be defeated a king must die) with 300 of the top Spartan fighting men, their helots and 11,000 Boetians, whose lands would be the first taken if the Persians got through. Curiously, in what is obviously an early example of good public relations, one rarely hears about anyone but the 300 brave Spartans, although to be fair they did represent a high proportion of Spartan fighting men, and their epitaph 'Go, tell the Spartans, thou who passest by, / That here obedient to their laws we lie' has echoed down the centuries. All left behind died in battle, and although central Greece was conquered, the Persians had already, in effect, lost the war. Their fleet, on which they depended for communication, had been badly damaged in a storm, and then defeated by the Athenian fleet in the Battle of **Salamis**, one of the first great naval engagements recorded in detail. Again an oracle comes into play, for the Athenians had been told by **Delphi** that they should put their trust in their wooden walls, and the great Athenian leader **Themistocles** had ordered the evacuation of Athenian lands and that everything should depend on protection from the wooden ships.

THERSITES [*Literature*]
Thersites, a character in both HOMER and Shakespeare's TROILUS *and Cressida*, is an ugly, foul-mouthed slanderer on the Greek side in the TROJAN WAR, constantly reviling and criticising his fellow-Greeks, until he is killed by ACHILLES for mocking him. Such is his reputation that there is even a rare adjective **thersitical**, meaning abusive and loud, derived from his name. 'Like the very first vulgarian, Thersites in *The Iliad*, a soldier who dares to talk back to his betters, she has received a sound beating for her vulgarity' (*Independent* 17.4.96).

THESEUS see ARIADNE, MINOTAUR, PROCRUSTES

THETIS see ACHILLES

THIRTY PIECES OF SILVER [*Religion*]
Thirty pieces of silver was the price JUDAS was paid for betraying

Christ, so has become the reward of treachery. Thus, on the rivalry between stout-brewers for customers, 'Their disloyalty, like that of Judas Iscariot, has been bought. Instead of 30 pieces of silver, they have been subverted to 20p a pint – the discount Beamish is offering' (*Times* 21.3.92).

THIRTY-NINE STEPS, THE see JOHN BUCHAN, RICHARD HANNAY

THOMAS THE TANK ENGINE see FAT CONTROLLER

THOMPSON TWINS see TIN-TIN

THOR [*Mythology*]
In Norse myth Thor is the god of thunder, after whom Thursday is named. In German he is **Donner** as in 'donner und blitzen' ('thunder and lightening'). Thor carries a hammer, **Mjollnir**, and T-shaped symbols of this hammer were worn by his worshippers much in the way Christians wear a cross. In myth he is often a figure of fun, with more brawn than brains, but in Iceland at least, he seems to have been a genuinely popular god, with more followers than, for instance, the more austere ODIN.

THOUGHT POLICE see 1984

THOUGHTS OF CHAIRMAN MAO see MAO

THREE GRACES see GRACES

THREE MUSKETEERS see D'ARTAGNAN

THREE-PIPE PROBLEM see HOLMES, SHERLOCK

THRUSH see MAN FROM UNCLE

THUMPER see BAMBI

THUNDERBIRDS [*Television*]
The most sophisticated and probably the most popular of Gerry

Anderson 'Supermarionation' puppet TV shows, *Thunderbirds* (1965–66) told the story of **International Rescue** run by the Tracy family in the 21st century. Millionaire **Jeff Tracy** hid everything on his Pacific island, for the secret of the people behind International Rescue must be kept, with the result that all the launch sites for the Thunderbirds were elaborately camouflaged beneath the buildings of Tracy island. The five Tracy sons, named after the first five Americans in space, piloted the Thunderbirds. **Scott** flew **Thunderbird 1**, a jet-rocket, used for reconnaissance and getting there fast. **Virgil** flew **Thunderbird 2**, a large transporter frame into which could be fitted various pods used for carrying necessary equipment such as the burrowing Mole or **Thunderbird 4**, the atomic submarine piloted by **Gordon**. **Thunderbird 3** was a space rocket, piloted by **Alan**, and used to keep in touch with **Thunderbird 5**, a space station in which **John** monitored the world for distress signals. See also LADY PENELOPE and PARKER.

THUVIA, MAID OF MARS see BARSOOM

TIANANMEN SQUARE [*History*]
In a year when Communist states in Europe were starting to convert peacefully to democracy, the events in China's Tiananmen Square, the major meeting place in Peking, came as a shock. In June 1989 the pro-democracy demonstration there was repressed with extreme violence, with the loss of hundreds of lives, many of them before the cameras of the world's press, and the events soon became called the Tiananmen massacre.

TIBER see HORATIUS

TIBERIUS, EMPEROR [*History*]
The Roman Emperor Tiberius (ruled 14–37 AD) is notorious for his sexual depravity and above all for his cruelty, summed up in his saying 'Let them hate me, so long as they fear me'.

TIGGER, see WINNIE THE POOH

TIGGYWINKLE, MRS [*Literature*]
The hedgehog laundress Mrs Tiggywinkle is one of the most pop-

ular of Beatrix Potter's creations, to the extent that 'tiggy' or 'tiggywinkle' has almost become another word for hedgehog. It has also been adopted as the name of the wild-animal rescue centre St Tiggywinkle's, which started off specialising in hedgehog rescues.

TIN WOODSMAN see WIZARD OF OZ

TINKER BELL [Drama, Film]
In J. M. Barrie's PETER PAN Tinker Bell (often written Tinkerbell) is his little fairy companion (in the original play just a moving spot of light). She is very jealous of Peter, and in her jealousy tried to kill WENDY, but loves him enough to sacrifice her own life by drinking the poison CAPTAIN HOOK has put out for him. The only way to save her life, in a shameless bit of audience manipulation by Barrie, is for all the children in the audience to show they believe in fairies by clapping their hands. 'Like Tinkerbell, standard-issue action movies only live if you believe in them' (*Guardian* 20.7.96).

TIN-TIN [Television, Popular Culture]
In the Belgian strip-cartoon series, Tin-Tin is a boy reporter-detective who has various unlikely adventures accompanied by his dog **Snowy** (Milou in the original French). Other regular characters in the series, which began in 1929, are the irascible CAPTAIN HADDOCK, the absent-minded PROFESSOR CALCULUS and a pair of identical comic British policemen, the **Thompson twins**.

TINY TIM see BOB CRATCHIT

TIR NA NOG see AVALON

TISIPHONE see FURIES

TITAN, TITANIC [Mythology, Transport]
In Greek myth the Titans were a race from before the Olympian gods, the children of the Sky (**Uranus**) and Earth (**Gaea**). Their offspring were giants and from this the word 'titan' came to mean 'giant', and the name came to be applied to such things as the Titan rockets used for early space-flight and so named to indicate

their size and power. The adjective from Titan is Titanic, and this was the name given to a vast new ocean liner that struck an iceberg near Newfoundland on its maiden voyage on the night of April 14–15 1912. Unfortunately, the ship had been advertised as unsinkable and there were not enough life-boats to take everyone on board, so that although the ship sank slowly and everyone could have got off, 1513 people died. This gave a whole new meaning to the word 'titanic'. The expression 'like re-arranging the deckchairs on the Titanic', a more modern equivalent of fiddling while Rome burns (see NERO), seems to be a fairly recent invention, dating only from the mid 1970s. 'Directing research funding into fewer and fewer universities ... brings to mind deckchairs and the *Titanic*' (*Independent* 22.4.96) See also STINGRAY.

TITFIELD THUNDERBOLT   [*Film*]
The 1952 Ealing comedy *The Titfield Thunderbolt* tells the story of a railway branch-line that is marked for closure. The locals thereupon take over running it, the Thunderbolt of the title being the name of the railway engine. The name is used for any comic aspect of a railway or for the pleasures of rail in the past.

TITHONUS see AURORA

TOAD OF TOAD HALL   [*Literature*]
The vainglorious, extrovert and wealthy **Mr Toad** of Toad Hall, owner of quite the finest house on the river, is an animal of strong and varied enthusiasms, until one day he is run down by a motor car, and it is love at first sight, as he sits in the road going 'poop, poop' in imitation of the horn. His friends, **Ratty**, who thinks that the only thing in life worth doing is just messing about on the river, the modest **Mole** and the brusque but kindly **Badger,** expect this enthusiasm to die out as rapidly as the others, but Toad buys and smashes up car after car. They decide to save him from himself and lock him up until the passion is burnt out, but he escapes, steals a car and is jailed. After he escapes from the deepest dungeon in all England, they have to get rid of the stoats and weasels that have taken over Toad Hall and drive them back to the **Wild Wood** where they belong. Kenneth Graham's novel *The Wind in*

the Willows (1908) is a hymn to rural England and has long been a favourite. It was turned into an equally popular musical play, *Toad of Toad Hall* in 1930, and such is the force of Toad's character that this name is often used instead of the official title.

TOBERMORY see WOMBLES

TOBY see PUNCH AND JUDY

TOBY, UNCLE see TRISTRAM SHANDY

TODD, SWEENEY [*Crime, Mythology*]
In the melodrama of Sweeney Todd 'the Demon Barber' of Fleet Street, Sweeney is a barber who murders his customers, cutting their throats instead of shaving them, and then disposing of the bodies through a trap door. The bodies are then robbed and passed into the pie shop next door where they are made up into pies and sold to the public, thus getting rid of the problem of how to dispose of the bodies. He gets his come-uppance when incriminating evidence is found by eaters of the pies. 'ITV continues to lose its Saturday night audience at an alarming rate (the network's lifeblood draining away faster than a haemophiliac's at Sweeney Todd's)' (*Evening Standard* 10.6.96).

TOLKIEN [*Literature*]
In 1997 J. R. R. Tolkien's *Lord of the Rings* was voted the most popular book of the twentieth century, but Tolkien himself is not that often alluded to. However, **sub-Tolkien**, as a disparaging term for some of the weaker Dungeons and Dragons novels or any fantasy involving elves, is well-established. See also BILBO AND FRODO BAGGINS, GANDALF, GOLLUM, MORDOR.

TOM AND JERRY [*Television*]
The cartoon cat and mouse series *Tom and Jerry*, first created in 1937, consists of little other than Tom, the cat, trying to catch Jerry mouse, and Jerry's attempts to thwart him and get his own back. The series has a fine reputation for extending the bounds of reality as only cartoons can do, but has been criticised by concerned parents for the violence it contains.

TOM, UNCLE [*Literature*]
Harriet Beecher Stowe's 1852 anti-slavery novel *Uncle Tom's Cabin* has as its hero a black slave whose mildness and patient forbearance despite all his tribulations earn him the respect of his white masters. Stowe meant Tom to be seen as a Christ-like figure, enduring all that is sent to him in this world, even being beaten to death by SIMON LEGREE, confident of his reward in the next world. However, it is hardly surprising that 20th-century civil-rights campaigners, fighting against such acceptance of discrimination, regarded UNCLE TOM with abhorrence, and **Uncle Tomism** – servile behaviour towards whites, or behaviour which supports white oppression – became an deadly insult. See also TOPSY.

TOMSK see THE WOMBLES

TONTO see LONE RANGER

TOPSY [*Literature*]
In Harriet Beecher Stowe's 1851 anti-slavery novel *Uncle Tom's Cabin*, Topsy is a little slave girl so deprived of a normal human background and kept in such benighted ignorance by her owners that she has no concept of God, let alone any idea of family. Asked where she came from she answers 'Never was born, never had no father, nor mother, nor nothing'. I 'spect I growed.' This has popularly become 'just growed' and so we find comments such as 'Like Topsy, Fantasy Football has just growed and growed' (PM, Radio 4, 24.9.96).

TORQUEMADA [*History*]
Tomás de Torquemada (1420–98) was a Spanish Dominican monk, the first Inquisitor-General of the SPANISH INQUISITION. He was responsible for the burning to death of some 2000 heretics, and has become symbolic of torture and remorseless questioning.

TORREY CANYON [*Technology, Ecology*]
In March 1967 the oil tanker the *Torrey Canyon* ran aground on the Seven Stones Reef between the Scilly Isles and Land's End, rupturing its tanks, and over 100 miles of some of Britain's most beautiful coastline was heavily polluted with crude oil. Pollution on

this scale had not been experienced before, and those coping with the problem had to learn as they went along. The public was made to realise for the first time the potential for destruction that major spills could have, and the *Torrey Canyon* became symbolic of this new awareness. The fame of the *Torrey Canyon* was eclipsed by that of the *Exxon Valdez* in 1989, when an even larger tanker spilt nearly 11 million gallons of crude in Alaska's Prince William Sound and thousands of miles of pristine coastline were damaged.

TORTOISE AND THE HARE [*Mythology*]
The fable of the tortoise and the hare tells of a race between the two. The hare was so confident of winning that rested half-way thorough and fell asleep, allowing his rival to amble across the finishing line with the comment 'Slow and steady wins the race'.

TORVILL AND DEAN [*Sport*]
The British ice skaters **Jayne Torvill** and **Christopher Dean** dominated competitive ice dancing from 1981to 1984. They often scored perfect marks for their interpretation, and their names have become used for dominance or perfection in a given field.

TOSCA see SCARPIA

TOTO see WIZARD OF OZ

TOULOUSE-LAUTREC see MOULIN ROUGE

TOVES, SLITHY see JABBERWOCKY

TOYTOWN see NODDY AND BIG EARS

TRACY, JEFF, SCOTT, VIRGIL, GORDON, ALAN AND JOHN see THUNDERBIRDS

TRANSPORTER see STAR TREK

TREASURE ISLAND see BLACK SPOT, CAPTAIN FLINT, BEN GUNN, ISRAEL HANDS, JIM HAWKINS, BLIND PEW, LONG JOHN SILVER

TREENS see DAN DARE

TRICKY WOO see MRS PUMPHREY

TRIGGER see ROGERS, ROY

TRILBY see SVENGALI

TRIM, CORPORAL see TRISTRAM SHANDY

TRIMALCHIO see PETRONIUS

TRISTAN AND ISOLDE [*Literature, Folklore*]
Tristan or **Tristram** and Isolde are two of the great lovers of
Medieval Romance. Tristan is the nephew of Mark, King of
Cornwall, and his greatest knight. When a marriage is arranged
between Mark and Isolde (also spelt **Isolda, Iseult** or beginning
with a Y), daughter of an Irish king, Tristan is given the job of
fetching the king's bride. On shipboard returning to Cornwall
Tristan and Isolde drink a flask of wine they find, not knowing
that it is a love potion brewed by Isolde's mother, and intended
for the newly married couple on their wedding night. Tristan and
Isolde are helpless under the effects of the potion, condemned to
tragic and adulterous love.

TROILUS [*Literature*]
Troilus's story is another medieval love tragedy. Troilus is a young
TROJAN price who falls in love with **Cressida**, a young widow left
unprotected in Troy when her father defects to the Greek side.
Cressida's uncle PANDARUS should protect her, but he is a friend of
Troilus, and determines to bring the lovers together. When
Cressida's father demands that she be exchanged for a captured
Trojan, there is nothing the lovers can do, although Cressida
promises to try to return. Instead she allows herself to be seduced
by the Greek Diomedes. She thus becomes a symbol of faithless-
ness, but Troilus remains true and becomes a symbol of fidelity.

TROJAN WAR, TROJAN HORSE [*Literature, Mythology*]
The Trojan War began after the Trojan prince, Paris, abducted

267

HELEN OF TROY. For ten long years the Greeks besieged Troy, trying to get her back, until ODYSSEUS had the idea of the Trojan Horse. This was an enormous, hollow wooden horse left on the sea shore when the Greeks pretended to abandon their siege. The Trojans were persuaded it was so large because it had been left as an offering to the gods. The Trojans therefore pull down part of the city wall to get it inside. At night the Greeks hiding inside climb out and let in the other Greeks, who had returned into the city, and Troy finally falls to the Greeks. Thus a Trojan Horse has come to mean a trap intended to undermine an enemy, and in computer jargon is a bug inserted into a program designed only to operate under certain circumstances. A Trojan has been used for a good companion or a hard, determined worker since the Middle Ages (presumably via the idea of a brave warrior).

TROTTER, DEL BOY AND RODNEY [*Television*]
In the immensely popular TV comedy *Only Fools and Horses* (1981–96), Derek 'Del-Boy' Trotter and his dim brother Rodney are two south London-market traders, wide-boys, surviving on their wits and always on the lookout for a fast buck. Del-Boy, a bit of an ARTHUR DALEY figure, has ambitions to enjoy the good life, and is the optimist, expecting each scheme to bring success. Rodney, who drives their RELIANT ROBIN truck, is the wet, dependent one.

TROY see TROJAN

TUCK, FRIAR see ROBIN HOOD

TUFTY THE SQUIRREL [*Popular Culture*]
Symbol of a long-running campaign to teach children road safety.

TUMNUS, MR see NARNIA

TURPIN, ARCHBISHOP see ROLAND AND OLIVER

TUVOK, MR see VULCANS

TWEEDLEDUM AND TWEEDLEDEE [*Literature*]
In Lewis Carroll's *Through the Looking Glass* (see ALICE IN WONDER-

LAND) Tweedledum and Tweedledee are identical, not very bright, twins. The term already existed for two virtually identical things or people, but most people nowadays know of it from Carroll.

TWEETY PIE AND SYLVESTER [*Television*]

Like TOM AND JERRY, Tweety Pie and Sylvester are combating cartoon characters. Tweety Pie is a canary who speaks in a baby voice ('I tort I tor a puddy tat') while Sylvester is a spluttering cat (favourite exclamation: 'Suffering succotash') who is constantly thwarted in his attempts to eat the bird.

TWIN PEAKS see AGENT COOPER, LAURA PALMER

TWIST, OLIVER [*Literature*]

Charles Dickens' 1838 novel *Oliver Twist* was an attack on the mistreatment of orphans in his day. Brought up in the workhouse where he is punished for asking for more food, farmed out as a virtual slave worker before falling into the hands of FAGIN and BILL SIKES, Oliver is lucky to find help and in the end even finds his family, although Dickens makes it clear that not all children were as lucky. Allusions to Oliver Twist are often to his request 'Please sir, I want some more.'

2001 see HAL

TYPHOID MARY [*History*]

Mary Mallon (c. 1879–1938), nicknamed Typhoid Mary, worked as a cook in the New York area. She was a carrier of typhoid, but immune to the disease herself, and her presence in a kitchen was linked with numerous outbreaks of the disease. This first happened in 1904 when a series of outbreaks of typhoid were found to be linked to houses where she had worked. Mary disappeared, was found again in 1907 still working as a cook, and was put in an isolation hospital until 1910 when she was released on condition she never worked in catering again. However, four years later new outbreaks of typhoid were found to be linked with her presence in the kitchen, and she was again put in isolation until her death. Her name has come to be used of anyone who persists in wrong-doing or is a source of contamination.

UBU [*Drama*]
Ugly, obscene, greedy, cowardly and generally repulsive, Ubu is the fantastical anti-hero of Alfred Jarry's 1896 satirical play *Ubu Roi* and of *Ubu Enchainé* (1899). Not the least horrific aspect of Ubu is that his character gradually took over the personality of his creator, this no doubt helped by Jarry's alcoholism. 'The strength of this well-researched biography is the often hilarious picture of Laing in full flight at conferences, a more grotesque **Groucho** MARX or Ubu, insulting all and sundry' (*Independent* 5.7.96).

UGLY DUCKLING [*Children's Literature, Mythology*]
Hans Andersen's story of the ugly duckling, mocked and reviled by the other ducklings until it turns into a beautiful swan is used both for someone physically ugly and for someone generally unpromising who turns into someone admirable.

UGLY SISTERS [*Folklore*]
CINDERELLA's Ugly Sisters who despise and oppress her, while remaining unaware of their own unpleasantness and ugliness, have become symbols of jealousy and self-delusion.

ULYSSES see ODYSSEY

UMBOPA see ALLAN QUARTERMAIN

UMSLOPOGAAS [*Literature*]
In Rider Haggard's ALLAN QUARTERMAIN novels Umslopogaas is a vast Zulu warrior whose fighting power lies in his beloved double-headed axe, which he calls 'Woodpecker' because of the ability of the sharply pointed weapon to peck holes in people's skulls.

270

UNCAS [*Literature*]
In James Fennimore Cooper's HAWKEYE novel *The Last of the Mohicans* (1826) Uncas is a young Indian brave, son of CHINGACH-GOOK, the last of the line of the Mohican chiefs. He is much more impetuous than his father, but is everything a young brave should be – perfectly formed, an incredibly fast runner, dutiful and obedient and intelligent. He is the truly noble savage who dies trying to save the life of Cora, the captive white girl, from the savage Indian **Magua**.

UNCLE see MAN FROM UNCLE

UNTOUCHABLES see ELIOT NESS

UPAS TREE [*Folklore, Natural World*]
In the eighteenth century a legend grew up about the upas tree, a fabulous tree found in Java that was so poisonous that is destroyed all living things up to fifteen miles around, and the name soon became more generally used for a noxious or destructive influence. In modern use *upas*, from the Malay word for poison, means a real Javanese variety of tree, the sap of which is used to poison arrows.

URANIA see MUSES

URANUS see TITAN

USHER, FALL OF THE HOUSE OF [*Literature*]
In Edgar Allan Poe's morbid tale *The Fall of the House of Usher* (1839) the last survivors of the ancient line of Usher are the brother and sister Roderick and Madeline Usher. Both are pale, sickly and at the very least, neurotic. Madeline wastes away and is buried in the vault beneath the house, but is in fact not dead but only in a cataleptic trance. Her highly sensitive brother can feel her knocking at the coffin and, her efforts to escape succeeding, she enters the room he is in, embraces him and falls dead. Roderick too dies, overcome by the effects of sharing his sister's exertions and by terror. The whole gloomy, ancestral mansion in which the events have taken place then sinks into the marsh on

which it stands. This story has become a useful label for the whole genre of morbid terror stories.

UTOPIA [*Literature, Philosophy*]
In 1516 Sir Thomas More (see MAN FOR ALL SEASONS) published a book in Latin called *Utopia* which described an imaginary island with a ideal society. From this the name has come to mean a vision of any such perfect society. More created the name from the Greek elements *ou*, 'not' and *topos*, 'place', meaning the name to be interpreted as 'nowhere' because such perfection could not exist. However, because of the very positive associations of the place, the word has come to be treated as if formed from the element *eu*, 'good, pleasant' and an opposite, **dystopia**, formed for a society in which everything is wrong.

VADER, DARTH [*Film*]

Darth Vader is the villain of the STAR WARS films. A renegade JEDI KNIGHT who has turned to the dark side of **The Force**, he now serves the evil Emperor as his chief henchman and terrifies all who come into contact with him. He always dresses in black, with a cloak billowing out behind him. So much of him has been replaced by artificial parts that he is now more machine than man, and has to wear a gleaming black protective helmet at all times, his breathing a bronchial rasp coming through the mouth-piece like that of some robot.

VALENTINE, SHIRLEY [*Drama, Film*]

Willy Russell's play (filmed in 1989) *Shirley Valentine* tells the story of a bored housewife, ignored by her husband, her children now flown the nest. She goes on holiday to Greece, and finds both romance and herself, and rediscovers pleasure in living. 'The Shirley Valentine Experience, in Surrey on 31 August, promises to "reawaken your passion to live, love and laugh again".' (*Guardian* 19.8.96).

VALENTINO [*Film*]

The American silent film star Rudolph Valentino (1895–1926) was the ultimate male sex symbol of his time, sending female filmgoers wild with such passionate roles as that of *The Sheik* (1921). Ever since his name has been used to indicate a certain brooding male sex-appeal.

VALHALLA [*Mythology*]

In Norse myth Valhalla is the great hall of the slain where warriors who fall in battle fight and feast with ODIN waiting for GOTTERDÄMMERUNG when they will fight as part of his army.

VALKYRIE [*Mythology*]
The Valkyries are ODIN's daughters who choose the slain on the
battle field who are to go to VALHALLA. These female warriors are
best known from Wagner's operas and are usually treated as
large, big-busted women with long hair, horned helmets and loud
voices.

VANDERDECKEN see FLYING DUTCHMAN

VANE, HARRIET see LORD PETER WIMSEY

VENUS see APHRODITE

VERA, AUNTIE see GILES

VIRGIL see INFERNO

VLADIMIR see GODOT

VOLUMNIA see CORIOLANUS

VRONSKY see ANNA KARENINA

VULCAN see APHRODITE

VULCANS [*Television, Film*]
In the STAR TREK series Vulcans are a race of wise but emotionless
people whose life is governed by logic. The best-known examples
of the race are MR SPOCK from the original series and Mr **Tuvok**
from *Voyager*. With both of these characters, conflict and humour
come from the mutual inability of emotional humans and logical
Vulcans to understand each other's motivations. The Conservative
MP John Redwood is often described as a Vulcan, though others
feel he is more like a **Romulan** (see KLINGONS).

WACKY RACES see DICK DASTARDLY

WADMAN, MRS see TRISTRAM SHANDY

WALKER, ANNIE AND JACK see ROVERS RETURN

WALL, MAX [*Entertainment*]
Max Wall (1908–1990) was a music-hall comedian with an extraordinary walk, cadaverous appearance, large head and black plastered-down hair who dressed in extraordinary clothes. Towards the end of his life his career, which had been in decline along with the music halls, had a final flourish as he took on serious, often experimental, acting roles. 'There are now certain clothes that I can no longer wear and when one has a collapsed bottom, very thin legs and gargantuan feet, leggings are in this group. I look very like Max Wall.' (*Guardian* 27.8.96).

WALLACE AND GROMIT [*Film, Popular Culture*]
Nick Park's prize-winning plasticine animations of the eccentric, cheese-loving, Lancashire inventor Wallace and his silent side-kick, Gromit the dog, always leave one with a nagging suspicion that although very much the assistant, Gromit is the more intelligent of the pair.

WALTER, SOFTY see DENNIS THE MENACE

WALTONS, THE [*Television, Film, Literature*]
Although they started life in a novel and film (1963), The Waltons are best known from the TV series showing the domestic crises of this close family in a poor area of Virginia during the Depression and the Second World War. All of these forms were written by Earl Hamner Jr, who based the stories on his own life. Events are seen

through the sentimental eyes of **John-Boy Walton**, the eldest son of the family, and the clean-living, idealised all-American family saga has been much parodied. 'Families so messed up they made the residents of BROOKSIDE look like The Waltons'. (*Guardian* 2.11.96).

WARP-FACTOR see STAR TREK

WASHINGTON, GEORGE [*History*]
Although it has long been proved that George Washington (1732–99) never cut down a cherry tree, so cannot have said 'I can't tell I lie, Pa; you know I can't tell a lie. I did cut it with my hatchet', this, and his remarkable wooden false teeth, are still the commonest type of allusion to Washington.

WATERLOO see NAPOLEON

WATSON, DOCTOR see HOLMES, SHERLOCK

WAYNE, BRUCE see BATMAN AND ROBIN

WAYNE, JOHN [*Film*]
The American film actor John Wayne (1907–79) is famous for his cowboy roles, films in which he seems to win wars single-handed and for his right-wing politics, but is alluded to most frequently for his distinctive, stiff-legged walk, most often seen in films as he goes to put the forces of evil to flight.

WEDNESDAY see ADDAMS FAMILY

WELLER, SAM see PICKWICK

WELLINGTON see WOMBLES

WENDY [*Drama, Film*]
Wendy Darling is the eldest of the three **Darling** children (the others being **John** and **Michael**) who go with PETER PAN to **Never Never Land**. Peter takes her there to be a mother to the lost boys, and this little girl happily takes on all the duties of a wife and

mother. As such she is most often cited as what girls today do not want out of life.

WESSEX [*Literature*]
Wessex is Thomas Hardy's name for the area of south-west England he wrote about in his novels. It is used to indicate all that is associated with his novels: wild, beautiful countryside and rural passions and tragedies.

WEST, MAE [*Film*]
The American actress Mae West (1892–1980), who wrote much of her own material, was the master of innuendo, and often found herself censored. With her platinum hair and hour-glass figure, she was the DOLLY PARTON of her day, hence the fact that when the US forces were issued with chest-covering inflatable life jackets they were immediately christened Mae Wests.

WHARTON, HARRY see BILLY BUNTER

WHISTLER'S MOTHER [*Art*]
The artist James McNeill Whistler (1834–1903) painted in 1871–72 a work he called *Arrangement in Grey and Black, No. 1: The Artist's Mother* but which is universally known as Whistler's Mother. It shows a rather grim-looking old woman sitting in profile lost in either thought or senility, and is one of the most parodied paintings around.

WHITE QUEEN [*Literature*]
The White Queen in Lewis Carroll's **Alice** story *Through the Looking Glass* (see ALICE IN WONDERLAND) is best known for her habit of crying over such things as pricking her finger before it happens, on the grounds that there is no point in crying about it afterwards; and for three quotes: 'The rule is, jam tomorrow and jam yesterday – but never jam today', 'It's a poor sort of memory that only works backwards' and 'Why, sometimes I've believed as many as six impossible things before breakfast'.

WHITE RABBIT [*Literature*]
In Lewis Carroll's ALICE IN WONDERLAND, Alice's curious adven-

tures start after she follows a white rabbit, neatly dressed and consulting his watch and exclaiming that he is late, down a rabbit hole. The White Rabbit exclaims 'Oh my dear paws! Oh my fur and whiskers!'

WHITEHOUSE, MRS MARY see ALF GARNET

WHO, DR [Television]
The children's TV series *Dr Who* has been enormously popular ever since it was first shown in 1963. The Doctor, a Time Lord who has appeared in several incarnations over the years, has varied in character, but has always been eccentrically dressed, barely in control of his ship, the TARDIS, and has above all used brains rather than brawn to overcome enemies such as the DALEKS. Although the series is notorious for its rocking sets and cheap special effects, good writing, especially those scripts written by Terry Nation, overcame the production values, and many children spent their Saturday evenings cowering behind the sofa while Dr Who saved the world. See also K9.

WHORE OF BABYLON see BABYLON

WICKED WITCH OF THE WEST see WIZARD OF OZ

WIDMERPOOL [Literature]
In Anthony Powell's *A Dance to the Music of Time* sequence of novels Kenneth Widmerpool is the ridiculous, ugly, charmless, pompous, but ruthlessly ambitious butt of all who know him. Despite all his disadvantages, and constant rejections, he has tenacity and he remorselessly climbs his way up the social ladder and becomes wealthy, a Labour MP and finally a life peer before dying relatively young in sexually scandalous circumstances.

WILD WOOD see TOAD OF TOAD HALL

WILDE, OSCAR [Literature, History]
The dramatist and poet Oscar Wilde (1854–1900) is famous for his quick wit and as a leader of style. He was a leading light in the literary world of his day, and was the model for BUNTHORNE in

Gilbert and Sullivan's *Patience*. He was imprisoned and later had to leave the country after he came into conflict with the Marquis of QUEENSBERRY who objected to Wilde's homosexual relationship with his son Lord Alfred Douglas, known as **Bosey**.

WILLIAM see WILLIAM BROWN

WIMSEY, LORD PETER [*Literature*]

Lord Peter Wimsey is the sensitive, book-collecting, aristocratic detective in Dorothy L. Sayers' books. He starts out a nervous wreck after his experiences in the First World War, but as the books progress he become tougher and more foppish. He loves the independent minded **Harriet Vane**, a writer of detective fiction, but only persuades her to marry him after he has provided the vital evidence that proves her innocent of a murder charge. His devoted valet, **Bunter**, is also a useful assistant in the detecting business.

WINNIE THE POOH [*Children's Literature*]

In A. A. Milne's *Winnie-the Pooh* (1926) and *The House at Pooh Corner* (1928) Winnie the Pooh is the teddy bear belonging to CHRISTOPHER ROBIN who lives in the Hundred Acre wood with his friends the timid **Piglet**, EEYORE the gloomy donkey, **Owl**, **Tigger** the bouncy tiger, the maternal **Kanga** and her baby **Roo** and the bossy **Rabbit**. Pooh is 'a Bear of Very little Brain, and long words Bother me', but he is good natured, has a lively imagination and is a keen maker of verses, or Hums as he calls them. He is also very greedy, especially for honey, and for him it is always 'time for a little something'.

WISE MEN OF GOTHAM see GOTHAM

WISTY, E. L. [*Television*]

E. L.Wisty is the sad little man in a grubby raincoat whose surreal rambling monologues were written and performed by the comedian Peter Cook (1937–95).

WIZARD OF OZ [*Film, Literature*]

Frank Baum's 1900 book *The Wizard of Oz* tells the story of how

Dorothy and her little dog **Toto** are carried off from dreary Kansas by a cyclone to the **Emerald City** of **Oz**. The MUNCHKINS direct Dorothy down the YELLOW BRICK ROAD to the city of Oz where they think the Wizard can help her get home. On her way she meets a **Cowardly Lion** who joins her in the hope that the wizard can give him courage, a **Tin Woodsman** who hopes for a heart and a **Scarecrow** who hopes for brains. They have to deal with the **Wicked Witch of the West**, who proves to be water-soluble, before they discover that the wizard is a fraud although a good psychologist who convinces the Lion, Tin Woodsman and Scarecrow that he has given them their gifts. Dorothy finally gets home with the help of **Glinda the Good** Sorceress. Baum wrote numerous sequels to this work in which the same characters often re-appear.

WODEHOUSE, P. G. see BERTIE WOOSTER, JEEVES

WODEN see ODIN

WOMBLES [*Television*]
Elizabeth Beresford's Womble children's books tells the adventures of a race of small, furry, rotund, burrowing animals who devote their lives to clearing up after humans and to recycling their cast-offs, first on Wimbledon Common and later in Hyde Park in London. Their leader is **Great Uncle Bulgaria**, with the mechanically minded **Tobermory** as his deputy. The senior female Womble is the cook **Madam Cholet**. Younger Wombles include the inquisitive **Bungo**; fat, lazy **Orinoco**; intellectual **Wellington** and the athletic **Tomsk**.

WONKA, WILLIE see MIKE TV

WOODENTOPS [*Television*]
The children's TV programme *The Woodentops* was made from 1955 until 1958 and was often repeated thereafter. It depicted the everyday farming life of a family of wooden-doll string puppets which moved jerkily about their business, the twin children getting up to mischief and playing with their dog **Spotty Dog,** 'the biggest spotty dog you ever did see', while Daddy Woodentop

looked after the cows and Mummy Woodentop worked in the kitchen.

WOODSTOCK [History]
The free music festival held at Woodstock, New York State, in August 1969 was attended by some 300,000 people, and was totally non-violent despite there being no form of supervision. This event has entered folk-history and was the high point of the Hippie peace and love movement, and seemed to show that a new way of doing things could be found. This idealism was shattered only months later at ALTAMONT.

WOOKIE see HAN SOLO

WOOSTER, BERTIE [Literature]
P. G. Wodehouse is widely regarded as one of the masters of English comic writing, especially when writing about the silly-ass type, and the best known of these chumps is Bertie Wooster, who has a heart of gold, but scarcely a brain in his head, although he does not recognise this. Luckily for Bertie and his friends at the DRONES club, Bertie's gentleman's gentleman, JEEVES, is usually at hand to rescue them from scrapes, although this can be difficult when Bertie's terrifying **Aunt Dahlia** or even more terrifying **Aunt Agatha** are involved (to quote Bertie 'It is no use telling me there are bad aunts and good aunts. At the core they are all alike. Sooner or later, out pops the cloven hoof'). Among Bertie's friends are BINGO LITTLE and timid, newt-loving GUSSIE FINK-NOTTLE who is in love with the drippy **Madeline Basset**. Among those he comes into conflict with are fierce **Sir Roderick Glossop** and the would-be fascist leader **Roderick Spode.**

WORF see KLINGONS

WORTHINGTON, MRS [Song]
Noël Coward's 1935 song *Mrs Worthington* tells of the mother of an untalented and unattractive, stage-stuck girl and begs 'Don't put your daughter on the stage, Mrs Worthington', so that Worthington has become a name used for anyone keen to go on the stage or for a theatrical, pushy mother.

WOTAN see ODIN

WRITING ON THE WALL see DANIEL

WUTHERING HEIGHTS see HEATHCLIFFE AND CATHY

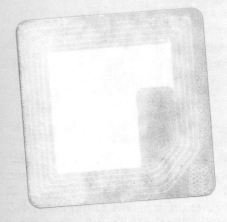

X FILES [*Television*]

The phenomenally successful television series *The X Files* tells of the encounters of FBI special agents **Dana Scully** and **Fox Mulder** with various preternatural, often extra-terrestrial, phenomena.

XANADU [*Literature*]

'In Xanadu' the poet Coleridge tells us 'did **Kubla Khan** / A stately pleasure-dome decree / Where Alph, the sacred river ran / Through caverns measureless to man / Down to a sunless sea'. The palace, we are told were set in gardens by a natural fountain, in utmost natural beauty 'It was a miracle of rare device, / A sunny pleasure-dome with caves of ice'. We never get a full description of this marvellous place as Coleridge was interrupted by the Person from PORLOCK, and by the time he got back to work had lost the vision that inspired the first part of *Kubla Khan*. However, the term Xanadu has been taken up to describe any fantastic, luxurious or mystical place, so that, for example the large, luxurious compound built by Sir James Goldsmith in the jungle has been described as 'his Xanadu-style mansion in Mexico' (*Independent* 17.4.96). When Orson Welles made the film **Citizen Kane**, based on the life of WILLIAM RANDOLPH HEARST the name used for the fictional version of Hearst's real-life luxurious castle of San Simeon was Xanadu.

XERXES [*History*]

Xerxes I was king of Persia from 485 to 465 BC and was responsible for the invasion of Greece that led to the Battle of THERMOPYLAE and the Persians' defeat at Salamis. He is most often cited for his actions on the way to invade Greece. A bridge of boats was built across the Hellespont to allow his troops to cross from Asia to Europe, but a storm sprang up and destroyed it. Xerxes had the sea whipped with chains before the bridge was re-built. This was meant to be a bit of public-relations work to show that Xerxes regarded himself as master of the land and sea and was not put out by this setback, but with his subsequent defeat at the hands of the relatively puny Greeks it looked more like hubris and arrogance.

YAHOOS [*Literature*]

In Jonathan Swift's satire *Gulliver's Travels* (1726) Lemuel **Gulliver**'s final set of adventures take place in the land of the **Houyhnhnms**; noble, wise and rational horses who are revolted by the savage, filthy Yahoos, a race of debased humans. Thus Yahoo has come to mean an uncouth, unthinking or degenerate person. Yahoo is now also the name of an internet search programme. See also BROBDINGNAGIAN, LILLIPUT.

YANKEE DOODLE [*Song*]

The term 'Yankee' is used of an American, or more particularly on a New Englander. The song *Yankee Doodle* has been adopted almost as a national song by the United States, and no-one seems particularly bothered that the words seem virtually meaningless. In fact, it was originally a song sung by the English to mock the shabbily dressed colonists: Yankee Doodle rides to town on a pony, not a horse, and his dress sense is so poor that he thinks just sticking a feather in his hat will make him a macaroni, a contemporary term for a dedicated follower of fashion.

YELLOW-BRICK ROAD [*Film, Literature*]

In the WIZARD OF OZ **Dorothy** and her friends are told to follow the yellow-brick road and, once they have found this, it will lead them to their goal, the city of **Oz**. Thus a yellow-brick road is a desirable path or a solution to a problem.

YELLOW JERSEY [*Sport*]

In France's national cycling race, the *Tour de France*, the yellow jersey (in French **maillot jaune**), is worn by the person who made the fastest time in the previous stage of the race. Thus a yellow jersey can be used to mean a symbol of success or sign that someone is the leader of the pack.

YES MINISTER see SIR HUMPHREY

YODA [*Film*]
In the STAR WARS films Yoda is a small, pointy-eared, cave-dwelling creature who gives the impression of being a bald furry animal, but is in fact a master of the ways of the **Force**, and the last one left alive who can instruct LUKE SKYWALKER how to become a JEDI KNIGHT. He speaks a version of English which puts the words in a very unusual order. This caused a small stir among linguisticians when the films first came out, for it is perfectly easy to understand Yoda, yet it has proved very difficult to find any human language that puts sentences together in the same way he does.

YOGI BEAR [*Television*]
The cartoon character of Yogi Bear was the bane of **Jellystone Park** (the series liked puns – Yogi's name is based on the baseball player Yogi Berra and Jellystone on Yellowstone Park). Yogi, who always wore a pork-pie hat and a tie, regarded himself as 'smarter than the average bear' and with his side-kick the bear cub **Boo Boo** devoted himself to outsmarting the **Ranger's** attempts to stop him stealing tourists' picnic baskets.

YOSEMITE SAM [*Television*]
In the **Bugs Bunny** cartoons Yosemite Sam is the rarin', tearin', hollerin', red-moustached, short-tempered, Wild West prospector type who is always in conflict with Bugs. He never stands a chance against the cunning rabbit, for Bugs knows that Sam has an incredibly short fuse, and the least thing will cause him to loose his temper to such an extent that he can be tricked into rushing blindly into almost anything.

YOSSARIAN see CATCH-22

ZARKOV, DR see FLASH GORDON

ZEBEDEE see DOUGAL

ZENDA, THE PRISONER OF see RURITANIA

ZEPHYR [*Mythology, Literature*]
A zephyr is a poetic term for a soft and gentle breeze, from the ancient Greek name for the west wind. It is one of those words that has such a strong association with artificial poetic language that it is now almost always used ironically.

ZEUS [*Mythology*]
In Greek myth Zeus was the king of the gods, whose weapon was the mighty thunderbolt with which he could strike down any who opposed him. His wife was HERA, but he had a habit of chasing other women, both mortal and immortal, often disguised as an animal. See also AEGIS, APHRODITE, ATHENE, DANAE, HERCULES.

ZIMMER [*Medicine, Popular Culture*]
The Zimmer frame, a trade name for a walking aid for the elderly, has now become a slang term for anything geriatric or elderly. 'Radio 2 is not as fuddy-duddy as it's painted ... all the old jokes about Radio Zimmer are misplaced.' (*Independent* 14.5.96).

ZINDERNEUF, FORT see BEAU GESTE

ZOLA, EMILE see ALFRED DREYFUS

ZORDON, ZORDS, see POWER RANGERS

ZORRO [*Television, Literature*]

Johnston McCulley's creation Zorro harks back to the days when California was Spanish and Hidalgos ruled. In a set-up very similar to that of the SCARLET PIMPERNEL Don Diego de la Vega is an apparently weak and foppish scion of one of the great houses. But secretly he is Zorro (The Fox), a mysterious masked stranger who goes about righting the wrongs of those oppressed by tyranny and rescuing fair maidens. His calling card is the letter Z, often inscribed by a dextrous flick of his rapier on the body on his enemy.